St. Louis Community College

Forest Park
Florissant Valley
Meramec

Instructional Resources
St. Louis, Missouri

W. H. Auden: 'The Map of All my Youth'

AUDEN STUDIES 1

W. H. AUDEN

'The Map of All My Youth'

EARLY WORKS, FRIENDS AND INFLUENCES

Auden Studies 1

EDITED BY KATHERINE BUCKNELL AND
NICHOLAS JENKINS

CLARENDON PRESS · OXFORD
1990

Oxford University Press, Walton Street, Oxford OX2 6DP

Oxford New York Toronto
Delhi Bombay Calcutta Madras Karachi
Petaling Jaya Singapore Hong Kong Tokyo
Nairobi Dar es Salaam Cape Town
Melbourne Auckland
and associated companies in
Berlin Ibadan

Oxford is a trade mark of Oxford University Press

Published in the United States
by Oxford University Press, New York

British Library Cataloguing in Publication Data
Auden, W. H. (Wystan Hugh), 1907–1973
W. H. Auden: 'The Map of All My Youth'. Auden Studies Vol. 1
1. Poetry in English. Auden, W. H. (Wystan Hugh) 1907–1973
I. Title II. Bucknell, Katherine III. Jenkins, Nicholas
821.912
ISBN 0–19–812964–5

Library of Congress Cataloging in Publication Data
Auden, W. H. (Wystan Hugh), 1907–1973.
The map of all my youth: early works, friends, and influences /
W.H. Auden; edited by Katherine Bucknell and Nicholas Jenkins.
p. cm.—(Auden studies; 1)
Includes bibliographical references and index.
. Auden, W. H. (Wystan Hugh), 1907–1973—Biography—Youth.
2. Poets, English—20th century—Biography—Youth.
I. Bucknell, Katherine. II. Jenkins, Nicholas, 1961– .
III. Title. IV. Series.
PR6001.U4Z47 1990   811'.52—dc20 [B]   90–7055
ISBN 0–19–812964–5

Typeset by Hope Services (Abingdon) Ltd.
Printed and bound in
Great Britain by Biddles Ltd.,
Guildford and King's Lynn

ACKNOWLEDGEMENTS

MANY individuals and institutions have been generous with materials and permissions and we would like to thank each of them on our own behalf and on behalf of our contributors: the Estate of W. H. Auden for permission to print all items by Auden which appear in this volume; the Estate of Louis MacNeice for permission to print unpublished and uncollected writings by MacNeice; Naomi Mitchison for permission to quote from a draft of her 'Foreword' to Auden's 'Writing' manuscript and from her letters to Katherine Bucknell; Stephen Spender for permission to quote from a letter to Kathleen Bell; John B. Auden for allowing us to quote from his brother's letters to him; Don Bachardy for permission to use manuscripts by Auden which belong to the Estate of Christopher Isherwood; Aurora Ciliberti for permission to quote from an Auden letter in her possession; the Henry W. and Albert A. Berg Collection of the New York Public Library (Astor, Lenox and Tilden Foundations) and the late Dr Lola L. Szladits for allowing us to publish a selection of Auden's letters to Spender as well as to quote from numerous other items in the Collection; The Bodleian Library, Oxford, for permission to publish a selection of Auden's letters to E. R. and A. E. Dodds, to quote from other letters also in the Dodds Bequest (MS Eng. lett. c. 464), and to quote from the John Hilton Papers (MS Don. c. 153); The Brotherton Library, Leeds, for permission to use manuscripts in their collection; The Edinburgh University Library for allowing us to print Auden's 'Writing' manuscript in its entirety (MS Gen. 2122/13); Faber and Faber Limited and Random House Inc. for permission to include Sonnet 'XVI' from 'The Quest' (US Copyright 1941 and renewed 1969 by W. H. Auden), reprinted from *W. H. Auden: Collected Poems*, edited by Edward Mendelson; Faber and Faber Limited for permission to include 'A Communist to Others'; and King's College, Cambridge, for permission to print a letter from Auden to Spender in its collection. Kathleen Bell is grateful to the British Academy for support of her work on the Dodds correspondence. We would like to thank Columbia University, the Commonwealth Fund, Magdalen College, Oxford, and Worcester College, Oxford, for support during our own work on this volume. At Oxford University Press Kim Scott Walwyn and Frances Whistler were at all times patient and encouraging. David Bradshawe, Lewis

Cooper, Caroline Gregg, Siri Huntoon, J. R. Maguire Jr., and Hugo Vickers have also given invaluable help.

Finally, we thank John Fuller and Edward Mendelson without whose generosity, energy, and intelligence this volume would not have appeared.

CONTENTS

INTRODUCTION

Auden Studies is a new series, in which a volume will appear once every two or three years. Broadly speaking, this first volume focuses on the earlier part of Auden's life, our next volume will concentrate on the later part, and subsequent volumes will likewise be centred on particular topics (although contributions of significance will not be excluded simply for failing to suit the announced theme).

Auden Studies will make available some of the unpublished writing by Auden that has been accumulating in libraries and collections over the last few decades. Here we include some little known poems written by Auden in German, the manuscript of an important early essay which was published in a heavily altered version, and the first two selections from Auden's letters to receive a scholarly presentation. All of these materials have been edited and commented on (and in the case of the German poems translated) by various hands, each in a slightly different way; no uniform style has been imposed.

They are followed by essays about Auden, about his teacher and friend Frank McEachran, and about Louis MacNeice. Every volume of *Auden Studies* wil be concerned not only with Auden but also with his friends and contemporaries, those who influenced him, and those by whom he was influenced.

Next is a 'Symposium' in which four critics spanning several generations discuss a single poem by Auden; this will be a regular feature in *Auden Studies*.

Finally, there are two contributions devoted to books and bibliography: an essay for amateurs about collecting Auden's works, and an extensive supplement to the second edition of the Auden *Bibliography*.

Auden Studies welcomes contributions from any viewpoint. Typescripts and an s.a.e. should be sent to: The Editors, *Auden Studies*, c/o The Academic English Books Editor, The Oxford University Press, Walton Street, Oxford OX2 6DP.

K.B.
N.J.

ABBREVIATIONS

Works by Auden cited in this volume

AT   *Another Time* (New York, 1940; London, 1940).

CP45   *The Collected Poetry of W. H. Auden* (New York, 1945).

CP76   *Collected Poems*, ed. Edward Mendelson (London, 1976; New York, 1976).

DBS   *The Dog Beneath the Skin or Where is Francis?*, with Christopher Isherwood (London, 1935; New York, 1935).

DD   *The Dance of Death* (London, 1933).

DH   *The Dyer's Hand* (New York, 1962; London, 1963).

DM   *The Double Man* (New York, 1941), see also *NYL*.

EA   *The English Auden: Poems, Essays and Dramatic Writings 1927–1939*, ed. Edward Mendelson (London, 1977; New York, 1978).

FA   *Forewords and Afterwords*, selected by Edward Mendelson (New York, 1973; London 1973).

FTB   *For the Time Being* (New York, 1944; London, 1945).

JTW   *Journey to a War*, with Christopher Isherwood (London, 1939; New York, 1939).

LFI   *Letters from Iceland*, with Louis MacNeice (London, 1937; New York, 1937).

NYL   *New Year Letter* (London, 1941), British edn. of *DM*.

O   *The Orators: An English Study* (London, 1932).

O³   *The Orators: An English Study*, 3rd edn., 1st American edn. (London, 1966; New York, 1967).

OTF   *On the Frontier: A Melodrama in Three Acts*, with Christopher Isherwood (London, 1938; New York, 1939).

PB   *Paul Bunyan: The Libretto of the Operetta by Benjamin Britten*, with an essay by Donald Mitchell (London, 1988).

PD   *The Prolific and the Devourer*, in *Antaeus*, 41 (Summer 1981), 4–65.

PDW   *Plays and Other Dramatic Writings 1928–1938*, with Christopher Isherwood, ed. Edward Mendelson, (Princeton, 1988; London, 1989).

SP   *Selected Poems*, ed. Edward Mendelson (New York, 1979; London, 1979).

SW   *Secondary Worlds*, (London, 1968; New York, 1969).

Other Abbreviations used in this volume

Berg   The Henry W. and Albert A. Berg Collection, New York Public Library (Astor, Lenox and Tilden Foundations).

Bibliography	B. C. Bloomfield and Edward Mendelson, *W. H. Auden: A Bibliography 1924–1969*, 2nd edn. (Charlottesville, 1972).
Bodleian	The Department of Western Manuscripts, Bodleian Library, Oxford.
Carpenter	Humphrey Carpenter, *W. H. Auden: A Biography* (London, 1981; New York, 1981).
CHK	Christopher Isherwood, *Christopher and His Kind 1929–1939* (New York, 1976; London, 1977).
Early Auden	Edward Mendelson, *Early Auden* (New York, 1981; London, 1981).
Farnan	Dorothy J. Farnan, *Auden in Love* (New York, 1984; London, 1984).
Finney	Brian Finney, *Christopher Isherwood: A Critical Biography* (London, 1979; New York, 1979).
Fuller	John Fuller, *A Reader's Guide to W. H. Auden* (London, 1970; New York, 1970).
LTC	Stephen Spender, *Letters to Christopher*, ed. Lee Bartlett (Santa Barbara, 1980).
Osborne	Charles Osborne, *W. H. Auden: The Life of a Poet* (New York, 1979; London 1980).
Tribute	Stephen Spender, ed., *W. H. Auden: A Tribute*, (London, 1974; New York, 1974).
WWW	Stephen Spender, *World Within World* (London, 1951; New York, 1951).

British and American editions are distinguished where necessary in the notes by the suffixes (L) for London or (NY) for New York. Further publication details of Auden's work may be found in the Bloomfield and Mendelson *Bibliography*.

The German Auden: Six Early Poems

TRANSLATED BY DAVID CONSTANTINE

AUDEN went to Germany in October 1928 and lived there, mainly in Berlin, until July 1929. In April 1930 he took up a teaching post at Larchfield Academy in Helensburgh on the Firth of Clyde. For the vacation that summer he went back to Berlin. It seems likely that these six poems in German, all published here for the first time, were written after his return from that holiday. The opening line of one, 'Es regnet auf mir in den Schottische Lände' (2), points definitely to Helensburgh, and others also have separation and absence as their given context. As was his habit with most of the poems that he wrote at this time, Auden sent them all to Christopher Isherwood who was still in Berlin.

Are these the poems Isherwood referred to in his 1937 essay 'Some Notes on Auden's Early Poetry'?

It is typical of Auden's astonishing adaptability that, after two or three months in Berlin, he began to write poems in German. Their style can best be imagined by supposing that a German writer should attempt a sonnet-sequence in a mixture of Cockney and Tennysonian English, without being able to command either idiom. A German critic of great sensibility to whom I afterwards showed these sonnets was much intrigued. He assured me that the writer was a poet of the first rank, despite his absurd grammatical howlers. The critic himself had never heard of Auden and was certainly quite unaware of his English reputation.[1]

If these *are* the poems, then Isherwood seems to be misremembering the date of their composition. The alternative is, of course, that his recollection is trustworthy, but that he has other, presently lost, poems in mind.

Auden's German is indeed an interesting mixture. There are at least half a dozen major grammatical errors—of gender, case, syntax, word order—in every poem. Thus: 'Mach Spass mit der die reichen sind' (4. 9) or 'Mein Kaffee auszutrinken und Dein Wein' (1. 2). And this *is* inaccuracy, not idiosyncracy or inventiveness. Sometimes the absence or wrongness of grammatical connections makes it impossible to be sure of the sense. Take, for example: 'O hab kein Angst der Zeit muss nicht vorbei, / Das Unbestimmt Bestimmt nicht werden muss' (5. 9–10).

---

[1] Repr. in *Exhumations* (London, 1966), 21.

Certain locutions are very lame or empty: '. . . und dass ich finde / Dass dieses Jahreszeit langweilig heisst' (5. 1–2), or 'Wir sprechen Namen aber nicht zu denken' (3. 12). By September 1930 Auden had lived some eleven months in Germany. Perhaps his German ought to have been rather better than it looks here? I have been told by people who should know, that although he came to understand the language perfectly, Auden never spoke or wrote it without mistakes.

Still, grammatical lapses are only one element in the mixture. There are also passages of ambitious and nearly successful syntax (2. 8–12) as well as moments of verbal agility and fun, especially in 'Chorale' (6). Elsewhere linguistic and grammatical simplicity produce a very strong effect: 'Weil ich kein Geld hab' komm ich nicht in Frage, / Du liebst dein Leben und ich liebe Dich' (1. 7–8). All in all, the language of these poems does amount to a coherent heterogeneous diction. Auden had learned more than a smattering of the vernacular of Berlin—its Cockney, as Isherwood suggests. You can hear the dialect in a phrase like: 'Ick bläb bei Dir' (6. 8). And naturally he knew the words that came with his sexual preoccupations: 'Eier', 'Trippe', 'Schwanz', 'Blubber', 'blasen'.

These poems remind one of Brecht. 'Chorale' is a contrafacture, in very Brechtian style: obscene new wine in sacred old bottles. ('O sacred head, surrounded . . .') Perhaps Auden knew of the 'Großer Dankchoral' in Brecht's *Hauspostille*? Certainly he had heard the 'Morgenchoral' with which Act 1 of the *Dreigroschenoper* begins. Brecht's own style was one in which his equivalents of 'Cockney and Tennysonian English' coexisted abrasively and amusingly, and in *Mahagonny* (with 'Moon of Alabama' and 'Benares-Song') he did to English rather what Auden is doing here to German. It is possible that Auden knew and was influenced by these things, but more likely that the contiguities are only accidental or 'of the times'. The whole ethos of the poems is similar to that of the *Städtebewohner* sequences that Brecht, on the threshold of Marxism, was writing in the late twenties. Auden would not like that comparison perhaps.

His city world is a bleak one, nevertheless. Absent from it, he remembers Berlin life without illusion. He wants to get back there for the sex, but he knows very well what these remembered relationships are like: mercenary. Associates in them remain essentially unconnected: one moves off to where the money is, to where the life is cushier, the other is left behind. There is very little complaint. The tone of voice is resigned: 'So kommt es immer vor' (2. 5), 'Du must' (2. 14). The constituent factors are abuse, estrangement, selfishness, and betrayal. That is how things are: 'Denn . . . jeder Art von Liebe denkt an sich'

(1. 5–6). The fundamental fact is loneliness. Auden inhabits (to my mind, at least) what Graves said a poet should at all costs avoid: loveless circumstances. But perhaps what he celebrates in 'Chorale' makes up for it?

Of the sonnets, all but one use the Shakespearean rhyme-scheme. Behind 'Jetzt bin ich faul' (4) there is the ghost of 'Being your slave, what should I do but tend' (Sonnet 57), and there are other, perhaps predictable, echoes of Shakespeare's obsessive enquiry into absence and dependence. The mercenary strain in Auden's sonnets, his sense of love as a commodity ('die Ware Liebe' as Brecht called it) is a bleaker equivalent of the financial and commercial imagery in Shakespeare's.

These poems are remarkable for their images, even though the language sometimes fails to present them clearly. A good deal crystallizes around the trains in 'Es regnet auf mir' (2) and likewise, if more obscurely, around the poor boy in 'Zu sagen Liebe' (3) who is being used and abused as a go-between by a loveless partnership. Moreover, there are many telling details which, being contained in single heavily end-stopped rhyming lines, linger in the mind as images. In fact, Auden himself went back to them; three lines from 'Lacrimae Rerum' (1. 5, 8, 12) were turned into English for the lyric 'Night covers up the rigid land' (1936), and line 4 of 'Ich weiss dass Du' (5) seems to have gone into 'Journey to Iceland' (also 1936).[2]

These poems in German are worth knowing. A good deal of the truth comes through, in the language in which it was experienced. That may be what the 'critic of great sensibility' detected.

A Note on the Text and Translations

The texts of the poems are taken from manuscripts that Auden sent or gave to Christopher Isherwood in the 1930s and which now belong to Isherwood's estate. Auden's punctuation, however unusual, has been left intact. For reasons given above, even the literal versions (printed here beneath the German) were not always easy to do. I went through the poems with a native speaker, who was himself sometimes nonplussed. In 5. 9–10, for example, it may be that an intended English sense is not only not being conveyed but is actually being contradicted by the German used. The unliteral versions are my own doing. I tried to make coherent readable verse. I am aware that in places they depart from the original German (by reference to the literal versions any reader can monitor where and how much) and that they do not read like Auden.

---

[2] Repr. in *EA*, 162 and 203–4.

[1] *Lacrimae Rerum*

Wir können uns ein Bischen sitzen stehen
Mein Kaffee auszutrinken und Dein Wein;
Nacher wir müssen auseinander gehen,
Lass' uns die letze Stunde sturmfrei sein.

Denn jede Liebe hat ihr eigene Lage
Und jeder Art von Liebe denkt an sich;
Weil ich kein Geld hab' komm ich nicht im Frage,
Du liebst dein Leben und ich liebe Dich.

Man wartet auf Dir in den feinen Dielen,
Die Stunde geht vorbei, beeil' Dich nun;
Von Kohlen haben diesen Dicken vielen,
Mein Traum von Dir mit Dir hat nicht zu tun:

Und dass ich traurig bin ist komisch blos;
Es schadet nicht, mit Dir ist gar nichts los.

[Sept. 1930?]

We can sit or stand around a bit / Drink up my coffee and your wine; / Afterwards we must part, / Let's have this last hour to ourselves. // For every love has its own situation / And every sort of love thinks of itself; / Since I've no money there's no question of me, / You love your life and I love you. // They are waiting for you in the fine parlours, / The hour is passing, hurry now; / Of money these fat people have a lot, / My dream of you with you has nothing to do: // And that I'm sad is funny merely; / It does no harm, you are not worth my while.

Lacrimae Rerum

So we can sit and stand around a bit.
I'll drink my coffee and you drink your wine.
Then say goodbye. Let's make the most of it:
An hour of yours that's still an hour of mine.

For every love has its contingency
And puts itself first. Loves of all kinds do.
I've got no money so you'll not want me.
You love your life and what I love is you.

They're waiting for you in the posh places.
Hurry along now or you'll miss your chance.
They are the loaded men, they feed their faces.
My dream of you is an irrelevance.

And if I'm sad that makes you laugh, I know.
But never mind: I'm not your business now.

[2]

Es regnet auf mir in den Schottische Lände
Wo ich mit Dir noch nie gewesen bin
Man redet hier von Kunst am Wochenende
Bin jezt zu Hause, nicht mehr in Berlin

So kommt es immer vor in diesen Sachen
Wir sehen uns nie wieder, hab' dein Ruh:
Du hast kein Schuld und es ist nichts zu machen
Sieh' immer besser aus, und nur wenn Du

Am Bahnhof mit Bekannten triffst, O dann
Als Sonntagsbummelzüge fertig stehen
Und Du einsteigen willst, kuk einmal an
Den Eisenbahnen die dazwischen gehen.

Sonst, wenn ein olle Herr hat Dich gekusst
Geh mit; ich habe nichts bezalt; Du must.

[Sept. 1930]

It is raining on me in the Scottish lands / Where I with you have never yet been / They talk here of art at the weekend / Am now at home, no longer in Berlin // Thus it always happens in these things / We'll never see each other again, peace be with you: / You have no blame and there is nothing to be done / Look better and better, and only when you // On the station meet with acquaintances, oh then / When the little local Sunday trains are standing ready / And you are about to get in, give a glance at least / At the trains which are going between them. // Otherwise, when an old gent has kissed you / Go with him; I haven't paid anything; you must.

It's raining on me in the Scottish lands.
I'm in a place where you have never been.
There's arty conversation at weekends.
I'm home again. I'm not still in Berlin.

But things like this, they always end the same.
We've said 'Auf Wiedersehen' for good, I know.
It can't be helped and you are not to blame.
Don't lose your beauty sleep. I wonder though

On Sundays when you all meet up to catch
Some little local train and you're about
To climb aboard, whether you'll turn and watch
The big transcontinentals pulling out.

But then: go with the gent who's kissing you.
I haven't paid. Do what you have to do.

[3]

Zu sagen Liebe ist es schon zu spät
Denn Du, mein Lieber, bist von Liebe satt
Der arme Junge der kein Verhältnis hat
Und nur als Konpter zwischen Menschen geht;

Der trägt Geschenke blos und unsern Namen
Und kommt zuruck und kann uns nur entfernen
Er kann uns küssen und nicht kennen lernen;
So sind wir nicht allein und nicht zusammen.

Lass' Ihm dann weg. Wir ohne Liebe schenken,
Wir brauchen jezt nicht mehr sein mies Figur,
Wir küssen aber uns zu grüssen nur
Wir sprechen Namen aber nicht zu denken:

Nun dann wir können so zusammen sein
In diesem glauben dass wir sind allein.

[Summer–Autumn 1930]

To say love it is already too late / For you, my love, are sick of love / The poor boy who has no relationship / And only as a transaction ['*Konpter*', *which I have not been able to find in any dictionary, may be a version of 'Konto', an account (such as a bank account), or 'Kunde', a client or customer*] goes between people; // He carries presents merely and our names / And comes back and can only distance us / He can kiss us and not get to know us / So we are not alone and not together. // Let him go away then. We without love give gifts, / We don't need any more now his miserable figure, / We kiss but only to say hello to one another / We speak names but not to think: // Now then we can be so together / In this belief that we are alone.

The time we might have called it love has gone.
You've had as much of love as you can stand.
We use a boy who hasn't any friend
But comes and goes when someone takes him on.

The gifts and names he bears are not his own.
He goes between, and we get more remote
And though he kisses us we keep him out
And we are not together and not alone.

We have no love to give. It's time he went.
There's nothing for us now in his misery.
The kisses we give are a formality.
The names we speak are not the ones we meant.

We cannot be together unless we know
We are alone with nowhere else to go.

[4]

Jezt bin ich faul so wie ein dummes Tier
Ich habe nichts zu tun wo Du nicht bist
Bin fleissig nur als dein Student, nach Dir
Mein einzige Geschäftliche Reise ist.

Früher hab ich von Anderen gesucht
Kein Pfennig hab verdient, war noch allein,
Wenn Du ein Stellung hast, bin ich vernugt
Ein ganz einfacher Arbeiter zu sein.

Mach Spass mit der die reichen sind und klug
Gib mir den schweren Arbeit; zu tragen Mehl,
Zu waschen oder putzen; ist genug
Dass Du befehlst und ich bin zum Befehl.

Weil, wenn Du kukst mir an, dann ist mir wie
Ich König wär ein grosses Industrie.

[Summer–Autumn 1930]

Now I am as lazy as a stupid animal / I have nothing to do when you are not there / Am diligent only as your student, to you / My only business journey is. // Earlier I looked for things from others / Never earned a penny, was still alone, / If you have an employment I'm content / To be a very lowly workman. // Have fun with those who are rich and clever / Give me the heavy work: to carry flour, / To wash or clean; it's enough / That you give orders and I'm at your command. // For when you look at me I feel as though / I were the king of a great industry.

I'm in an idle brute stupidity
For in your absence what is there to do?
I cannot learn unless you tutor me
And all my business dealings are with you.

I've never had to earn a living wage.
Others kept me. I was on my own.
But if you have employment I'll engage
To be your menial without a moan.

Have fun then with the rich and clever crowd.
Give me the heavy work. I'll hump your stuff,
I'll wash and clean for you. If I'm allowed
To do your bidding that will be enough.

For when you look at me you make me feel
I own the Ruhr with all its coal and steel.

[5]

Ich weiss dass Du bist weg, und dass ich finde
Dass dieses Jahreszeit langweilig heisst:
Im Dorf die dofen Bauern machen Kinder,
Der Held auf einem Todfahrt ist verreisst

Weiss aber nicht was jezt dein Körper macht
Warum die Stunden heute bremsen doll;
Weiss aber nicht der Stunde von der Nacht
Das Traum von mir und Dir beginnen soll.

O hab kein Angst der Zeit muss nicht vorbei,
Das Unbestimmt Bestimmt nicht werden muss:
Das schmales Bett, es soll erhalten zwei
Die brauchen nicht zu warten auf ein' kuss

Dann soll ich wissen dass ich bin bei Dir
Und wissen nicht wenn du muss weg von mir.

[Sept. 1930?]

I know that you are away, and that I find / That this time of the year is called boring: / In the village the stupid peasants are fathering children, / The hero on a death-trip has gone away // But don't know what your body is doing now / Why the hours today are slowing down so much / But don't know the hour of the night / The dream of me and you shall begin. // Oh don't be afraid the time must not go by / The uncertain must not become certain: / The narrow bed, it shall receive two / Who do not need to wait for a kiss // Then I shall know that I am with you / And not know when you must go away from me.

I know you've gone. You left me vegetating.
The vacant season bores me worse and worse.
The yokels here are busy copulating.
Our local hero's travelling (in a hearse).

But what your body's doing now I don't know
Nor why the hours are slowing down today
Nor when tonight my dream of you should go
To meet your dream of me somewhere halfway.

Don't be afraid: time won't abandon you
And doubtful things will pass beyond a doubt.
Your narrow bed is wide enough for two.
We'll have the kisses we have done without.

And I shall know that you are with me then
And not know when you'll go away again.

[6] *Chorale*

(*To the Passion Chorale tune*)

Der ist ein schöne Junge
 Er wohnt jezt in Berlin
Wo ich in vier Monaten
 Soll wieder kehren hin.
Er hat kein' schwere Trippe
 Er ist nie nep bei mir
Er hat kein Englisch Onkel
 Er sagt 'Ick bläb bei Dir.'

Er hat zwei nette Eier
 Ein fein Schwanz auch dazu
Wenn wir ins Bett uns liegen
 Dann gibt es da kein Ruh;
Und alle Art von Küssen
 Kann er, und blasen gut
Wenn ich bin weggefahren
 Hab ich geweint von Wut.

O warte nur, mein Junge,
 In England bin ich fromm
Blubber und Geld zu sparen
 Bestimmt ich wieder komm.

[Aug.–Sept. 1930]

He is a lovely boy / He lives now in Berlin / Where I in four months / Am to go back again. / He's got no serious VD / He's never over-pricey with me / He has no English uncle / He says 'I'll stay with you.' // He has two nice balls / A nice cock too / When we get into bed / Then there's no peace and quiet there / And all sorts of kissing / He's good at, and good at sucking / When I went away / I wept with rage. // Just wait, my boy, / In England I'm well behaved / To save blubber and money / Certainly I'll come again.

Chorale

(To the Passion Chorale tune)

Oh he's a lovely laddie
  His home is in Berlin
Another four months here and
  I'll be back there again.
His clap is nothing serious
  He never rips me off
He's got no English uncle
  He tells me I'm enough.

The balls on him are beauties
  His cock's a beauty too
When we're in bed together
  We find plenty to do;
At kissing and at sucking
  I give him alpha plus
And when it came to parting
  I made an awful fuss.

It won't be long, my darling,
  In England I go straight
I save my spunk and money
  Then I'll be back: you wait!

Auden's 'Writing' Essay

EDITED BY KATHERINE BUCKNELL WITH
A FOREWORD BY NAOMI MITCHISON

Editor's Introduction

'WRITING, or the Pattern Between People' was composed during the first three months of 1932 at the request of Naomi Mitchison. She included it in her children's guide to the modern world, *An Outline for Boys and Girls and Their Parents*, published by Victor Gollancz the same year.[1] The essay endeavours to describe, for a readership of school-children, the nature and origin of language and the forms in which it is spoken, written, and read. Auden's original manuscript, entitled 'Writing' and printed here for the first time, was altered for publication perhaps more than any other essay he ever wrote.

The original version of 'Writing' sheds fresh light on the nature and origin of Auden's ideas as well as on his personal outlook at the time. It also illuminates his subsequent development, since many of the themes first addressed in 'Writing' were to be taken up again, and in some instances dealt with quite differently, in later essays. 'Writing' was first made prominent by Edward Mendelson, who called it 'a manifesto of [Auden's] private ideology';[2] however, the manuscript version of the essay helps to make clear that the 'ideology' is not nearly so systematic as the word implies and that it is mostly borrowed—from I. A. Richards and Gerald Heard, with a smattering of T. S. Eliot, Freud, and others. This doesn't mean that Auden did not believe what he wrote in the essay: on the contrary, the influence of Richards, Heard, and some of the others was profound and enduring in part because Auden discovered in their work ideas with which he agreed or which seemed to offer resolutions to problems with which he was already struggling on his own.

'Writing' is centrally concerned with the relation between the writer and the society in which he lives, and it marks the birth in Auden of a self-conscious desire to communicate with his audience. After the

---

[1] (London).   [2] *Early Auden*, 15.

obscurity of *The Orators* (completed late in 1931), Auden now wished to be understood, perhaps remembered, and even loved by his readers. Some of the reasons for this were personal; indeed the essay itself is in many ways remarkably personal. By the time he returned from Germany in 1929, Auden had broken off his engagement with Sheilah Richardson and he had given up hope of eventually making a conventional heterosexual marriage. For a time he was equally pessimistic about romantic relationships with men. His poems from this period are obsessed with loneliness, solitude, and absence. Towards the end of 1931 his mood began to change, partly due to the 'therapeutic' effect of writing *The Orators*,[3] and partly due to the start of a new love affair.[4] In the months that followed, Auden began to look for emotional sustenance less in private, sexual relations and more in public, social ones; he came to believe, under the influence of Gerald Heard, that some kind of group life would best satisfy him. 'Writing' was commissioned for an audience of schoolchildren, and it is no accident that this released in Auden a new kind of communicative ease, for a school was the community to which, at the time, Auden belonged. 'The simple sentences and homely style' Edward Mendelson has described[5] came to Auden because he was speaking to the members of the kind of society in which he was living from day to day.

In the manuscript of 'Writing', the section entitled 'History of literature' begins with the statement that 'A book is the child of a marriage between a writer and the group or society in which he lives.' This does not appear in the published essay, but the word 'marriage' is one key to the desires behind 'Writing'. As a poet, Auden wished to forge a permanent, intimate relation with the society in which he lived. In later essays, he was to use a similar image of the family, but in a different way. In 1948 he wrote: 'The poet is the father who begets the poem which the language bears',[6] and then in 1962 (in another essay also called 'Writing'): 'The poet is the father of his poem; its mother is a language: one could list poems as race horses are listed—*out of L by P*.'[7] These formulations make clear that his focus was eventually to shift away from the human beings that make up society to a more abstract spouse, words themselves (and, interestingly, the idea of marriage was to

[3] In the 1966 'Foreword' to O^3 (L), Auden said that his 'unconscious motive' in writing the work had been 'therapeutic', 8.

[4] Carpenter, 123, 131.   [5] *Early Auden*, 15.

[6] 'Squares and Oblongs', *Poets at Work: Essays Based on the Modern Poetry Collection at the Lockwood Memorial Library, University of Buffalo* (New York), 172.

[7] *DH* 22.

give way to the biological relationship). Although 'Writing' concludes without any clear sense of how to bring about in the contemporary world the ideal relation between writer and society, and the good writing that should result from this relation, the poems that began to appear shortly after the essay was completed express a sense of great optimism. Auden was launching upon the most popularly successful and perhaps happiest phase of his career.

A comparison of the manuscript printed here with the essay that was published in *An Outline for Boys and Girls and Their Parents* reveals minor changes in phrasing (mostly for brevity or clarity), the loss of a few examples and amplifications, the addition of one paragraph to the section on 'Verse Form', and the addition of four cross-references to other essays in the volume (two of these were to Gerald Heard's contribution to the *Outline*, entitled 'The History of Ideas or How We Got Separate'). Also, a list of 'Books to Read' was appended at the end of the published essay (as at the end of almost all the essays in the *Outline*), which included I. A. Richards's *Science and Poetry* but not his *Practical Criticism* from which Auden borrowed more directly.[8] A few apparent mistakes were made in transcribing Auden's manuscript for the 1932 book; these mostly affect scattered individual words, but a notable error occurs at the opening of the section entitled 'Meaning' where, in the published version of the essay, the first paragraph was wrongly included at the end of the preceding section, 'Speech'.

Most important among the differences between the two versions of the essay, three substantial passages were cut from Auden's manuscript and a fourth entirely rewritten. No evidence survives to suggest that Auden made any of these changes himself. His letters to Mrs Mitchison during this period *could* refer to successive drafts of his piece: in January 1932 he wrote, 'I have actually started your article', then in March, 'Here is the article. I hope over and done with for good', *perhaps* implying that he had been made to rework it.[9] But no intermediate draft of the essay is known to exist. Mrs Mitchison recalls that 'the "Books to Read" were his idea'[10] (among them is a favourite book of poetry from adolescence, de la Mare's *Come Hither*), but if Auden ever wrote out the

---

[8] Neither cross-references nor reading list appear with the essay as reprinted in *EA* 303–12. Cross-references are described below in my footnotes to the manuscript. 'Books to Read' were listed as: 'P. H. B. Lyon, *The Discovery of Poetry*; T. Warner, *On the Writing of English*; W. de la Mare, *Come Hither*; A. Quiller-Couch, *The Art of Writing*, L. A. G. Strong, *Common Sense about Poetry*, I. A. Richards, *Science and Poetry*', 868.

[9] ALS both from Larchfield Academy, Helensburgh, Scotland (Berg).

[10] Letter to me, 28 Oct. 1988.

list for her, it has apparently not survived. Perhaps any revisions he might have made were lost with such a list; on the whole, though, it seems more likely that Mrs Mitchison made the changes herself, the rewriting as well as, most definitely, the cutting. She notes that 'In my copy I head this chapter "slight re-write". I couldn't leave a lot of the really depressing parts.'[11] Still, she is certain that although Auden may not have made the revisions himself, he had an opportunity to reject them:

If any bits were taken away or added to any of the articles in the book, it was always in consultation and usually written by the author . . . We all discussed things a good deal, but I think Auden was not in London at this time. But everyone had proofs and no doubt spotted things they didn't like.[12]

The first of the substantial passages to be cut from the 'Writing' manuscript appears in the opening section, 'Speech'. It presents a conversation between a man and a girl on a train which is ostensibly about the weather but which, the passage argues, is really about the possibility of becoming friends, maybe even lovers. The passage begins: 'Self conscious as we are, much of our speech is like a tunnel under which the currents of feeling can pass unseen.' It goes on to dramatize the way in which speech attempts to communicate feelings even as it veils them, and it exemplifies the recurring theme of 'Writing', that language tries to bridge an emotional gap between isolated individuals.

A second substantial passage was cut from the section entitled 'Different kinds of writing'. It makes a distinction by their use between writing as literature—a work of art—and other kinds of writing. Literature is read only for its own sake, 'as a single act, confined to the reading and understanding of the writing itself'; it has no relation to the processes of life, and no further purpose. Though he concedes that, according to this distinction, an absolutely pure work of literature does not exist, Auden makes no attempt to reconcile the claims of this passage with the overriding implication of his essay that all writing, including literature, serves an emotional purpose in trying to unite isolated individuals. Interestingly, the absoluteness of this distinction between art and other kinds of writing looks forward to Auden's later view that 'All art is gratuitous'.[13]

---

[11] In an abandoned draft of her 'Foreword' (in my possession).
[12] Letter to me, 28 Oct. 1988.
[13] *SW* 62. Auden also said the same thing less definitely in 'Squares and Oblongs' twenty years before *SW*: 'In my opinion, the public is partially right . . . in thinking that the writing of art is gratuitous', 166.

A third passage was cut from the section entitled 'Why people read books'. Here Auden explains how metaphor works and why it is different from untruth. The passage borrows directly from *Practical Criticism*, conflating Richards's arguments about metaphor with his arguments about doctrine in poetry. Auden writes:

For example if a friend says 'So and so is a swine.' We don't say 'Thats absurd. He is a man so he cant be a pig'. We know perfectly well he means that he has the same feelings of disgust towards so and so as he [would] feel towards swine.

This example is taken from Richards's definition of metaphor:

A metaphor is a shift, a carrying over of a word from its normal use to its new use . . . If you call a man a swine, for example, it may be because his features resemble those of a pig, but it may be because you have towards him something of the feeling you conventionally have towards pigs, or because you propose, if possible, to excite those feelings.[14]

Auden goes on to cite (inaccurately) some lines from 'The Rime of the Ancient Mariner' which are the very lines that Richards uses later in his argument to demonstrate the problem of belief which arises when supernatural machinery is introduced into poetry.[15]

The problem of belief in poetry troubled Auden throughout his career. He was greatly attracted to the distinction put forward by Richards in *Science and Poetry* between a 'statement' and a 'pseudo-statement', but he was never fully at ease with it. (Auden first read *Science and Poetry* at Oxford, probably at the suggestion of Christopher Isherwood who as a Cambridge undergraduate attended Richards's lectures with Edward Upward.) In Richards's definition 'a pseudo-statement . . . is justified entirely by its effect in relieving or organizing our impulses and attitudes' while 'a statement . . . is justified by its truth'.[16] Richards argued that 'it is not the poet's business to make true statements'.[17] Rather, he urged that we must

cut our pseudo-statements free from belief, and yet retain them, in this released state, as the main instruments by which we order our attitudes to one another and to the world . . . poetry conclusively shows that even the most important among our attitudes can be aroused and maintained without any belief entering in at all . . .[18]

---

[14] *Practical Criticism: A Study of Literary Judgement* (London, 1929), 221–2.
[15] See ibid. 272.
[16] *Science and Poetry* (London, 1926), 59.
[17] Ibid. 56.   [18] Ibid. 61.

By this argument, Richards made lies in poetry not merely acceptable but necessary; we know they are lies, but lies can satisfy a need that makes us turn to poetry. But Richards was really describing the effect of lies, or pseudo-statements, on the reader; Auden was eventually to see them as a grave danger to the poet. The poet, far more than the reader, must give himself up emotionally to the lie in order to write his poem. For Auden this meant taking the lie seriously. In his 1962 essay, 'Writing', he put the danger clearly:

What makes it difficult for a poet not to tell lies is that, in poetry, all facts and all beliefs cease to be true or false and become interesting possibilities. The reader does not have to share the beliefs expressed in a poem in order to enjoy it. Knowing this, a poet is constantly tempted to make use of an idea or a belief, not because he believes it to be true, but because he sees it has interesting poetic possibilities. It may not, perhaps, be absolutely necessary that he *believe* it, but it is certainly necessary that his emotions be deeply involved, and this they can never be unless, as a man, he takes it more seriously than as a mere poetic convenience.[19]

Auden's preoccupation with the problem of belief took varying forms throughout his career. It probably accounts in part for his ambivalence towards Yeats, whom he emulated and criticized by turns. And it was a major reason for his controversial revisions to his own early work. In his 1965 'Foreword' to *Collected Shorter Poems 1927–57* he said that he had omitted some poems 'because they were dishonest', explaining that 'A dishonest poem is one which expresses, no matter how well, feelings or beliefs which its author never felt or entertained.'[20] It is hardly surprising that in his 1932 'Writing' essay he failed to deal conclusively with this difficult theme; in any case, the passage introducing it was dropped. But other manuscript passages based on the theories of Richards were retained in the published essay. The account of 'Meaning', with its division into four kinds—'Sense', 'Feeling', 'Tone', 'Intention'—is taken from Richards's chapter in *Practical Criticism* on 'The Four Kinds of Meaning' (in some instances even the examples and the phrasing are from Richards).[21] And the first three paragraphs of 'Writing', which remained virtually unchanged in the published essay, draw on Appendix A of *Practical Criticism*, 'Further Notes on Meaning'. Also, Auden's assertion in the second paragraph that 'the earliest use of language was . . . to express the feelings of the speaker' derives from Richards's

[19] *DH* 19.   [20] (London, 1966; New York, 1967), repr. in *CP76* 15.
[21] See *Practical Criticism*, 179 ff.

statement that 'Originally language may have been almost purely *emotive*'.[22]
But this is an idea which Auden himself reiterates in other forms
throughout the essay and which seems to have been entirely in harmony
with his own convictions at the time. To a certain extent, the network of
borrowings from Richards suggests the way in which Auden, when he
encountered a useful idea, somewhat indiscriminately took up other
ideas attached to it, for instance Richards's teaching on metaphor and
belief, and became entangled in theories that he would only eventually
recognize as unacceptable to him. In 1947 he told Alan Ansen that he
still thought *Practical Criticism* an important book, reportedly saying: 'I
know it can be very misleading, but it does ask the right questions even if
it comes up with the wrong answers. It makes one think about what
actually does happen when you read a poem, which people hadn't
thought about before.'[23]

The most significant difference between the manuscript and
published versions of 'Writing' comes at the end where, in the
manuscript, there is a long passage entitled 'History of literature'
followed by a 'Summary' of the whole essay. These are combined in
the published essay into a single two-paragraph section with the title
'Books and Life'. The central idea of the published version of this
passage is that good writing emerges from a society that is small and
unified in its interests but that contemporary society is stratified and
fragmented so that literature has turned in on itself and away from real
life. This idea, probably derived from T. S. Eliot's 1929 essay, 'Dante'
(where, incidentally, Eliot discussed in a 'Note to Section II' some of
the similarities and differences between Richards's theory of poetic
belief and his own),[24] is carved out boldly from the much longer
manuscript version and has the memorableness that comes with
concision. But many revealing sentences are dropped and Auden's
historical account of the way literature has arrived at its present pass is
lost. The manuscript version is not thoroughly worked out (the city-
state, for example, does not fit into the historical evolution and has to
be presented on one side as a special example), but it is apparently the
germ for the more fully developed history of literature that was to
appear in Auden's 1938 Introduction to *The Oxford Book of Light Verse*.

[22] Ibid. 353.
[23] Ansen, *The Table-Talk of W. H. Auden*, ed. Nicholas Jenkins (New York, 1989), 44.
[24] (London), repr. in *Selected Essays*, 3rd edn. (London, 1951), 237–77. 'Note', 269–
71. Auden apparently knew the essay well. Years later he described it to Ansen, referring
in particular to the part that mentions Richards (see *Table-Talk*, 53).

There, as in 'Writing', it again served as the basis of an attempt to analyse the relation between artist and society.

In later years, Auden was to back away from this difficult task of analysis, regarding the relation as something of a mystery. In a sense, this was the natural extension of the distinction he tried out in the 'Writing' manuscript, but then put aside for many years, between art and the processes of life. In the 1932 manuscript Auden called the relation between artist and group or society a 'marriage' whose progeny was books, and he went on to say that 'Books provide a kind of a history of society'; by 1968 he was to have adopted an emphatic and carefully qualified ambivalence:

All art is gratuitous, so that one can never say that a certain kind of society must necessarily produce a certain kind of art. On the other hand, when we consider a certain society and the literature which it actually did produce, we can sometimes see reasons why it was possible for such a society to produce it.[25]

His 1969 poem 'Pseudo-Questions', whose title raises again the issues associated with Richards's doctrine of the 'pseudo-statement', suggests that it is a mistake even to address the question of the relation between '*Art and Society*'.[26]

The final sections of the 1932 manuscript also illuminate links between 'Writing' and Auden's other work of the period, as well as shedding further light on the way in which he responded to his reading. For instance, his suggestion that heroic literature was produced by a bachelor group devoted to a leader looks back to the heroic band and leader at the centre of *The Orators* and, like *The Orators*, owes much to Auden's reading during his time in Berlin of Freud's *Totem and Taboo* (1913) and *Group Psychology and the Analysis of the Ego* (1921).[27] Also, the abandoned 'Summary' in particular highlights Auden's fascination during this period with the ideas of Gerald Heard. Its opening sentence, 'Man writes and reads because he is lonely and wants to be re-united with a group', alludes to Heard's theory that individual human consciousness evolved from a primitive group consciousness. In his *Social Substance of Religion: An Essay on the Evolution of Religion*, Heard argued that primitive man had lived and thought as a member of a small, closely

---

[25] *SW* 62.
[26] *CP76* 634.
[27] Auden probably read the English translations of these works which first appeared in Britain in 1919 (London, trans. A. A. Brill) and in 1922 (London, trans. James Strachey) respectively.

united group.[28] The emergence of the self-conscious individual had fragmented the group, and Heard theorized that religion was man's institutionalized attempt to recapture the feeling he had once experienced within it. In his 'Summary' Auden hints that language endeavours to play a similar role, and, although he despairs of its success, this is indeed a central theme of his essay.

Near the start of 'Writing', in a passage that was retained essentially unchanged in the published essay, Auden describes a moment in human history when 'man became self-conscious, he began to feel, I am I, and You are Not-I; we are shut inside ourselves and apart from each other.' This new self-conscious man still remembered the time when he had been part of a group and had felt at one with the world around him. Auden argues that language originated with man's attempt, by making noises once made by the group together, to recapture the feeling of oneness:

Before he had lost it, when he [was] doing things together in a group, such [as] hunting; when feeling was strongest, as when, say, the quarry was first sighted, the group had made noises, grunts, howls, grimaces. Noise and this feeling he had now lost had gone together; then if he made the noise, could he not recover the feeling? In some way like this language began . . .

This original scene—of a group of primitive men making noises and sharing a feeling while hunting together for food—derives from Heard's description of the powerful group emotions from which religion began. Drawing on contemporary accounts of the behaviour of the Great Apes, Heard imagined a 'proto-human circle that thrilled, gesticulated, grunted and hopped, while the leaders effected some common purpose'. For Heard's proto-human circle, the energy of concentration produced a special kind of emotional unity. Most often the experience began with a food-getting effort (as in Auden's hunting scene), but soon the feeling of unity was sought after for its own sake:

When with one mind in one place they approached food (they must have felt the same unity as they gathered snarling out behind their protagonists when attacked, but that situation must have been rarer than a food unity even in man's most troubled times), they would have had a sense of communion. For this emotional experience, this revivifying of the community sense, they must have begun to value as an end in itself, and the food must have become increasingly an occasion rather than a cause.[29]

[28] See also *The Ascent of Humanity: An Essay on the Evolution of Civilization from Group Consciousness through Individuality to Super-Consciousness* (London, 1929).
[29] *Social Substance of Religion: An Essay on the Evolution of Religion* (London, 1931), 89–90.

The focus upon food in Heard's argument, and in Auden's, is important because Heard placed hunger as an instinct at the centre of his theory of the primal group. This was in deliberate contrast to Freud's emphasis upon the sexual instinct. Heard took issue with Freud's belief, shared in various forms by Bronislaw Malinowski and other anthropologists, that group life had evolved from family life. Instead, he insisted that group life was equally primitive; moreover he argued that the group was a more stable unit on which to found a society. In Heard's view, the family, based on parental domination and filial subservience, could only provoke social revolution. He took issue in particular with Freud's *Totem and Taboo* because it suggested that culture originated in a sexual dispute between father and sons. The behaviour of the Great Apes, Heard argued, showed that food, companionship, and the group were more important than sex. Heard theorized that group life had failed not only as a result of the emergence of the self-conscious individual but also for economic reasons. In order to survive, the group had grown larger, and it had ceased to provide emotional sustenance to its members. Furthermore, it had come into competition with the family, which drained off devotion due to the group. All of these ideas are reflected in the loosely formulated observation of Auden's 'Summary' that contemporary social conditions make it impossible for a group to exist of the right size to nurture literature:

The larger the group the harder to unite it and the cruder the feelings which do. But it is impossible for people now to exist in small groups *only*. Like the city state such groups cannot earn the money to live; they become competitive and unequal like the family.

For Auden, steeped in the theories of Freud and convinced that the relations among the members of his own family were a primary cause of his psychological ills, Heard's must have seemed a liberating mythology. It ended the necessity of trying to find happiness in conventional family life, holding out group life not just as an alternative to it, but as something better. Moreover, it said that sexual relations, the source for Auden of much unhappiness, were not centrally important. Indeed, Auden was so attracted to Heard's theory of the primitive group mind that he overlooked some convincing arguments against it. In *Sex and Repression in Savage Society*, which Auden read in the late twenties, Malinowski insisted that more careful observation of primitive societies 'will rule out from sociology such words as "group intinct", "consciousness of kind", "group mind", and similar verbal panaceas'.[30] Nevertheless, in the opening section of 'Writing' Auden invokes a story told by W. H. R. Rivers about a group of Melanesians setting out in a boat without having to discuss who should take which oar and who steer; Rivers had offered this story as proof of the existence of group communication among primitive people. For Malinowski such behaviour would be explained by custom: the men were simply doing what they saw done around them and what had always been done in the past.[31] Malinowski believed there was a high level of individualism amongst the Melanesians which was not initially apparent to Western observers, and he wished to explode what he regarded as the myth promulgated by Rivers of the group mind.[32] Although Heard tried, at the start of *Social Substance of Religion*, to distinguish his conception of the group mind from the one criticized by Malinowski, he was not entirely persuasive. Still, Auden borrowed what he found useful at the time and, as with the theories of Richards, this meant that he took on board some ideas that might not have withstood his careful, long-term scrutiny.

In a section of the 'Writing' essay itself entitled 'Writing', Auden theorizes that not only spoken language but also written language originated with man's sense of separation from the primal group. In the second paragraph of this section he asserts: 'The urge to write like the urge to speak came from man's growing sense of personal loneliness, of the need for group communication.' This section (only one paragraph was altered for publication) goes on to describe 'Primitive people, living in small groups' who had a strong sense of 'the life of the tribe'. As in Heard's account of prehistoric man, the rupture in the group experience coincides with the emergence of individual self-consciousness; this in turn leads to a new awareness of individual mortality. Man 'loses this sense of the continuously present group life', and so he turns to writing to prolong his own individual life: 'he wishes to live forever'. Finally, Auden goes on to suggest that, like speech and writing, even poetry itself emerges from the excitement of the primal group. He begins his section on 'Verse Form' with a description of group excitement increasing until it becomes the measured movements of a dance:

---

[30] (London, 1927), 239.
[31] See for instance *Argonauts of the Western Pacific: An Account of Native Enterprise and Adventures in the Archipelagoes of Melanesian New Guinea* (London, 1922), 327.
[32] See for instance *Crime and Custom in Savage Society* (London, 1926), 48–9.

Speech originated in noises made during group excitement. Excitement seems naturally to excite movement. When we are excited we want to dance about. Noise was thus in the beginning associated with movements of a group, perhaps dancing round food or advancing together to attack. The greater the excitement, the more in sympathy with each other each member of the group is, the more regular the movements; they keep time with each other; every foot comes down together.

Again imagine a circle of people dancing; the circle revolves and comes back to its starting place; at each revolution the set of movements is repeated.

The passage recalls Heard's 'proto-human' group which had also moved in a circle. And Heard had described just such a ritual dance evolving from their excitement and then being prolonged for its own sake:

the addition of rhythm permits the performers to keep up their practice longer. Instead of the surrounding group straining and grunting in sympathy, and with attention riveted while the one or the few are actually engaged in 'getting there', now once they are all 'in time', and in step everyone can sink into the rhythm which expresses urgency, but which also, because it can keep the urgency up, has a momentum of its own, carries along the congregation with it. This is an important change. Owing to this, they are able to go on chanting and gesticulating when the leaders are no longer immediately striving to achieve an object just out of reach. The rhythm will thus end by becoming itself an end. The group will find that it enjoys ritual for its own sake . . .[33]

In 'Verse Form' Auden compares the 'circle of people dancing' to verse: 'When words move in this kind of repeated pattern, we call the effect of the movement in our minds the metre. Words arranged in metre are verse.' He goes on to say that the excitement of the poet as he is writing gives the pattern to the words which the excitement of the primal group once gave to the dance:

When a poet is writing verse, the feeling as it were excites the words and makes them fall into a definite group going through definite dancing movements, just as feeling excite[s] the different members of a crowd and makes them act together.

The myth which Auden discovered in Heard's work of the primal group and the ritual dance made its way also into Auden's poetry. In April 1932, not long after he completed 'Writing', Auden wrote a poem, beginning 'The chimneys are smoking', which evokes the feelings of a happy love affair (probably the one he had begun in the

---

[33] *Social Substance of Religion*, 91.

previous autumn). The poem calls the lovers 'the belovèd group' even though they are only two, and its final stanza elaborates upon the imagery of the dance to suggest the way in which the lovers' joy participates in a universal 'wish to be one':

> Then dance, the boatmen, virgins, camera-men, and us
> Round goal-post, wind-gauge, pylon, or bobbing buoy;
> For our joy abounding is, though it hide underground,
>   As insect or camouflaged cruiser
>   For fear of death sham dead,
>   Is quick, is real, is quick to answer
>   The bird-like sucking tread
>   Of the quick dancer.[34]

A month later in the poem beginning 'O Love, the interest itself in thoughtless Heaven', the emotional intensity represented by the universal group dance is called by a simpler, more familiar name, love, and Auden expands his hopes for the benefit of its power beyond the 'belovèd group' outward over the whole community of England. Like the 'Summary' of the 'Writing' manuscript, the poem calls for a return to a 'simpler' emotional condition. It asks 'Love' to enliven man's thoughts in the same way that natural joy creates a pattern in the movement of a group of starlings; the 'bird-like' tread of the earlier poem's dancer is now transformed into flight:

> O Love, the interest itself in thoughtless Heaven,
> Make simpler daily the beating of man's heart; within,
> There in the ring where name and image meet,
>
> Inspire them with such a longing as will make his thought
> Alive like patterns a murmuration of starlings
> Rising in joy over wolds unwittingly weave . . .[35]

Since Heard believed religion was man's attempt to recapture the unity of the primal group, and since Auden felt language could play a similar role, it is suggestive that the poem takes the form of a prayer. Indeed, the original 'Writing' manuscript has a surprising religious dimension. Auden's 'History of literature' looks back to medieval Europe as a society united by the Catholic Church, much in the way he wished contemporary society were united. Then, members of different nations shared a universal language, Latin, and members of different classes could speak as freely across class boundaries as do, for

---

[34] *EA* 116–18.   [35] *EA* 118–19.

example, the pilgrims in Chaucer's *The Canterbury Tales*. In his
'Summary' Auden observed that contemporary society needed a
similar unifying force: 'We shall do absolutely nothing without some
sort of faith either religious like Catholicism or political like
Communism.' These and two other mentions of Christ and the
Church (in the section 'Spoken and Written language') were cut from
the published essay, and in the new final section 'Books and Life', the
medieval Church was described as 'the universal religious State'[36] a
phrase perhaps worthy of a truer leftist than Auden. Mrs Mitchison's
views on the Church, then and now, are much more pronouncedly
against it than Auden's, and these changes in his manuscript probably
reflect her position more than his. In fact, when the *Outline* was
published, a group of churchmen and educators nominally led by the
Archbishop of York and the Bishop of Durham protested its overall
failure to mention Christ and its apparent endorsement of Bolshevism;
many adverse reviews focused on the same issues. Auden wrote to Mrs
Mitchison, 'The Outline raised the wind. I agree with the Bishops that
Xrist should not have been omitted. Why not attacked.'[37] But this
seems like false enthusiasm calculated to impress a senior correspondent with his willingness to outrage authority and his nonchalance
toward the outcry against the book on which they had both worked. In
any case, Eliot's ideas about the benefits to literature of a Europe
united by religious faith and a common language appealed to Auden at
this time, as did, more particularly, the group unity associated in
Heard's work with the primitive Christian church.

Certainly Heard was not promulgating Christianity, but he did
attribute to the early Christians a brief revival of the genuine group
feeling. In that context Heard, like Auden in the poem beginning 'O
Love, the interest itself . . .' gave the feeling its familiar name, love. He
argued that there was 'at the core of the Gospel a love so intense that it
is more than self-forgetful, it is more even than self-destructive, it
takes the self and expands it over a whole community'.[38] Heard argued
that this love among the early Christians was generated by the ritual of
a communal meal, the agape, shared by a group of an ideal small size:

It began with a real meal. Food, as the nucleus of the group, is therefore
retained. After the feast there was singing. Rhythm is added, as we have seen it

[36] *EA* 311.
[37] ALS from the Downs School, Colwall, 10 Oct. 1932 (Berg). See Mrs Mitchison's
'Foreword' and my Endnote for the attack on the *Outline*, led by Arnold Lunn.
[38] *Social Substance of Religion*, 209.

was added to the food interest in the building up of religion. The Primitive Church in its dynamic rite is recapitulating the history of religion's evolution. The small group of about a dozen lent over the cushion of the pulvinus, or sigma, and so formed an inward-looking group—perhaps a ring. There was a great cry of Sursum Corda (probably the oldest part of the Eucharist). It was the outbreak of exultation as the worshippers realised they were in the formed psychic field. Then there was the kiss of peace, the manifestation of psychophysical tenderness, the love that is an intensity of serenity.[39]

Heard went on to describe the outburst of spiritual exercises following the agape when 'inspired persons began to speak', transporting the whole congregation; finally, in a third phase, 'the whole culminates in the ecstatic dance'.[40]

The experience evoked in Auden's June 1933 poem beginning 'Out on the lawn I lie in bed', and which he referred to years later as a 'Vision of Agape',[41] was partly modelled on Heard's description of the experience of the early Christians. Heard's emphasis on equality among the small, closely united group (in contrast to the unequal relations of the family) and the image of the ring (looking back from the agape to the proto-human circle of dancers) are preserved in the lines:

> Equal with colleagues in a ring
> I sit on each calm evening,
> Enchanted . . .

The love described in the poem expands the self, like the love Heard described at the centre of the Gospel, over a whole community, 'North and South and East and West'. In addition, the moon that 'climbs the European sky'[42] may recall Heard's theory that at primitive religious feasts, the rise of the moon signalled an end to the monthly vigil of self-denial and anticipation and the release of pent-up energies in group enthusiasm.[43] Even the dedication to Geoffrey Hoyland, headmaster of the Quaker Downs School where Auden was teaching when he wrote the poem, points to Heard's work. Heard argued that the seventeenth-century Quakers, when their movement was still new, had briefly revitalized the spirit of the first Christians. The charged meditative silence shared by the Quakers at their Meeting for Worship had, in Heard's view, recaptured the feeling of unity of the primitive group.[44]

[39] Ibid. 213–14.   [40] Ibid. 214, 217.
[41] See the 'Introduction' to Anne Fremantle, ed., *The Protestant Mystics* (1964), repr. in *FA* 69 ff.
[42] *EA* 136–7.
[43] See *Social Substance of Religion*, 115–16.   [44] See ibid. 303.

And, in fact, Heard himself apparently visited Auden at the Downs around the time the poem was written, or perhaps shortly afterwards. In a letter to Stephen Spender, probably written in late June 1933, Auden mentioned that, 'Gerald is coming to morrow to talk to the boys', which suggests just how closely in touch with Heard he was at the time.[45]

Auden's vision of agape was in a sense both sought after and prepared for. It found its form, actually and poetically, in Heard's mythology of the group because this mythology satisfied poetic and personal needs which Auden had had for some time. The poem beginning 'Out on the lawn' reformulates some of the themes first addressed in 'Writing' over a year earlier, and makes Auden's hopes for the future clearer and more ambitious. The lost unity of the primal group is recaptured in the poem's ring of colleagues, although language plays no role in this; now language takes on a larger social task. In the form of the poem, it attempts to bridge the broader gap between the small group of colleagues and 'The gathering multitudes outside'.[46] At the end of 'Writing' Auden was uncertain how to achieve a community that might nurture and be nurtured by good writing. In 'Out on the lawn', a 'creepered wall' continues to divide the poet from the larger society in which he lives, and, although the poem's final stanzas seem more confident that the wide-reaching changes called for in the 'Summary' of 'Writing' will soon come about, in fact it is only Auden's writing that has progressed, not the world. His poetry is now able more clearly to articulate the nature of the change that he longs for, but this does not guarantee an answering real change in society. Later this was to lead to a different kind of change, a change in Auden's attitude toward the task of writing, that turned him gradually toward a stricter separation between poetry and the world.

A Note on the Manuscript and the Text

The 'Writing' manuscript is in Special Collections, Edinburgh University Library (Gen. 2122/13). It consists of nine sheets, one used as a title-

---

[45] ALS from the Downs School, Colwall, dated only 'Monday' (Berg). Nicholas Jenkins places it not before 14 June 1933, and possibly as late as July. See his 'Eleven Letters from Auden to Stephen Spender', Letter 2, in this volume. Whether Heard played any direct role as catalyst to Auden's vision cannot be argued, however tempting, since the dates of the vision, Heard's visit, and the composition of the poem cannot be fixed precisely. Mendelson observes that 'The astrological and meteorological details in the poem are consistent with those recorded for 7 June 1933 and a day or two before and after' (*Early Auden*, 161), which would make Heard's visit, probably, after the vision.

[46] *EA* 137.

page, of cream-coloured paper, foolscap size (8″ × 13″, 20.3 × 33 cm.), wide-ruled with a margin at the left. The sheets are densely written in blue-black ink on both sides of the paper starting on folio 2^r and finishing on folio 9^r. There are occasional insertions and deletions and a few ink blots and smudges. After the title-page, the sheets are numbered in Auden's hand on the recto only, but counting each side as one. Thus the number '1' appears on folio 2^r, the number '3' on folio 3^r, the number '5' on folio 4^r, and so forth. However, this odd-number sequence is interrupted on folio 8^r where Auden has written the number '12' instead of '13'. After this, the number '14' appears on folio 9^r. Despite the misnumbering, the manuscript does not appear to be missing any pages.

Some question marks have been pencilled in the margins alongside corresponding underlinings in the text; these were apparently not made by Auden (see Mrs Mitchison's 'Foreword' and n. 4). The obscurity of Auden's handwriting at these junctures suggests a reader who found some words illegible. In one or two instances, the queried words or phrases were cut from the published essay. There are also two parallel lines in the margin beside the conversation between a man and a girl on a train, which was dropped.

Since we already have an edited version of 'Writing', I have tried in transcribing the manuscript to retain the feel of Auden's draft. I have not regularized spelling, punctuation, or capitalization, and I have not normalized idiosyncrasies except in the very few instances where they might prove confusing. Any such emendations are indicated by square brackets. Quotations and parentheses are silently closed, and single quotations and round brackets are used uniformly although Auden erratically introduced double quotes and square brackets as well. Under-linings are rendered in italics. Also, I have indented wherever Auden clearly intended to start a new paragraph, except for those paragraphs which open a new section of the manuscript and require no further demarcation. All other changes and additions are indicated by square brackets, with a few exceptions discussed below. Uncertain readings are also indicated by square brackets and preceded by a question mark.

This transcript does not attempt to show everything that the manuscript shows, for example, Auden's interlineations or revisions. Frequently when Auden made a change, he did not complete it, although it is usually clear from the manuscript what he intended. For instance, in the section called 'Speech', he wrote 'We are not in the group'; then, in changing it to 'We are outside the group', he crossed out 'not' and left 'in', so that the manuscript actually says 'We are outside in the group'. I have emended this and a very small number of similar cases without using square brackets which would be more clumsy than helpful. In another instance, Auden indicated in the manuscript that the section on 'Verse Form', which he wrote out after the section on 'Different Kinds of Writing', was to be inserted in front of it. I have silently followed his instructions; accordingly, where in the section on 'Different Kinds of Writing' he refers to a distinction made in the section on 'Verse Form' saying 'See below', I have altered this to 'See [above]'. I have dealt with other insertions in the same way.

Wystan Before Editing

NAOMI MITCHISON

I LOOK again on what Wystan wrote and what I as editor published in *An Outline for Boys and Girls and Their Parents*. That was in 1932, a long time ago, and I had rather a fight to get this scarcely well-known young writer accepted as the author of the piece about writing in the section which I called 'Values' rather than 'Arts'. The other authors in this section were, so to speak, grown-ups, men and women already with a considerable reputation. Wystan was only just acquiring a reputation and a following and was at the moment teaching in Helensburgh.

All the contributors were given a word limit. Few kept to it. I had a very difficult job, trying to control my flock, and of course made some mistakes. But I was very determined to publish something which could be gulped down fairly easily by my young audience. This *Outline* was one of Victor Gollancz's great ideas, to get what was going on in the world, from Physics to Parliamentary Democracy to Music, across to a young audience, hungry, we hoped, for real knowledge. Many of the authors were enthusiasts for the idea; some went on to brilliant careers. But none got any of the money which Victor and I hoped for and almost promised.[1]

Why? The book was attacked by religious vultures, going for me and my authors for our neglect of Christianity. Of course the *Outline* was a thoroughly moral book; we all cared deeply for things like truth, understanding, and compassion. But it had nothing to say about the Church which at that period had considerable power of the kind which we now see in the depths of the Moral Majority, fortunately without influence in this country. The attack was successful; there was no second edition. I was extremely upset, for my contributors as well as myself. Victor wrote to Temple, the Archbishop of York, asking him to edit a book on Christianity and the Crisis. That didn't work, but something of the kind was produced by Canon Dearmer, so all was not lost—to the firm.[2]

[1] The hope must have been vivid, since Auden subsequently recalled that he had been paid for his piece. See Robert A. Wilson, 'Collecting W. H. Auden', in this volume, p. 201. All footnotes by Bucknell.

[2] See Endnote.

Wystan's manuscript is full of brackets, sometimes no doubt as afterthoughts when he was displeased with his first sentence. Sometimes I cut them, often edged them into the text, for they might be solid bits of relevant information. I see that I cut out a rather improbable conversation with a girl about self-consciousness. He was much interested in what, like the rest of us, he called the wireless and the talkies. He feels and tries to express the difference between 'langue' and 'parole', but can't quite get it down. But he is wrestling with major problems about writing; there are still uncertainties and he brings in unlikely little bits of science. Every now and then he says something which perhaps seems uninteresting now, but was fresh in the thirties.

He wrote a long section about epic poetry which I cut heavily. He said that it was essentially masculine. 'Women are not of much importance in it except as causers of trouble.' He had of course read his Homer, but there are other epics from further north or further east. Then he goes off into aspects of history, bringing in Dante, Chaucer, and so on. He stresses unity: 'Whenever a society is united . . . it has a great outburst of good writing.'[3] I remember thinking uneasily that there were people in the increasingly Nazi Germany of that date who felt the same way. He was against class divisions, naturally, but there is rather a dangerous feeling for oneness.

I felt he was getting into depths where he was unsure and so did whoever else was reading the manuscript—I often got in other of my authors to help or make suggestions which I could pass on. The small marks on the edge of Wystan's manuscript might have been made by Dick Gleadowe or perhaps Olaf Stapledon.[4] Anyhow by page thirteen of his draft he was well over his word limit. He comes up with 'I am also inclined to think we read far too much.' Then he calls on his readers 'to stop learning to read and write, and stop moving from place to place, and let literature start again by oral tradition'. It was about the same time that he said the same kind of thing in a poem which you will remember:

---

[3] This appears in the published essay only, *EA* 311.

[4] For a description of these marks, see my 'A Note on the Manuscript and the Text'. R. M. Y. Gleadowe and William Olaf Stapledon were both contributors to the *Outline*. Gleadowe's essay, 'Visual Art or the Pattern Set Down', reflects his artistic talents; he was then drawing master at Winchester and Slade Professor of Fine Art at Oxford. Stapledon was a philosopher and science fiction writer. His essay for the *Outline*, 'Problems and Solutions, or the Future', was later incorporated into *The Waking World* (London, 1934). Mrs Mitchison recalls that Stapledon 'helped me a lot with the *Outline*' (letter to me, Apr. 1988).

> All of the women and most of the men
> Shall work with their hands and not think again.[5]

Well, I let him have the last words in the printed piece: 'Forests are cut down, rivers of ink absorbed, but the lust to write is still unsatisfied. What is going to happen? If it were only a question of writing it wouldn't matter; but it is an index of our health. It's not only books, but our lives, that are going to pot.'

Not very encouraging for the boys and girls or even their parents; however, I thought it would be something to chew over, as well as being somewhat different from anything they could have expected.

Endnote

In *You May Well Ask: A Memoir 1920–1940* (London, 1979) Mrs Mitchison recalls, 'the *Outline* was torpedoed by a vicious attack from Arnold Lunn on behalf of the Church', 170. Lunn wrote to *The Church Times* the week the *Outline* was published (108. 3636 (30 Sept. 1932), 364) and apparently orchestrated the protest, which appeared in *The Morning Post* the following week, signed by the Archbishop of York, the Bishop of Durham, the Headmasters of Eton and Harrow, and fourteen other prominent Christians (clergymen of several denominations, educators, politicians, and others). Lunn's own name did not appear, but his father's (Henry S. Lunn, until 1930 editor of *The Review of the Churches*) did, and the protest used many phrases from his letter to *The Church Times*, again criticizing the *Outline* for its atheism, Bolshevism, and undermining of the family. See my 'Editor's Introduction' for Auden's response to the protest (p. 30).

The 'viciousness' of Lunn's attack was apparently motivated by the fact that among the many endorsements which Gollancz had succeeded in getting for the *Outline* in advance of its publication, and which he used to advertise the book (see the almost full-page advertisement with sixteen quotations from Lloyd George, Bertrand Russell, Aldous Huxley, and many others in *The Sunday Times* (25 Sept. 1932), 13), were enthusiastic remarks by distinguished churchmen such as H. R. L. Sheppard, a former Dean of Canterbury, and Percy Dearmer, Canon of Westminster and Professor of Ecclesiastical Art at King's College, London. Lunn felt they had been trapped into recommending the *Outline* without thoroughly reading it. Actually, the protest was lodged against this aspect of Gollancz's publicity scheme: 'It is necessary that a protest should be recorded against the commendation by Christian men and women of a volume which professes to give an outline of history, and mentions Mohammed, Buddha, and Lenin, but does not mention Christ', *The Morning Post* (6 Oct.

---

[5] *O*, Book 3, Ode 4 ('Roar Gloucestershire'); repr. in *EA* 105. John Fuller has suggested that Auden got these ideas from D. H. Lawrence's *Fantasia of the Unconscious* (London, 1923), 83, 77. See Fuller, 71.

1932), 11. Lunn went on to write a more thorough critique for *The English Review* in which he revealed that his father had been among the advance recipients of the *Outline* and was so appalled by its contents that he returned the book to Gollancz without comment, 'The Scandal of the *Outline*', 55 (Nov. 1932), 471–84.

In an interview with *The Sunday Times*, Gollancz counter-attacked, suggesting that the attitude of the signatories of the protest, 'who denounce a book . . . because of a phrase or two to which they may object', was itself far less Christian than the *Outline*. He pointed out that the book did mention Christianity—if not Christ—several times and positively, as a force which had contributed to 'the gradually increasing unity of the world' (9 Oct. 1932), 12. This 'unity', in his view, was the real theme of the book. He insisted the *Outline* did not subvert the family, but simply presented it objectively with some of its alternatives. He did not mention Bolshevism.

Other reviewers were also derisive of the *Outline*'s unconventional account of history and culture. The reviewer for *The Times Literary Supplement* said it neglected not only Christianity but all the great religions of the world and most of the great men of European art, literature, and philosophy: 'the writers of this 'Outline' prefer on the whole to talk as little about great men as they reasonably can . . . But Lenin gets his full laurels, with an illustration—we had almost said icon—showing the worshipping crowds at his tomb' ('An Outline for Youth' 1602 (13 Oct. 1932), 722). The influence of Gerald Heard on the *Outline* was widely noted.

Interestingly, from Oct. 1931 to Nov. 1934 Lunn was engaged in a polite but combative correspondence with J. B. S. Haldane (the geneticist and Mrs Mitchison's brother), in which the former defended Christianity and the latter science. During this time, Lunn was received into the Roman Catholic Church. The letters were published as *Science and the Supernatural: A Correspondence Between A. Lunn and J. B. S. Haldane* (London, 1935).

In 1933, Gollancz published *Christianity and The Crisis*, edited by Dearmer, who was a prolific author on both secular and religious subjects. The book included contributions, as Dearmer says in his Preface, from 'distinguished . . . philosophers and statesmen, theologians and economists' (13), among them William Temple, then Archbishop of York. By 1936, the *Outline* itself had sold about 36,000 copies, according to Gollancz (see *Bibliography*, 123).

Writing

W. H. AUDEN

Speech

If an Australian aborigine were to sit down on a pin he would say 'Ow'.
Dogs with bones growl at the approach of other dogs. English, Russian,
Brazilian, all mothers 'coo' to their babies. Sailors at any port, pulling
together on a hawser; watch them and listen—Heaving they grunt
together 'Ee-Ah'

This is the first language.

We generally think of language being words used to point to things, to
say that something is *This* or *That*, but the earliest use of language was
not this; it was used to express the feelings of the speaker; feelings about
something happening to him (the prick of the pin) or attitudes towards
other things in his world (the other hungry dog; the darling baby) or
again as a help to doing something with others of his own kind (pulling
the boat in) The first two uses are common to many animals but the last
is peculiar to the most highly organized and contains more possibilities
of development.

Life is one whole thing made up of smaller whole things which
themselves are made up of smaller whole things and so on. The largest
thing we can talk about is the universe, the smallest the positive
electrons of the atom which run round its central negative electron,
already a group. So too for us, nucleus and cell, cell and tissue or organ,
organs or tissues and the human individual, individual and family, family
and neighbours, neighbours and nation, nation and world, always
groups linked up into larger groups, each group unique, an individual
thing, different from every other thing, but without meaning except in its
connection with other things. The whole cannot exist without the part,
nor the part without the whole; and each whole is more than just the sum
of its parts, it is a new thing. (eg $2H_2 + O_2 = 2H_2O$, but the behaviour of
water is not just the result of adding the behaviour of hydrogen to the
behaviour of Oxygen)

But suppose the part begins to work not only as if it were a whole
(which it is) but as if there were no larger wholes, there is a breakdown
(eg. a cancer growth in the body). And This is what has happened to us.

At sometime or other in human history, when and how is not known exactly, man became self-conscious, he began to feel, I am I, and You are Not-I; we are shut inside ourselves and apart from each other. There is no whole but the self.[1]

The more this feeling grew, the more he felt the need to bridge over the gulf, to recover the sense of being as much part of life as the cells in his body are part of him. Before he had lost it, when he [was] doing things together in a group, such [as] hunting; when feeling was strongest, as when, say, the quarry was first sighted, the group had made noises, grunts, howls, grimaces. Noise and this feeling he had now lost had gone together; then if he made the noise, could he not recover the feeling? In some way like this language began, but its development must have been very slow, like the development of full self-consciousness. Among savage tribes for example news travels much quicker than a messenger could carry it, by a sympathy which we, ignorant of its nature and incapable of practising, call telepathy. Dr Rivers tells a story somewhere of some natives in Melanesia getting into a rowing-boat. There was no discussion as to who should stroke or steer. All found their places as we should say by instinct.[2]

Even among ourselves two friends have to say very much less to understand each other's meaning than two strangers. Their conversation is often unintelligible to a third person. Even when we are listening to anyone it is not only the words themselves which tell us what he means but his gestures, (Try listening with your eyes shuts. It has been suggested that speech consists of movements of the larynx and other organs of speech which correspond to what were once movements of the hands) and also the extent to which he is talking to us personally (It is always difficult to understand what people are saying at another table in a restaurant. We are outside the group)

Self conscious as we are, much of our speech is like a tunnel under

---

[1] Here the version of the essay published in the *Outline* gives a cross-reference to Heard's essay: '(See *History of Ideas*, p. 431).' The passage describes an apparent decline in early man's ability to draw pictures which coincided with his growing ability to distinguish between different things and a corresponding increase in his linguistic resources. On the preceding page (430) Heard describes early man's lack of a self-conscious sense of himself as a separate individual.

[2] Rivers tells this story in *Instinct and Unconscious: A Contribution to a Biological Theory of the Psycho-Neuroses* (Cambridge, 1920), 94–5; however, the fact that Auden does not give the exact source of the story suggests that he may have been recalling it from Heard's telling in *The Ascent of Humanity* (see p. 51). In any case, whether it proved the existence of a group mind was controversial; see my 'Introduction', pp. 26–7.

which the currents of feeling can pass unseen. For example take the kind of conversation one hears in railway carriages

> Man. Its very cold for this time of year
> Girl. Yes it would be warmer if the sun were to come out.

What is really going on is something quite different, something like this

> Man. What a nice looking girl you are. I hope you dont mind my speaking to you like this but I should like to know if your voice is as nice as your hat. Journeys are dull are'nt they unless one finds somebody nice to talk to. I expect you have your difficulties too, like me. We all have. Lets be friends.
> Girl. You look nice but a girl has to be careful. You can never tell what men will be like if you encourage them too much. I hate trains too. Have you ever been in love. What was she like. Alright. We'll try and see how we get on.

Meaning.

Words then are a bridge between a speaker and a listener. What the bridge carries, ie what the speaker gives and the listener receives, we call the *meaning* of the words

In anything we say there are four different kinds of meaning; any one of them may be more important than the other three, but there is generally something of all four.

(1) *Sense* (typical case. Fat stock prices on the wireless)
We say *something* or expect *something* to be said to us about something 'Stinker is a man'. We now know that there is a thing called Stinker and that thing is a man and not a dog or anything else.

(2) *Feeling* (typical case. The conversation of lovers)
We generally have feelings about the things of which we are talking. 'There's that horrible man Stinker'. We now know that the speaker does not like Stinker)

(3) *Tone* (typical case. An after dinner speech)
We generally have an attitude to the person we are talking too. We say the same thing in different ways to different people, 'There's that swine Stinker' 'There's Mr Stinker; of course I expect he's charming really, but I dont like him very much, I'm afraid.'

(4) *Intention* (typical case. A speech at a General Election)
Apart from what we say or feel, we often want to make our listeners act or think in a particular way. 'There's that man Stinker. I shouldnt have much to do with him if I were you'. The speaker is trying to stop us seeing Mr Stinker.

Language and Words

Language as we know it consists of words, that is a comparatively small number of different sounds (between forty and fifty in English) arranged in different orders or groups, each sound or group of sounds standing for something, an object, an action, a colour, an idea etc.

To go back to our sketch of the origen of language; before language we have the people who feel something, (the hunting group), the feeling (feeling of unity in the face of hunger or danger etc), the object which excites the feeling (the hunted Bison), and the noise which expressed the feeling. If the noise was later used to recover the feeling, it would also present to the memory, the idea or the image of the animal or whatever it was excited the feeling. Thus sounds would begin to have sense meaning, to stand for things, as well as having meaning as feeling

It is unlikely therefore even at the first that language was entirely onomatopoeic, that is that words were sounds imitating the sounds of things spoken about. Many words no doubt did, just as they still do (eg. hissing, growling, splashing). It is only possible to imitate in this way actions or objects which make a noise. You could never for example imitate the sound of a chair. In fact most of the power of words comes from their *not* being like what they stand for. If the word 'ruin' for instance was only like a particular ruin, it could only serve to describe that one solitary building; as it is the words conjures up all the kinds of ruin which we know and our various feelings about them, ruined churches, ruined houses, ruined gasworks, loss of money etc.

Inflection

All languages are originally inflected, that is to say, the sound standing for a particular object or action changes slightly according to how we are looking at it. eg. The Roman said

Homo amat canem
but Canis amat hominem.

He felt that the man is a different man and the dog is a different dog if he is loving or being loved.[3] But as people get more self-conscious, more aware of what they are feeling and thinking, they separate their feelings and thoughts from the things they are feeling or thinking about. They show the difference in attitude either by changing the word order or by using special words like prepositions. Thus in English, the least inflected language

> The man loves the dog
> The dog loves the man.
> The man gives a bone *to* the dog

All languages show some inflection. (*I love him. He* love-*s me*)

Writing.

Writing and speech are like two tributary streams, rising at different sources, flowing apart for a time until they unite to form a large river. Just as it is possible for sounds conveying their meaning by the ear to stand for things, pictures conveying their meaning through the eye can do the same.

The earliest kinds of writing, such as Egyptian Hieroglyphs, or Mexican writings, are a series of pictures telling a story, as a sentence tells a story. The urge to write like the urge to speak came from man's growing sense of personal loneliness, of the need for group communication. But while speech begins with the feeling of separateness in space, of I-here-in-this-chair and You-there-in-that-chair, writing begins from the sense of separateness in time of 'I'm here to day, but I shall be dead to-morrow and you will be alive in my place and how can I speak to you'.

Primitive people, living in small groups, have very little idea of death, only a very strong sense of the life of the tribe which of course never dies. The moment man loses this sense of the continuously present group life, he becomes increasingly aware of the shortness and uncertainty of the life of the individual. He looks round desperately for some means of prolonging it, of living into the future, of uniting the past with the present. The earliest writings of which we know tell the exploits of dead kings. The writer is like the schoolboy who carves his initials on a desk; he wishes to live for ever.

How early speech joined up with writing it is impossible to say, but since sounds stood for things, they must have also as the sense or

[3] Here the *Outline* gives a second cross-reference to the same passage in Heard's essay '(See *History of Ideas*, p. 431).'

intellectual use of language developed, have stimulated visual images in the minds of the listeners, which would not have been very difficult to connect with real pictures. Just as sounds must soon have stopped imitating sounds of real objects, writing must soon have stopped being purely pictorial, drawings of each seperate object. A language of this kind would have had to contain thousands of letters and would have been very difficult to learn and slow and clumsy to write.

Further abstract ideas would be impossible to represent by pictures (How, for example, could you draw a picture of 'habit'). Luckily the fact that the marks of different sounds which it is possible to make are comparatively few, presented a solution to this difficulty. By inventing an alphabet or code where one kind of mark stands for one kind of sound, any word could be written by arranging the marks or letters in the order in which the sounds were made. (Our own alphabet comes originally from Eygpt through Phoenicia Colchis and Italy).

Spoken and Written language

As long as the people are living in small societies, and living generation after generation in one place, they have little need of writing. Poems, stories, moral advice are learnt by heart and handed down by word of mouth from father to son. Oral tradition has certain advantages and certain disadvantages over writing. Generally speaking, the *feeling* meaning is transmitted with extraordinary accuracy, as the gestures and the tone of voice which go with the words are remembered also. With a statement in writing it is often impossible after a time to decide exactly what the author meant. (Think how easy it is to misunderstand a letter, or how many different interpretations have been made of Christ's saying 'Thou art Peter. Upon this rock will I build my church'.) On the other hand the sense meaning is apt to get strangely distorted It is easy not to catch or to forget the exact words told to one, and to guess them wrongly; again we may be asked to explain something and add our own explanation which is passed on with the story. eg. this message was once passed back from the front lines from mouth to mouth to the officer commanding the reserve[:] 'Send reinforcements; the regiment is going to advance'. What actually reached him was this: 'Send three and fourpence; the regiment is going to a dance.'.

But as communities got larger and government became more centralised writing became more and more important. Still however as long as copying of original manuscripts had to be done by hand, books were rare and too costly for any but the few. The invention of printing in the fifteenth century (it began with the printing of playing cards and religious pictures off wooden blocks) greatly increased the power of the written word, but the cost of books still limited their circulation. Popular printed literature during the sixteenth and seventeenth century, apart from some religious books, was confined to broadsheets and pamphlets peddled in the streets. The eighteenth century saw the rise of the magazine and the newspaper, and the introduction of steam power at the beginning of the nineteenth century, by cheapening the cost of production, put printed matter within the reach of anyone who could read or write. (.N.B also, the introduction of the penny post; and the effect of universal education. Strangely enough, the last five years, with the wireless and the talkies have witnessed a revival in the use of the spoken word.)

The effect of this has been a mixed one. On the one hand it has made the language able to deal with a great many more subjects, particularly those which are abstract like some of the sciences, to be more accurate, to draw finer distinctions of meaning. Words written down in one language can be translated into another. Thus the worlds knowledge can be pooled, and words borrowed from another language for which the borrower has no word in his own with the exact shade of meaning which he wants (cf clock—chronometre: stranger—alien etc). On the other hand increase in vocabulary makes a language more difficult to learn, not only just to learn the words, but to learn how to use them. When communities are small and their interests common to all their members, mere acquaintance with each other is enough to make people use their language well, but as communities increase and interests become specialised, the past history of the language gets bigger and heavier, education in the use of language becomes more and more necessary. Such an education is at present almost entirely lacking. The speech of a peasant is generally better, ie more vivid, better able to say what he wants to say, than the speech of the average University graduate. Its like juggling with balls. You may be able to juggle fairly well with three but if you try six without careful practise, you will probably drop them all. It is not the language that is to blame but our skill in using it.

Verse Form

Speech originated in noises made during group excitement. Excitement seems naturally to excite movement. When we are excited we want to dance about. Noise was thus in the beginning associated with movements of a group, perhaps dancing round food or advancing together to attack. The greater the excitement, the more in sympathy with each other each

member of the group is, the more regular the movements; they keep
time with each other; every foot comes down together.[4]

Again imagine a circle of people dancing; the circle revolves and
comes back to its starting place; at each revolution the set of movements
is repeated.

When words move in this kind of repeated pattern, we call the effect
of the movement in our minds the metre. Words arranged in metre are
verse.

Just as in a crowd we are much more easily carried away by feeling
than when alone, so metre excites us, prepares us to listen readily to
what is being said. We expect something to happen and therefore it
does[.] When a poet is writing verse, the feeling as it were excites the
words and makes them fall into a definite group going through definite
dancing movements, just as feeling excite[s] the different members of a
crowd and makes them act together.

Metre is group excitement among words a series of repeated movements. The weaker the excitement, the less the words act together and
upon each other. Rhythm is what is expected by one word of another. In
scientific prose for example, what words do is only controlled by the
sense of what is being said. They are like people in a street on an
ordinary day. They can be or do anything they like aslong as they keep to
the left on the pavement, and dont annoy each other. But even here this
much is expected. There is always some degree of rhythm in all
language. The degree depends on the power of feeling.[5]

Language may be ornamented in various ways. The two most familiar
ornaments are alliteration (eg In a *summer season* when *soft* was the
sun[6]) and rhyme (Old King *Cole* was a merry old *soul*)

Alliteration is found in the early verse of the teutonic people and
rhyme beginning perhaps in the marching songs of the Roman soldiers,
was adopted by the early Christian hymn writers and so came into
modern verse. Alliteration is the effect produced by an arrangement of
words beginning with a similar sound, rhyme that produced by an
arrangement of words ending in a similar sound. The sounds are similar
but belong to different words and therefore have different meanings in

---

[4] Here the *Outline* gives a cross-reference to the title-page of the essay on 'Dancing and
Drama or The First Pattern of Life' by Beryl de Zoete '(See *Dancing*, p. 757).'

[5] Here the published essay has an additional paragraph on 'Accents, long and short
syllables, feet and all that . . .' which is followed in the *Outline* by a cross-reference to
J. B. Trend's essay 'Music or The Last Pattern': '(See *Music*, p. 876).' This passage on
rhythm compares rhythm in poetry with rhythm in music.

[6] William Langland, *Piers Plowman*, Prologue, 1.

each place. Through the likeness, thoughts and feelings hitherto distinct in the mind are joined together. They are in fact sound-metaphors.

Different kinds of Writing.

The difference between different kinds of writing lies not so much in the writing itself but in the way we look at it (and of course in the way the author wished us to look at it; but we often know very little about that). Literary forms do not exist outside our own minds. When we read anything, no matter what, a description of a scientific experiment, a history book, a ballad, or a novel, in so far as we pay attention only to what things are happening one after another to something or somebody it is a story; in so far as we read it only to learn the way in which something or someone behaves in certain circumstances, it is science; in so far as we read it only to find out what has actually happened in the past it is history.

People have often asked what is the difference between poetry and prose. The only difference is in the way the writer looks at things. (there is another difference between prose and verse. see [above]). For instance the novelist starts with a general idea in his mind; say, that people are always trying to escape from their responsibilities and that escape only lands them in a worse mess. Then he writes a story about what happened to Mr and Mrs Smith. He may never say in so many words that they tried to escape, never mention his idea, but this idea is the force which drives the story along. The poet on the other hand hears people talking in his club about the sad story of Mr and Mrs Smith. He thinks 'There now. Thats very interesting. They are just like everybody else; trying to get round life. Its like those sailors who tried to get to India by the North West Passage. On they go, getting further and further into the ice, miles from home. Why, thats a good idea for a poem'. He writes a poem about explorers; he may never mention Mr and Mrs Smith at all. The novelist then goes from the general to the particular, the poet from the particular to the general, and you can see this also in the way they use words. The novelist uses words with their general meaning and uses a whole lot of them to build up a particular effect; his character. The poet uses words with their particular meanings and puts them together to give a general effect, his idea. Actually of course, nearly all novels and all poems except very short ones, have both ways of looking at things in them (eg. Chaucer's Canterbury Tales are more like novels in verse; Melville's Moby Dick is more like a poem in prose). All you can say is that one way is typical of the novelist and the other of the poet.

Another question. What is the difference between writing as a work of Art, what we call literature, and other kinds of writings. Again, it depends how you choose to look at it.

We are treating any piece of writing as a work of art when we regard our reading of it as a single act, confined to the reading and understanding of the writing itself, and not as one of a series of acts extending before or after our reading. I mean that, suppose I take up a bulb catalogue and just read it and do nothing more, I'm treating it as a work of art. If on the other hand, as is more likely, my reading of the catalogue is only one small part of a long process which began with my writing to the bulb grower for one, and will end only when the bulbs chosen from it, ordered from the grower, planted and watered in my garden, come to flower, I am not treating it as a work of art.

The absolutely pure work of art in this sense doesnt exist. The most we can say is that there are some kinds of writing which we know all the time we are reading them, why we are, and other kinds which we dont.

Why people write books.

People write in order to be read. They would like to be read by everybody and for ever. They feel alone, cut off from each other in an indifferent world where they do not live for very long. How can they get in touch again; how can they prolong their lives. Children by their bodies, live on in life they will not live to see meet friends they will never know, and will in their turn have children, some tiny part of them too living on all the time. These by their body; books by their minds.

But the satisfaction of any want is pleasant: we not only enjoy feeling full; we enjoy eating; so people write books because they enjoy it, as a carpenter enjoys making a cupboard. Books are written for money, to convert the world, to pass the time, but these reasons are always trivial beside the first two—company and creation.

How people write books.

We know as much and no more about how books are made as we know about the making of babies or plants. Suddenly an idea, a feeling, germinates like a seed in the mind of the author and begins to grow. He has to look after it, manure and water the soil with his own experience, all that he knows and has felt, all that has happened to him in his life, straightening a shoot here, pruning a bit there, never quite certain what it is going to do next, whether it will just wither and die, come up in a single night like a mushroom, or thicken gradually into a great oak tree.

The author is both soil and gardener, the soil part of him does not know what is going on, the gardener part of him has learnt the routine. He may be a careful gardener but poor soil; his books are then beautifully written but they seem to have nothing in them: we say he lacks inspiration. Or he may be excellent soil but a careless gardener. His books are exciting but badly arranged, out of proportion, harsh to the ear: we say he lacks technique. Good soil is more important than good gardening but the finest plants are the product of both.

Why people read books.

When we read a book it is as if we were with a person. A book is not only the meaning of the words inside it, it is the person who means them. In real life we treat people in all sorts of ways. Suppose we ask a policeman the way. As long as he is polite we do not bother whether he beats his wife or not, in fact if he started to tell us about his wife, we should get impatient: all we expect of him is that he should know the way and be able clearly to explain it: When we go to the music hall we want the comedian to amuse us; we dont want to go for a walking tour with him. But other people we treat differently; we want more from them than information or amusement; we want to live with them, to feel and think with them. When we say a book is good or bad we mean that we feel towards it as we feel towards what we call a good or bad person. (Remember though that a book about bad characters is not therefore bad, anymore than a person is bad because he talks about bad people)

Actually we know that we cant divide people into good and bad like that; everyone is a mixture; we like some people in some moods and some in others and as we grow older our taste in people changes. The same is true of books. People who say they only read good books are prigs. We all like some good books and some bad. The only silly thing to do is to pretend that bad books are good. The awful nonsense that most people utter when they are discussing or criticising a book, would be avoided if they would remember that they would never think of criti[ci]sing a person in the same way. For example if a friend says 'So and so is a swine' we dont say 'Thats absurd. He is a man so he cant be a pig'. We know perfectly well he means that he has the same feelings of disgust towards so and so as he [would] feel towards swine. Yet you often hear people criticizing lines in poetry like

'The new horned moon
With one bright star within the nether tip' for being untrue.[7]

[7] Auden recalls these lines slightly wrongly from Samuel Taylor Coleridge's 'The

Or they will say that they dont like a book because they dont agree with it. We think it rather silly when people can only be friends with those who hold the same views on everything. Or again they dislike it because they dislike the author, which is liking saying you dislike a man because you disliked his father.

Reading is valuable just because books are like people and make the same demands on us to understand and like them. Our actual circle of friends is generally limited and all of us, I think, feel that our living, our relations with them are not as good as they might be, more muddled, difficult, unsatisfying than necessary. Just as a boxer exercises for a real fight with a punch ball or a sparring partner, so you can train yourself for relations with real people with a book. Its not easy, and you cant begin until you have some experience of real people first (any more than a boxer can practise with a punch ball until he has learnt a little about boxing), but books cant die or quarrel or go away as people can. Reading and living are not two watertight compartments. You must use your knowledge of people to guide you when reading books and your knowledge of books to guide you when living with people. The more you read the more you will realise what difficult and delicate things relations with people are but how worth while they can be when they really come off; and the more you know of other people, the more you will be able to get out of each kind of book, and the more you will realise how good a really good book can be, but that great books are as rare as great men.

Reading is valuable when it improves our technique of living, helps us to live fuller and more satisfying lives. It fails when we cant understand or feel with what we read, either because of ignorance of our own, or obscurity in the writing.

It is a danger when we only read what encourages us in lazy and crude ways of feeling and thinking; like cheap company (Too many people only read what flatters them; They like to be told they are fine fellows and all is for the best in the best of all possible worlds; or they only want to be excited, or to forget to-morrow's bills). It is also dangerous when it becomes a substitute for living; when we get frightened of real people

Rime of the Ancient Mariner'. Most editions available in 1932 (following the revised 1800 version of the poem) have 'The hornéd Moon, with one bright star / Within the nether tip' (3. 210–11). In fact, Auden is almost certainly remembering the lines from Richards's *Practical Criticism* (see my 'Introduction', p. 21); Richards quotes more accurately, though also without the accent on 'hornéd'.

and find books safer company: they are a rehearsal for living, not living itself. Swots and 'bookish' people have stage fright.

History of literature.

A book is the child of a marriage between an individual and the group or society in which he lives. Books provide a kind of a history of society.

Unfortunately we have almost no examples from the literatures of any but comparatively modern civilisations, none for example from the great megalithic matriarchal civilisation which starting in Egypt and Mesopotamia overan the entire world previous to our era. (except that is for what has filtered down to us distorted and overlain with later additions in folk tales and fairy stories). The earliest literatures we have belong to the Heroic age, a stage in the development of societies already patriarchal when increase in size forces them to migrate in small bachelor groups under a leader to find a wife and home elsewhere on conquered soil. Heroic literature consists of epics, long stories in verse of the exploits of these small groups of fighters, which were chanted in the halls of chiefs in the evenings. The size and bachelor nature of these groups, with their common devotion to a leader, and their common interests in fighting, sailing, and farming produces a character[ist]ic literature. In the epic there is no division between 'prosaic' and poetic (because there is no second-hand experience). Though often complicated in verse form (appreciation of technique is only possible in a leisured community. These people were conquerors forcing the people they conquered to work for them) yet the actions and emotional situations described are simple, fighting, eating, loving, farming, sleeping. It is essentially masculine; women are not of much importance in it except as causers of trouble, setting up a conflict between loyalty to the family and loyalty to the bachelor group. This theme of divided loyalties and the fight against hopeless odds in a narrow place are the commonest tragic situtions in the epic. But the appearance, at least the writing down, of these poems is in itself a sign that the day of that kind of society is passing: the migrant group has already begun to settle down: the bond between leader and his men to relax. Listening to these poems they recover for a moment the old feeling of unity; are one with their forefathers; but the moment passes. The group is growing into the feudal state.

The feudal state is too large to exist as a single group; it becomes stratified in layers, King, baron, knight, freeman, serf, each layer having little in common with another. Literature too becomes class-conscious. Instead of a common literature we have one for the 'gentle' and one for the 'simple'. The latter lacking the necessary degree of leisure and economic security, becomes crude in feeling and rude in form: the former becomes increasingly complicated in form and refined in feeling, but the feelings have no guts, no contact with the earth, full of feeling about feeling.

But the feudal system was international, common to all Europe, professing one religious faith, and Latin as a universal language for scholarship; poems were freely translated from one language into another, and the Catholic Church did its best to unite all classes. If you read Chaucer's Canterbury Tales you cant help being struck by the freedom with which pilgrims of every class talk to each other and laugh at each other's jokes. True, a pilgrimage, like a sea voyage, is a special occasion; but to-day cabin would not be so free with steerage.

We must go back for a moment to look at a special kind of society which has arisen at various times in history, and has seldom failed to show great literary activity, the city state (eg. Athens—Aeschylus. Florence Dante). It is easy to see why this should be so. The group is a small one, they are all neighbours sharing each others interests, and near enough to the country not to lose contact with reality. Leisure gives opportunities for the development of an intricate and difficult art. But the city state has never lasted very long. A few years of feverish activity and then—phut. Why, because its leisure is extorted from colonies or a slave class. It is economically parasitic. Sooner or later war or revolution kill it.

To return to the main current of history. The Feudal system broke down and the Reformation broke up religion. Europe became disunited. Not only [were there] classes, there were nations. And the Renaissance in Italy with its sense of the importance of learning, produced the highbrow, the man who thinks books are everything, and despises those who do not read them.

When nations are forming themselves, they always show great artistic activity (eg During the reign of Elizabeth in England). There is something to be done, a state to be re-made, an Armada to defeat, a religion to reform. But in time these aims are reached. The nation as a group is too large to be united except by exceptional circumstances like a war. In peace time its sense of unity evaporates very quickly and then the isolation is worse than before. Not only are there upper and lower classes; there are English upper and lower classes and French upper and lower classes; all out of sympathy with each other: a French literature and an English literature. Drama, always a sign that a community is united, disappears. Literature gets more and more shut up in little circle[s] of clever people. Dryden and Pope are very fine poets but they wrote for a highly cultured few, for a rentier class.

But there is worse to come. The Industrial Revolution taking the people from the country and herding them into the towns, destroys what folk culture and literature there was. The workers uprooted and oppressed cease to be creative.

People cease to be people to one another. They are algebraical symbols expressing money values. 'How much wages can I get out of x'. 'How many hours a day can I make y do'. You are either an employer or an employee; or a shopkeeper doing your dingy little best to cheat both.

What is literature doing? Either losing its nerve, it turns its back on life and begins to eat itself, becomes bookish, writing about writing, impossible to understand unless you have first read all the other books, or else soured and hysterical, prophesies disaster, or turns just nasty.

Summary.[8]

Man writes and reads because he is lonely and wants to be re-united with a group. Writing must do two things. It must affect the whole group and the way in which it affects it must be valuable, assisting the group towards a completer and more discriminating life. The larger the group the harder to unite it and the cruder the feelings which do. But it is impossible for people now to exist in small groups only. Like the city state such groups cannot earn the money to live; they become competitive and unequal like the family. I cannot see that such groups are possible except as short-lived oddities except in a one-class state where the distribution of money and leisure is more or less equal, and where industries [have] become decentralised so that we are not

---

[8] This follows an abandoned first version of the summary:

Summary
Man wants to write because he is lonely, and wants to be reunited in a group, and he reads for the same reason. Writing must do two things: it must move the whole group; and the way in which it moves them must be valuable, assist the fuller and more discriminating life of the group.

The larger the group the harder it is to affect it, and the cruder the feelings which do. What is to be done?

The best conditions for writing are the same as those for living. Small groups linked up into larger groups. To bind the former to the latter you must have faith either a religious one like Catholicism or a political one like Communism. The family which is essentially a group based on unequality will have to diminish in power and importance. (It is probable that living in communal dwellings will be no better. We must have equality of leisure. We shall have to choose. Its not only a question of literature but our future happiness.. We cant sit on the fence much longer. Well?

compelled to herd together in unmanageable masses Towns must be smaller[.] I am also inclined to think we read far too much; that if literature is to revive, most of us will have to stop learning to read and write, and stop moving from place to place, and let literature start again by oral tradition. One thing is quite certain. We shall do absolutely nothing without some sort of faith either religious like Catholicism or political like Communism. Its not only literature but our lives that are going to pot. We cant sit on the fence much longer. Well.

Eleven Letters from Auden to Stephen Spender

EDITED BY NICHOLAS JENKINS

AUDEN had no objection in principle to collections of writers' letters. He reviewed, generally approvingly, eighteen separate editions of correspondence, and his own poems are mined with allusions to other letter writers from Voltaire to Henry James. Although he instructed his executors to publish a notice after his death requesting that his friends burn their letters from him, it seems clear that this was mainly an effort to impede a biography—or at least to register a protest against one—and was not intended simply to preclude a future edition of his correspondence.[1] Whenever Auden complained about certain letters being published, as, for example, he did in the case of Keats's letters to Fanny Brawne, the thrust of his argument was literary critical rather than moral.

He defined a 'born letter writer' as one for whom 'a letter is as much a literary genre as a novel or a poem; he uses it to describe people and events, to make general reflections on life, etcetera, and it is almost an accident who receives the letter.'[2] In this sense, Auden was only occasionally a 'born letter writer.' Not surprisingly, a great deal of his correspondence is made up of short, declarative items that provide information, fix appointments, or thank their recipients. Moreover, Auden, who wrote some of his finest poems under the inspiration of a particular death or anniversary, sent most of his best letters to people who were in some way important to him and who therefore influenced the content and tone of his letter. This was evidently the case with Stephen Spender.

The correspondence between them, as it survives, is completely one-sided: Spender's letters to Auden seem to have gone into the rubbish

---

[1] See Edward Mendelson's 'Authorized Biography and Its Discontents' in Daniel Aaron, ed., *Studies In Biography* (Harvard English Studies 8; Cambridge, Mass., 1978), 10.

[2] 'The Untruth about Beethoven', *The Spectator*, 207. 6959 (10 Nov. 1961), 672.

along with Stravinsky's, Eliot's, and MacNeice's. However, 100 letters and postcards to him (twenty-one addressed jointly to Spender and his wife, and one to 'Stephen and Christopher and Walter') constitute one of the largest extant runs in Auden's correspondence. It spreads—with one unexplained hiatus between 12 April 1942 and 14 June 1951— across virtually the whole length of one of his longest friendships, although the bulk of the letters date from the 1960s and 70s when the Spenders were frequently Auden's hosts in London, and so needed to know when to pick him up from the airport.

The obvious strains of love, embarrassment, and exasperation in Auden's attitude to Spender seem to have been essential stimuli to the rather formal self-disclosures in these eleven letters. Auden, by turns bullying and flirtatious, returned almost reflexively to the differences between himself and his 'varsity chum', as though he considered Spender to be his personal antitype. It has probably always been clear that two contemporaries could hardly have been more perfectly antithetical as poets: Auden sought to base his writing on larger and more impersonal structures than the patterns produced by his own mind, while Spender, as an autobiographer and a connoisseur of self-consciousness, explored all the weakest, most solitary moments of the 'I'. Auden, though, went beyond the literary, and, continuing his search for doubles, opposites, and alternative lives for himself, found oppositions in almost every facet of their existences, from their blood-pressure to their political views. Labelling Spender was, however, a roundabout way to self-definition, because Auden was forced to fill in both sides of the equation, and pin himself down, too.

A Note on the Text of These Letters

Each letter writer offers unique problems and, like a rich invalid, demands a special treatment. In Auden's case, the main difficulties are with normalization and regularization. He was a prolific, often rushed correspondent, and the letters are speckled with single parentheses, uncrossed *t*s, and spaces in the middle of words. All such disorienting or ineffable deviations from printed norms have been corrected here. However, Auden himself approved of editions that were, broadly speaking, full and unregularized. In a review of Keats's correspondence, he praised the fact that 'all the important letters are included and without cuts ... the letters are printed in their original spelling and punctuation, which is more important than one might think, for normalization of such matters ruins Keats's peculiar epistolary style.'[3] My aim, then, has been to retain the idiosyncracies of spelling and punctuation in Auden's own 'peculiar epistolary style', while rinsing away any one-off lapses due not to habit or unconscious word-play, but to clumsy fingers or haste. Take, for instance, misspellings. Where there is no discernable enrichment of meaning in a misspelt word I have followed a simple rule. Throughout his life Auden regularly got wrong some words, 'Beaudelaire', for example, which remain readily comprehensible in his versions. As with anyone else, though, his mind often outran his muscles, and some misspellings, like 'phropetic' (for prophetic) or 'buisness' (for business), words which usually gave him no trouble, make less or no sense as they stand, and so they have been corrected here. (In most instances, this is a distinction between what can be understood easily when it is read aloud, and what cannot.) With Auden's punctuation, I have been as passive as I reasonably could. His habits, such as that of placing a parenthesis outside a sentence, have nearly always been retained, but a very few full-stops have been added silently where fruitless confusion would otherwise have been possible.

Doubtful readings are put into brackets and preceded by a question mark—[?now] in Letter 1 is an example—and apparently missing letters or words are also supplied in brackets. Because it is usually impossible to know when an interlineation was added, they have all been dropped into the text, on the principle that the sequence of words on the printed page page reproduces the sequence followed by the eye of someone reading the original manuscript. All postscripts, then, are reproduced where they occur (in Letter 2, for instance, at the head of the letter), rather than at the end where a transcription based on the (unknowable) order of composition would place them. All marks which lose their significance when the text of a letter is transferred into print have also been omitted. These include cancellations (except for the case of a few possibly meaningful deletions which are recorded in the footnotes), false starts, and page numberings. Underlined words are reproduced in italics, and I have made the start of a new paragraph clear by adding an indentation wherever it was missing in the original. Dates, addresses, and signatures have all been assigned a regular slot at the top left, top right, and bottom right of a letter respectively. This treatment, which attempts to be unobtrusive, preserves the distinction, perhaps an important one in the case of a writer who had quite severe standards of

[3] 'Keats in his Letters', *Partisan Review*, 18. 6 (Nov.–Dec. 1951), 701.

literary propriety, between what Auden himself chose to submit to print, and what had, so far as he was concerned, reached its final form once he had written it out.

The conventions of the minimal editorial apparatus will be obvious. A heading gives, as nearly as possible, the date of each letter, while the details of the manuscript (ALS for autograph letter signed, etc.), the instrument used, and the location of the original are shown at the foot of each letter. If a substantial extract has been printed before, that information follows. Auden's enormous range of reference and his unflagging practicality filled his letters with allusions and mundane ephemera. The footnotes, while assuming a basic knowledge of Auden's life and work, attempt, then, to supply a context for each letter and to give in short form whatever information a reader might need or be interested in. When that involved references to Spender's career, these too have been provided.

1. *17 October 1930*[1]

17.10.30

Larchfield Academy | Helensburgh | Dumbartonshire | N.B.[2]

My dear Stephen,

Thank you very much for your letter and your nice remarks about the book. No 2 is trash but I was too late to remove it. The long poem in four parts I think you will like better on acquaintance.[3] I hope you have got the book by now. I sent it but Winifred[4] wrote and said that she was keeping it till she knew where you were.[5]

I have not unfortunately seen the October Criterion yet. I am too poor but shall buy it next week when I get my half-term's pay.[6]

Of the two you send, I like the first two verses of 'What I expected was' very much, [?but] not the next one, and I hate the word 'poem' in a poem.[7]

What is wrong with the third verse and also with the other poem, I find

---

[1] Auden (referred to hereafter as WHA) had been in Berlin with Isherwood during July 1930. Then in Aug., after a brief visit to the so far unidentified 'Father Parker's Scout Camp', he went to his parents' cottage at Threlkeld in the Lake District. The Larchfield term started on 4 Sept.

[2] 'N.B.' is the abbreviation of North Britain, an old name for Scotland, at that time still occasionally used in postal addresses.

[3] WHA's *Poems* was published by Faber & Faber in London on 18 Sept. 1930. Poem II begins 'Which of you waking early and watching daybreak' (*EA* 41–2); WHA dropped it in the second edn. of his book, *Poems* (London, 1933). The 'long poem in four parts' is XVI, 'It was Easter as I walked in the public gardens' (*EA* 37–40).

[4] Winifred Paine, a family friend of the Spenders', who cared for Stephen Spender (referred to hereafter as SS) and his sister Christine after their parents died. She is 'Caroline' in *WWW*.

[5] SS was in Germany throughout the summer of 1930. He lived for most of the time in Hamburg, but he also visited Isherwood in Berlin.

[6] SS published 'Four Poems' in *The Criterion*, 10. 38 (Oct. 1930), 32–4. The batch, dedicated to WHA, consists of 'The Port', 'The Swan', 'Lines Written When Walking Down the Rhine' (later retitled 'In 1929'), and 'Not to you I sighed. No, not a word'. All were later collected in SS's first commercially published book, *Poems* (London, 1933). As an Assistant Master at Larchfield, one of five salaried members of staff, WHA earned £200 per year.

[7] SS's poem 'What I expected was' is XI in his *Poems* (1933). As published, the first two stanzas of the poem dramatize the speaker's naive expectations of a heroic personal life and the frustration of those expectations. In the third stanza, the attention turns outwards from self-pity towards extravagant compassion as the speaker sees cripples and their 'pulverous grief'. The fourth stanza ends with a hope for 'some final innocence . . . / Like the created poem / Or the dazzling crystal.'

a little difficult to explain. (by the by, 'Puffed and spreading in the chemist's jar' is a good line)[8]

Perhaps I can put it this way. All[9] poetry in our time is comic. There are two modes

(1) The drunken prophetic
(2) The legal disclaimer.

In that of your poetry which I have seen you are better at 2 than 1. Verse 1 and 2 of 'What I expected' is a successful legal poem, a scotch joke. Verse 3 is an unsuccessful, ie serious, attempt at the prophetic style, the Shakesperian joke.

I dont think the latter is any more natural to you than making obscene jokes. You become heavy, German.

No, [?now] I remember a prophetic line of yours which is very successful

'The new bronzed German
The young Communist and myself, being English.'[10]

As an example of the opposite error I would take my poem 'Which of you waking, early, and watching daybreak,'[11] which ought to have [been] written in the prophetic style and was done in the legal instead. Result a pompous old gentleman.

Have I made myself clear or am I talking complete nonsense. In my life by this wonderful pontic sea[12] one gets egocentric mania. We live ghoulishly in the past, the flag at the Golf-house flutters and nothing matters. I love it.

I know nothing about Vienna except that I wont go there.[13] There are Turkish baths for the mutually attracted middle-aged, I believe.

---

[8] The line WHA quotes here does not seem to be in SS's published work, so the 'other poem' was presumably abandoned.

[9] After 'All' WHA deleted 'verse'.

[10] From 'Lines Written When Walking Down the Rhine' (see n. 6 above), collected with revisions as 'In 1929' in *Poems* (1933).

[11] See n. 3 above. Mendelson dates the poem 'October 1929' in *EA* 42.

[12] *Othello* 3.3. 453–5: 'Like to the Pontic Sea, / Whose icy current and compulsive course / Ne'er knows retiring ebb'. Helensburgh overlooks the Firth of Clyde. By 1930, Larchfield was in financial and academic decline.

[13] WHA had already been to Austria several times in the middle twenties, but he did not, apparently, visit Vienna until 28 Aug. 1934 when he passed through during his 'Dracula trip'. SS seems to have first visited the city in the early summer of 1934. In 1930 Austria was on the brink of Civil War, and the capital, known as 'Red Vienna', was the centre of Social-Democratic power in the country. It also enjoyed a similar sexual reputation to Berlin's.

I teach rugger here. Every day I rush about in shorts telling people not to funk.[14]

> best love
> Wystan.

I have just finished a draft of a new play.[15]

ALS (Fountain Pen) Berg.

2. [? *late June–early July 1933*][1]

Monday   Downs School | Colwall | N^r Malvern.

Please write and say you have had this.

Dear Stephen,
    You letter arrived this afternoon. I am very glad you wrote.
    I must say at once that I had nothing whatever to do with Madge's article. He told me that he was writing a reply to your one in New Country, and asked permission to quote some verse or other of mine. I have not seen the article. He personally is a nice overcultured rather repressed young man who has had T.B of the intestines.[2]

---

[14] In his autobiography, Cecil Day-Lewis (1904–72), WHA's predecessor at Larchfield, describes the dangers of teaching rugger there: 'in a school of only sixty or so boys the first XV were giants compared with the second XV, who could give them no sort of a game unless I myself played for the pygmies. Many a gruelling hour I spent chasing all over the field, plastered with Scottish mud, trying to tackle the whole first XV one after another.' (*The Buried Day* (London, 1960), 189.)

[15] WHA started *The Fronny* in mid-Aug. 1930. On 8 Dec. that year, he sent it to T. S. Eliot at Faber & Faber. Most of the play has been lost, but *PDW* 464–89 contains the surviving fragments and full details of the play's history.

[1] Some time during the early summer of 1933, WHA abandoned 'In the year of my youth when yoyos came in' (repr. in *The Review of English Studies*, NS 29. 115 (Aug. 1978), 281–309). He continued working on *DD*, and, probably in early June, had the experience which has become known as his Vision of Agape.

[2] Charles Madge (b. 1912), poet, journalist, and sociologist. From 1935 to 1936 he was a reporter on *The Daily Mirror* and in 1937 founded the Mass Observation project with Tom Harrisson. Madge published two books of poems, *The Disappearing Castle* (London, 1937) and *The Father Found* (London, 1941). In 1939, after his marriage to Kathleen Raine had been dissolved, Madge began an affair with Inez Pearn (d. 1976), whom SS had married in 1936. (See Letter 4, n. 3, and Letter 9, n. 3.)
    In March 1933, an essay 'Poetry and Revolution' by SS appeared in Michael Roberts's

As to all this job versus means business; it makes me sick that people should try to use one to beat the other with.[3] As the one who has to have a job, *I* am naturally jealous of you and Christopher who can do as you please.[4] I dont think you know all the humiliations and exploitation of ones weakness that a job like mine involves, how hard it is to preserve any kind of integrity.

If I ever sound complacent about it, it is because as compensation I exagerate its occasional exquisite moments of satisfaction.

Of course I think you absolutely right to do as you are doing, though that, as you must know far better than [I] has its dangers, though I doubt if they are as insidious as mine.[5]

Good god if I were you I should always be abroad. This country would be intolerable without a fixed occupation.

I entirely agree with you about my tendency to National Socialism, and its dangers.[6] It is difficult to be otherwise when ones surroundings, and emotional symbols are of necessity national emblems.

I'm no more of a communist than you are but to acheive the kind of society I think we both wish for, it is fatal to ignore the national psychological factor.[7] The number of the completely disinterested is never quite large enough.

The success of fascism seems to show that if people have any share; even only a cultural one, (eg the secondary school clerk,) He responds to

anthology *New Country* (London), 62–71. It argued that 'if a poem is not complete in itself and if its content spills over into our world of confused emotions, then it is a bad poem'. Madge replied to this with 'Poetry and Politics' in *New Verse*, 3 (May 1933), 1–4. In the course of his piece, Madge quoted from 'A Happy New Year' Part II (*EA* 115–16) and 'A Communist to Others' (see pp. 173–7 of the present volume).

[3] Madge's article suggests that there are two kinds of poet: 'separatists' (like SS) who are 'to be found with a knapsack in the Tyrol or sitting in a Café at Perugia' and those (like WHA) 'who have got jobs, mostly as schoolmasters' and whose 'poems are not separate from the rest of their activity'.

[4] At the time of this letter, Isherwood, supported by an allowance from his 'Uncle Henry', was on the Greek island of St Nicholas with the boy called 'Heinz' in *CHK*, and SS was travelling in Italy with T. A. R. Hyndman ('Jimmy Younger' in *WWW*).

[5] SS was padding out a small private income by writing reviews. In early 1933 he had also contracted with Cape to write the book on Henry James that metamorphosed into his critical survey of modernism, *The Destructive Element* (London, 1935).

[6] In his 1966 preface to *O³*(L), WHA, looking back on the original 1932 edn., wrote, 'My name on the title-page seems a pseudonym for someone else, someone talented but near the border of sanity, who might well, in a year or two, become a Nazi' (7).

[7] SS did not begin to develop an explicitly socialist literary position until later in 1933; and he actually became a member of the Communist Party for just a few months in late 1936 and early 1937. As the thirties wore on, his commitments shifted back towards the personal and the private, where, since then, they have remained.

the national call and if the right appeal is not made, the wrong one will be.

Personally I think that the more internationally you can think and feel, the more I admire you.

For myself, I know my temperament and necessity, force me to work in a small field.

I wish I could see you. When are you returning.[8]

Many thanks for the dedication.[9]

It has been very hot here[10] and I am wildly in love with the enclosed, who is going to be a good painter.

Those swine at Oxford never sent me the Outlook so I havent yet seen your story.[11]

Gerald is coming to morrow to talk to the boys.[12]

Forgive this muddled letter. It will be alright if it convinces you

    (a) That I really had nothing to do with Madge's article

    (b) That I dont[13] dissapprove of internationlism.

    (c) That I admire you and your work very much

best love
Wystan

You got a lovely puff from Dobrée in the Listener. I hear we were all slated by Leavis in Scrutiny.[14]

ALS (Pencil) Berg. Cited in *Early Auden* (dated 'Summer 1934'), 337.

[8] SS was back in England by early Aug. 1933.

[9] SS does not seem to have published anything dedicated to WHA at around this time. It is possible, though, that he had already promised his volume of short stories, *The Burning Cactus* (London, 1936), of which WHA and T. A. R. Hyndman are joint dedicatees (see Letter 3, n. 12).

[10] The school magazine, *The Badger*, 1. 2 (Autumn 1933), 31, recorded a June of 'extreme heat and drought' with temperatures rising as high as 85°, and many days in the eighties.

[11] WHA contributed his poem 'To a Young Man on his Twenty-First Birthday' (*EA* 120) and SS his story 'The Burning Cactus' to the first issue of *New Oxford Outlook*, 1. 1 (May 1933).

[12] Gerald Heard (1885–1971) was famous throughout Britain during the early thirties as a broadcaster on popular science. At the same time, as the author of books on philosophy and psychic phenomena—including *The Ascent of Humanity* (London, 1929) and *The Social Substance of Religion* (London, 1931)—and as a highly coloured metropolitan personality, he enjoyed great prestige among London intellectuals. He lived in a modernistic West End flat with his boyfriend, the painter Chris Wood. WHA seems to have met Heard through Naomi Mitchison in 1929 or 1930. He is the model for Samson, the Virgilian guide, in 'In the year of my youth when yoyos came in'. (See also Letter 8, n. 16, and Letter 10, n. 7.)   [13] After 'dont' WHA deleted 'agree with'.

[14] Bonamy Dobrée (1891–1974), a close friend of T. S. Eliot, was in 1933 one of

3. [28 June 1935][1]

Friday   Downs School | Colwall, | N^r Malvern.

Dear Stephen,
  Thanks so much for your extremely interesting and valuable letter.
To take your points one by one.

  (A) Certain of the faults, though not excused, are partially explained
       by the circumstances of writing for dramatic performance. eg.

       (1) The audience. The theatre going audience is a bourgeois
            one. I must not let them yawn, I must not keep their minds
            too long at a stre[t]ch (ie scenes like the financier and the
            poet must intersperse more serious stuff).[2] The average
            level of appeal must not be much higher than the average
            level of response. There must even be something to keep
            the young man who has come with his girl by mistake,
            thinking it was a detective story.

       (2) The Performers. I have to write for a company, all
            of whom are young, and not particularly talented or
            intelligent, but well trained at movement. I cant give them
            heavy parts, or complicated characters to portray. As it is,
            the Vicars sermon makes much too great demands on
            them.[3]

  (B) Collaboration between a realist writer like Christopher and a[4]
       parabolic writer like myself leads to some uncertainty. It might
       interest you to know about the authorship of different scenes.

Scene I.   W.H.A.
Steamer scene.   C.I. (except song)

London's most influential literary journalists. He later became Professor of English at
Leeds University. His omnium gatherum review of books by the new generation of
writers, 'New Life in English Poetry' in *The Listener*, 9. 231 (14 June 1933), 958, praises
SS as 'the most evident singer of them all'. Leavis's attack is 'This Poetical Renascence' in
Scrutiny, 2. 1 (June 1933), 65–76, where he accuses WHA of 'undergraduate cleverness'
(70) and laments SS's attraction to the 'glamorous-ineffable-vague' (71).

  [1] On 30 May 1935, during the term in which WHA gave up his job as a master at the
Downs School, *DBS* had been published.
  [2] See *PDW* 237–40 and 241–3.
  [3] *DBS* was written by WHA and Isherwood for the Group Theatre, and first performed
by its members on 12 Jan. 1936 at the Westminster Theatre in a version which omitted the
Vicar's Sermon in the final scene (see *PDW* 554 and 575–9).
  [4] After 'and a' WHA deleted 'sy'[mbolic].

Ostnia scenes.	W.H.A.
Red Lamp scene.	W.H.A.
Asylum scene.	All except the Leaders speech. C.I.
Financier scene.	C.I. (except song)
Paradise Park. ⎫ Operation scene. ⎭	mostly, W.H.A.
Feet scene.	Poetry. W.H.A. Foot Dialogue. C.I.
Nineveh Hotel scenes.	Destructive Desmond, quarrel with dog, and dialogue after Francis discovery. C.I. The rest. W.H.A.
Last scene.	Vicars sermon. W.H.A. The rest. C.I.

(C) *Satire.*

For satire as a purely external thing, I have very little interest (eg. Dryden). Swift is different because he is satirising Mankind and is therefore included himself.

I dont say for a moment I succeed in doing it, but my whole theory of satire, I have tried to express in the poem in scene I which you once said you liked.

> Enter with him
> These legends love, etc.[5]

ie to convert one must be ones opponent and so make him convince himself.

If as you say I not only present them themselves but also their *own view* of themselves (judging not by the words only but by the whole context, which is what I always try to work comment by) Then of course I fail.

The Red Lamp song is not an exception really.[6] That kind of life actually has a genuine tragic *verbal* poetry of its own of which the song is meant to be an example. The Hotel addicts have lost contact with live words and so havent.[7]

(D) *Lack of Mature standards*

If these are not found in the choruses, which is the one place I've tried to set them (not possible for the characters for reason, A.2) it is a very serious criticism indeed. If I havent been explicit enough about the necessity to 'think willfully,' that is partly at any rate, because the part of the audience which will listen to poetry

---

[5] See *PDW* 201–2. The poem was actually written in Dec. 1931.
[6] *PDW* 219–20 and 223–4.   [7] *PDW* 223.

at all, are thinkers rather than actors. Creation is obviously thought + act, both of which I suppose are equally important except that the first is extremely rare, and those who do it, rarely do anything else.

In general however if you dont feel a standard there, it must be because I havent got one—the bugger's trait. In which case I can only say that I cant talk further ahead than I am. Actually the moral I tried to draw is always, 'You have the choice. You can make the world or mar it.' Free-will means you can choose either to fear thought or love and understand.[8]

Your remarks about my kind of satire incidentally reminds me of the reaction of my authorities to the letter I forwarded to you. I said 'That is what the boy's like. Therefore I write like that, and will do something for him.'[9] This completely nonplussed them as an idea.

Anyway, Stephen, I am most grateful for your letter. The moment one gets anything of a name, real criticism is almost impossible to secure, and you and Christopher and Edward[10] are the only people I can trust to control one. Not that we're so universally praised. eg. I.M. Parson's (who is he?) review of Dogskin in to-day's *Spectator*.[11]

---

[8] The passage from 'Actually the moral' to 'love and understand' was an afterthought by WHA, added at the foot of the page with an arrow drawing it into the main body of the letter. In *The Destructive Element*, published in April 1935, SS had written that WHA's best work stemmed from a 'loving attitude of mind: the writer does not write from hatred, not even when he writes satire, but from a *loving understanding* . . . The peculiar kind of experience which his poetry offers is an organic, living experience, made up sometimes of contradictions, and which is sometimes irresponsible and evasive. It is a mistake to suppose his poetry is primarily one of ideas: it is a chameleon poetry which changes its colour with the ideas which it is set against' (276) [my italics].

[9] This is presumably the letter WHA went in April to an ex-pupil, Michael Paget-Jones, who was at Bryanston. It contained the 'unfortunate exhortation to put an onion in the chalice' (Carpenter, 174) in honour of the Downs School's headmaster Geoffrey Hoyland, who was coming to preach at Bryanston. The staff there discovered the letter and sent it back to the Downs School. The offer of a job for WHA at Bryanston in the autumn was immediately withdrawn.

[10] Edward Upward (b. 1903), who, like WHA, was employed as a schoolmaster. He had joined the Communist Party, had published some short stories, and was working on a novel, *The Border Line*, which he eventually brought out in 1938 as *Journey to the Border*. On 6 Oct. 1930 WHA had sent him his *Poems* saying 'I shall never know how much in these poems is filched from you via Christopher.'

[11] I. M. Parsons (1906–80), an expert on WWI poetry and the editor of *The Collected Works of Isaac Rosenberg* (London, 1979), was a Partner (and later a Director) of Chatto & Windus. In the *Spectator* on 9 Nov. 1934 he had given a generally favourable review to SS's *Vienna* (London, 1934), but in the same magazine on 28 June 1935 he called *DBS* a 'shoddy affair, a half-baked little satire which gets nowhere'. In their 'Last Will and

I shall be delighted to receive a dedication.[12] Thanks. Will write to Gorer when I have a moment.[13]

My news.

(1) I am going in Sept to work for Grierson in G.P.O. Films.[14] £3 a week. (Please dont send p.c's to my house in which is written 'have you got a job yet' because my people thought I chucked up Bryanston of my own volition.)

(2) On June 14th I married Erika Mann, Thomas Mann's eldest daughter, to give her a new passport.[15] I didnt see her till the ceremony and perhaps I shall never see her again. But she is very nice. (Be very discreet about this if you hear about it anywhere. Officially it is perfectly genuine)

Best love
Wystan

ALS (Fountain Pen) Berg. Cited in *Early Auden*, 279–80, and *PDW* 555.

4. [? *30 January 1937*][1]

Saturday

Stephen darling,

What bad luck I do have. Off to-day for Sarinyena for I think about 1 month at Arragon Front.[2]

Testament' WHA and MacNeice returned the compliment: 'May the critic I. M. Parsons feel at last / A creative impulse' (*LFI* 247).

[12] This was almost certainly the dedication of SS's *The Burning Cactus* to WHA and T. A. R. Hyndman. It is just possible that SS had already promised this two years earlier (see Letter 2, n. 9). If so, both WHA and SS seem to have forgotten the fact.

[13] Geoffrey Gorer (1905–85), anthropologist and sociologist. His first book, *The Revolutionary Ideas of the Marquis de Sade*, was published in 1934.

[14] WHA started work as an assistant director in the GPO Film Unit run by John Grierson (1898–1972) on 1 Sept. 1935.

[15] In early 1935, Erika Mann (1905–69) learned that the Nazis were planning to take away her German citizenship because of her anti-Nazi cabaret, the 'Pfeffermühle'. In Amsterdam, she asked Isherwood to marry her so that she could get a British passport. He declined, but WHA, when asked, cabled back 'DELIGHTED'. The wedding actually took place in Cheltenham on 15 June, the day before Erika Mann lost her German citizenship. During 1940–1, WHA saw her with her family on a number of occasions in Princeton and Los Angeles, but after that they were rarely in touch.

[1] SS has written 'This letter was left for me at my hotel in Barcelona, 1937 I suppose SS' in ink across the top of this note. For the dating, and its bearing on WHA's journey around Spain, see the Appendix 'Auden and Spain'.

[2] A small town between Saragossa and Barbastro, about 200 km. NW of Barcelona.

I did so want to see you to argue with you about what Louis said you said about real and unreal love.[3]

> with lots of whichever you approve of just now
> from
> your devoted and sex starved
> Wystan

ALS (Pencil) Berg.

5. [c. 2–c. 12 July 1938]¹

Hotel San Jacino | 18 E. 60 Street.

Dear Stephen,

Thank you so much for your long chatty letter and poems. The Design for Living gets more baroque every day. I look forward to meeting Pat.[2]

We have been re-reading and re-reading Trial of a Judge.[3] Fabers with typical meaness sent one copy between us. As a result I am feeling rather low. It makes me feel that almost everything I've written is shabby superficial trash. Stephen, with all seriousness, I say that I'm certain it is

[3] In the autumn of 1936, SS broke off his relationship with T. A. R. Hyndman; shortly afterwards he met Inez Pearn at an Aid-to-Spain meeting in Oxford, and before Christmas 1936 they were married. On 22 Nov. SS wrote to Isherwood: 'I'm just not capable any more of having "affairs" with people. . . . I am sure that you will understand this necessity for a permanent and established relationship' (LTC 125–6). Because WHA was in London during the first half of Dec. 1936, working with Britten on The Way to the Sea (1937) and finishing off LFI with MacNeice, it seems plausible that he wanted to take up a remark by SS—relayed to him by MacNeice—about the difference between marriage with a woman and an affair with a man.

[1] WHA and Isherwood left England on 19 Jan. 1938 to gather material for their book JTW. On the way home from China, they stopped off in New York at the beginning of July. It was the first visit to the city for both of them.

[2] Design for Living is Noel Coward's play about a bohemian ménage à trois. It was published in England in 1933, but not performed (because of the Lord Chamberlain's objections) until 1939. SS states in a letter (12 Nov. 1988) that 'Pat' is Patrick de Maré. De Maré (b. around 1915) went to Wellington, where he became a friend of Gavin Ewart, and then read medicine at Cambridge. Afterwards he trained as a psychologist and went into practice in London. SS's poem 'Three Days' in The Still Centre (London, 1939) reflects on their short affair. De Maré is the author of, amongst other books, Perspectives in Group Psychology (London, 1972).

[3] SS's play Trial of a Judge was published by Faber & Faber in Mar. 1938.

the greatest poem of our time. I dont *feel* that it is a play at all, but then I havent seen it even with Boopydoop's spittle on it.[4] God, why doesn't he DIE. I dont see how we shall ever be rid of him without [that], chiefly because of Robert whom I cant bear to quarrel with.[5]

As a play I think it is much too serious and subtle. Drama to me is essentially a crude music like a roundabout, because, like the film, it is only intended to be seen once, when one is a little tight.[6]

I dont feel quite happy about what you say of poetry, as having to affect like propaganda for Spain, at least not in our time and with your make-up.[7] I think you expect too much of poetry and at the same time too little.

You seem to me to be realy a reflective, if you like, philosophical poet, indeed much more so than I am, and I think you will lose if you try to deny that nature. Eg. I dont like the poem on Lorca and De falla. Quoting from memory,

> The police took down
> The words from his mouth
> They found in his pocket
> A letter from the South,[8]

is in my style, the comic tradition, and doesnt suit you. Rilke is much nearer to you than Lorca.[9] But I must talk to you about all this.

---

[4] *Trial of a Judge* opened on 18 Mar. 1938 at the Unity Theatre, London, in a Group Theatre production directed by Rupert Doone—Boopydoop—(1904–66).

[5] WHA and Isherwood had a series of disagreements with Doone, culminating in a fierce quarrel in Aug. 1937 over whether they should allow their next play, *OTF*, to be performed by the Group Theatre. Robert Medley (b. 1905), the painter and stage designer, who was at Gresham's with WHA and who prompted him to begin writing poetry, lived with Rupert Doone.

[6] In his article 'Poetry and Expressionism', published in the *New Statesman & Nation*, NS 15. 368 (12 Mar. 1938), 407–9, SS had argued that a 'serious play' *was* very close to being a poem, but he insisted that this was because drama as a form was capable of a similar subtlety and depth.

[7] In the Introduction to *Poems for Spain*, an anthology he edited with John Lehmann and published in Mar. 1939, SS wrote that 'in a revolution, a national resurgence, a war against an aggressor, there is a revival of the fundamental ideas [of liberty, justice, etc.] and there is actually an identity of the ideas of public policy and poetry' (10). However, in the Foreword to his collection *The Still Centre*, published in May 1939, he said that 'one day a poet will write truthfully about the heroism as well as the fears and anxiety of today; but such a poetry will be very different from the utilitarian heroics of the moment' (10).

[8] The poem was, apparently, never published. F. Garcia Lorca (1898–1936), the playwright and poet, and Manuel de Falla (1876–1946), the composer, were prominent symbols of the Spanish Republic's struggle with Franco's Nationalist forces.

[9] During 1938 SS was translating both Rilke and Lorca. With J. B. Leishman, he published Rilke's *Duino Elegies* (London, 1939) and with J. L. Gili, *Poems: F. Garcia Lorca* (London, 1939).

We have been giving *On The Frontier* new fittings which improve it,
but still feel rather uncomfortable. The subject is too contemporary for a
semi-realistic play.[10]

love to all
Wystan

ALS (Fountain Pen) Berg.

6. *20 July 1938*[1]

20.7.38   42, LORDSWOOD ROAD, | HARBOURNE, | BIRMINGHAM.

Dear Stephen,

Thank you so much, my dear, for your charming letter. I too very
much want to see you and talk about poetry; I am so rarely in London,
and you are so rarely alone that we dont see as much of each other as we
should.

As to poetry and the public,[2] I think

(a) There is a complete scale of poetry from the most direct and popular
to the most difficult, from

> He had two daughters and a song
> The one went to Denver and the other went wrong[3]

to the Duinesien Elegies.

(b) That this is right, right in the same way that the Catholic church was
right in extending from the pagan superstition of the peasant's religion
to the Henry James subtlety of Aquinas or St Theresa.

[10] A first version of *OTF* was completed on 6 Sept. 1937. Almost immediately WHA
and Isherwood began to make revisions, and they worked intensively on the play during
their journey from Shanghai to New York in June 1938. *OTF* was published on 27 Oct.
1938 and had its first performance on 14 Nov. 1938 at the Arts Theatre, Cambridge, in a
production directed by Rupert Doone. In 'Poetry and Expressionism', SS called for a
'realism with a wide range of reference to contemporary problems, and with an approach
which can evade the surface naturalism of the prose drama and the whims of the censor'
(409).

[1] WHA and Isherwood docked on 17 July 1938. WHA then spent a few days at his
parents' home in Birmingham before he left for Brussels at the start of Aug. to work on the
poems for *JTW*.

[2] The points WHA makes in this letter are an extension, and in some ways a
qualification, of the argument in his Introduction to the *Oxford Book of Light Verse*
(probably written in 1937, though published in 1938, repr. in *EA* 363–8).

[3] An unidentified, presumably American, folk-song.

(c) That certain things can be said and only said in a popular way, and others only in a difficult way. Both ways have their limitations. The development of highbrow art in the 19th and 20th centuries has not been only bad. Problems have been attacked which were never touched in earlier less economically specialised ages.

(d) That certainly at the moment, and I am inclined to think, probably always, there are interests and experiences which are the property of only a few. Under any social system there are different levels of consciousness. Large-scale works, on major themes of vital importance to society as a whole, can of course have a very wide range, with a popular appeal in the mass and a particular appeal in the detail. But no artist creates only major works.

(e) That while our feeling that we want to write for many people is sound, we must beware, and I much more than you, of imagining

     (a) That everything we want to write can be popular

     (b) That if it isnt, we shouldnt want to write it.

(a) is untrue and (b) is cowardice. One has both to fight and accept one's isolation.

Christopher and I made up a Goethe-esque aphorism in the train.

> Poems are written with the head for the heart.
> Novels are written with the heart for the head.

Do you agree?

I like the three poems, particularly *Fall of a City*, but can something be '*pressed*' on a shelf?[4]

Much love
Wystan

ALS (Fountain Pen) Berg.

---

[4] SS's poem 'Fall of a City' appeared in *The New Statesman & Nation*, NS 16. 389 (6 Aug. 1938), 219, containing the lines, 'But somewhere some word presses / In the high shelf of a skull'. When SS collected the poem in *The Still Centre* (1939), the lines had been changed to, 'But somewhere some word presses / On the high door of a skull'.

7. [? *late April–early May 1940*][1]

1 Montague Terrace | Brooklyn Heights | N.Y.

Dearest Stephen,

Thank you so much for your letter and the poems. I like 'From a tree choked by ivy' very much indeed. 'Dearest and nearest brother' I dont like very much; I think my objection is the diction. A phrase like

> Orpheus maker of music
> Clasped his pale bride
> Upon that terrible river

reads like a translation from some other language.[2]

What you say about 'centre' is probably true.[3] I believe it to be there but am very shy about revealing it, partly because the nearest I can get now to expressing it directly is Kierkegaard's statement '*Before God we are always in the wrong*', and carelessly made such a remark appears misleading and defeatist.[4]

As you know my dominant faculties are intellect and intuition, my weak ones feeling and sensation.[5] This means I have to approach life via the former; I must have knowledge and a great deal of it before I can feel anything. People imagine that I absorb things easily and quickly: this is true only in the most superficial way. On the contrary I am really someone who has to grow very slowly; I develop slower than most people.

I've just finished a philosophical poem of 1700 lines which is part of a book for John Lehmann called *The Double Man*. The rest is partly verse

[1] WHA moved into the Montague Terrace apartment, which had a view across the East River to Manhattan, at the start of Oct. 1939. His collection *AT* was published in the United States on 7 Feb. 1940.

[2] The first poem mentioned is 'Tod und das Mädchen', collected in *Ruins and Visions* (London, 1942). The second, addressed to Humphrey Spender (b. 1910), is part II (and 'Tod und das Mädchen' becomes part III) of the sequence 'Elegy for Margaret' printed in *Poems of Dedication* (London, 1947). After a long battle with Hodgkin's disease, Margaret Spender, Humphrey's wife, died on Christmas Day 1945.

[3] In 1938 to 1939, as SS became disillusioned with his involvement in international politics, his thinking about poetry reached a point where he believed that his writing should become more revealing and personal. He frequently—as, for example, in his poem 'Darkness and Light' in *The Still Centre* (1939)—used the diagrammatic image of a circle's centre and circumference to illustrate his view of the self's relation to the outer world.

[4] *The Journals of Søren Kierkegaard*, ed. Alexander Dru (New York, 1938), 114.

[5] The main source for these categories is C. G. Jung's *Psychological Types*, trans. H. Godwin Baynes (London, 1923).

partly prose pensées.[6] I enclose a poem for *Horizen*. [7] Of course I wasnt offended by the editorial which I thought very fair.[8]

I wish you were over here, not because I dont support the allies—which in spite of everything I do—but because there doesnt seem anything that you cannot do just as well here as there—(unless it be suffering)—and for selfish personal reasons.

Just been reading Neville Henderson's book.[9] What emerges most strongly I feel is that the basic weakness of the democracies is the[10] failure to realise that if you give up Catholicism—and I think we must—one has to discover ones base again and that is a very long and very exhausting job. Henderson is the typical lazy protestant living off the fat of his Catholic past and imagining that metaphysics and mysticism are unnecessary—the virtues will be kept alive by good form. When therefore he meets [a] real heresy like Fascism, he is puzzled. He cannot understand that a rather nice man like Goering can behave in such an extraordinary way.[11]

But enough of all this

Much love to all,
Wystan.

ALS (Fountain Pen) Berg. Cited in Osborne, 204.

[6] WHA wrote 'New Year Letter' (*CP76* 161–93) between early Jan. and the middle of Apr. 1940. It was published in the United States, together with his 'Notes' to the poem, the sonnets 'The Quest' (*CP76* 224–31), a 'Prologue' (see n. 7 below), and an 'Epilogue' (*CP76* 222–3), as *The Double Man* on 21 Mar. 1941. In 1938 John Lehmann (1906–86), on behalf of the Hogarth Press in London, had commissioned a travel book on the States, to be called *Address Not Known*, from WHA and Isherwood. It was never written, and so, because he owed Lehmann a book, WHA had promised him the English edn. of *DM*. However, T. S. Eliot stopped the arrangement by exercising Faber & Faber's rights to WHA's work. The book was retitled *New Year Letter* and published in England by Faber on 20 May 1941.

[7] SS was associate editor of *Horizon* from 1939 until 1941. The poem WHA sent is 'Spring in Wartime', which became 'Prologue' in *DM* (see n. 6 above). It appeared in *Horizon*, 1. 7 (July 1940), 529–30.

[8] In *Horizon*, 1. 2 (Feb. 1940), the 'Comment' by the editor, Cyril Connolly (1903–74), discussed WHA and Isherwood's emigration to the United States, and noted that: 'They are far-sighted and ambitious young men with a strong instinct of self-preservation, and an eye on the main chance, who have abandoned what they consider to be the sinking ship of European democracy, and by implication the aesthetic doctrine of social realism that has been prevailing there' (69).

[9] *Failure of a Mission*, published in New York in mid-Apr. 1940. Sir Nevile Henderson (1882–1942) was the British ambassador in Berlin from 1937 to 1939, and his book is an account of his dealings with the Nazis.

[10] After 'is the' WHA wrote 'same as that of the Nazis', crossed that out, wrote 'lack of believ', and then also deleted that before continuing with the letter as it is printed here.

[11] Henderson describes Göring as suffering 'comparatively little from the personal

8. [?] 13–[14] March 1941[1]

13/3/41   7 Middagh Street | Brooklyn Heights | N.Y.C

Dearest Stephen,

People ring me up from time to time to ask me if I am going to answer what they describe as an attack by you in Horizen.[2] As I have not read it and dont intend to, I cant. I did happen by chance to see your review of my book (I liked *Dusk* very much) and was, I must confess a little hurt.[3] Your passion for public criticism of your friends has always seemed to me a little odd; it is not that you dont say acute things—you do—but the assumption of the role of the blue-eyed Candid Incorruptible is questionable. God knows it is hard enough to be objective about strangers; it is quite impossible with those whom one knows well and, I hope, loves. Personally, I will never write a review of a friends work, nor even a review of a contemporary poet if I can possibly help it. As to your review of me, what you say is probably accurate enough, but the tone alarms me. 'One is worried about Auden's poetic future'. Really, Stephen dear, whose voice is this but that of Harold Spender, M. P.[4] 'I hope, if I am

resentments which so often inspired Hitler and Ribbentrop, and up to the last I was inclined to believe in the sincerity of his personal desire for peace and good relations with England' (74).

[1] On 2 Oct. 1940 WHA moved into 7 Middagh St. and, during the same month, he returned to the Anglican Communion. *DM* was published on 21 Mar. 1941.

[2] The piece, 'Letter to a Colleague in America', is actually in *The New Statesman & Nation*, NS 20. 508 (16 Nov. 1940), 490 and is mainly an attack on Isherwood. However, at one point SS tells Isherwood: 'When another friend of ours writes to me that European Civilisation is "done for," and that we must get away and start something somewhere else, I must say I begin to wonder how much of value can be created, even in America, if the conditions in which we are living are so completely misunderstood.'

[3] *Horizon*, 3. 14 (Feb. 1941) contains SS's poem 'Dusk' (95–6), collected in *Ruins and Visions* (1942), as well as his essay 'The Year's Poetry, 1940' (138–48), which is partly a review of WHA's *AT*. Neither of WHA's quotations is verbatim, but the gist of both is accurate.

[4] Harold Spender (1864–1926) was SS's father. He was a journalist and author, but although he contested Bath in 1922 for the Liberal party, he was never elected to Parliament. SS's writing in the thirties is frequently critical of his father. His poem 'The Ambitious Son' (in *New Writing*, NS 3 (Christmas 1939), 55–7) plays on his father's 'megaphone voice', and in his novel *The Backward Son* (London, 1940) he published a severe portrait of Harold Spender as the MP 'Mr Brand'. In *WWW* (NY), SS wrote that 'just as Midas turned everything he touched to gold, so my father turned everything into rhetorical abstraction, in which there was no concreteness, no accuracy . . . A game of football ceased to be just the kicking about of a leather ball by bare-kneed boys. It had become confused with the Battle of Life. Honor, Integrity, Discipline, Toughness and a dozen other qualities haunted the field like ghostly footballers' (7).

bombed, he will write some sapphics about me' is funny and a good criticism, but for you to say it seems to me in shocking taste, suggesting that my only interest in you is as potential elegiac material. Your concluding sentence about being tired of receiving vague advice from America contains more than a trace of suggestio falsi.[5] You know quite well that practically all the poems were written before the war; even the one you quote was finished the day before England actually entered the war, yet you suggest that the book is my American Message to the British People in their Hour of Peril.[6] As to your accusation of vague abstractions when I might have got closer to Reality, you are on firmer ground. I unfortunately lack your great gifts of sensual perception but they are not in my nature and I shall never have them. (in Jungs terminology, I am a Thinking-Intuitive type, not a Feeling-Sensation type like you)[7] Accordingly I can only develop along the abstract systematic formalist line (like Henry James & Valery). The dangers of this I know very well are of the abstract losing all contact with the particular; it also often means that a single poem is incomplete and vague considered without relation to other poems. The sensation type of artist had just the opposite difficulties; his danger is that he observes the sensual facts but either cant abstract them into a significant pattern (photo-montage poetry) or has only one pattern which he repeats and does not develop. What I object to in your criticism is the opposition of Abstraction and Reality, as if Reality were Sensual Fact alone, and not a Pattern of Facts, as if the flight from reality could not be in two directions, to the uncoordinated meaningless fact and to the abstraction that has no relation to fact at all. This is the Time-Magazine-G-P-O-Film-Unit line.[8] If you dont mean this, then you seem to mean that Reality is now a

---

[5] 'This book is too general, too abstract, too vague, too scattered and too diffuse; all too often. Of course, in England we are being blasted by the concrete and the particular, so perhaps this makes us over-conscious of the abstractedness of many of the books of advice from America' (142). The OED defines suggestio falsi as 'a misrepresentation of the truth whereby something incorrect is implied to be true.'

[6] SS quotes from 'September 1, 1939' (EA 245–7). Britain declared war on Germany on 3 Sept. 1939.   [7] See Letter 7, n. 5.

[8] In 1936, criticizing Documentary Film (London, 1936) by Paul Rotha of the GPO Film Unit, WHA had written that the documentary began by saying, '"The private life is unimportant. We must abandon the story and report facts, i.e., we must show you people at their daily work, show you how modern industry is organised, show you what people do for their living, not what they feel". But the private life and the emotions are facts like any others, and one cannot understand the public life of action without them' (EA 354–5). In magazine publishing, Time Inc., founded in 1923 by Henry Luce (1898–1967) and Briton Hadden (1898–1929), followed a similar formula, especially with its photojournalistic weekly Life (started in 1936), where the picture was given much greater prominence than the accompanying text.

property of the English which is strangely close to the statement which once amused us all so much 'Spender is Pre-Jubilee'.[9]

But what really alarms me is that in a crisis of this time, you should be so bothered about what other contemporary writers are up to. What has to be done to defend Civi[li]sation? In order of immediate importance: (i) To kill Germans and destroy German Property. (2) to prevent as many English lives and as much English property as possible from being killed and destroyed. (3) to create things from houses to poems that are worth preserving. (4) to educate people to understand what civi[li]sation really means and involves. Literary criticism is a very small and negative part of the last. With your gifts for creation and education there is more than enough for you to do. (Even in criticism there are the great figures of the past to illuniate [*for* illuminate]) For God's sake, Stephen, dont become a literary version of your uncle, or a Dorothy Thompson of the Arts.[10]

I dont see how my own attitude about the war can be of any interest except to myself, but here it is. If I thought I should be a competent soldier or air-warden I should come back to-morrow. It is impossible for me to know whether it is reason or just cowardice that makes me think I shouldnt be of much military effectiveness. All I can do, therefor is to be willing to do anything when and if the Government ask me. (which I told the Embassy here).[11] As a writer and a pedagogue the problem is different, for the intellectual warfare goes on always and everywhere, and no one has a right to say that this place or that time is where all intellectuals ought to be. I believe that for me personally America is the best, but of course the only proof lies in what one produces. (Even then if it is bad one cant say it would not have been as bad had one lived

---

[9] The source of this statement, which SS says in a letter was made by a 'literary elder-statesman', has not been located, but the remark refers to George V's Silver Jubilee in May 1935 and was a comment on SS's *The Destructive Element*, published in April 1935. In *WWW* (NY), SS remembered a reviewer saying that 'if I had not gone abroad so much, but had stayed in England during the year of the Royal Jubilee, I would realize that England could not possibly be affected by forces of chaos which disturbed continental countries' (129).

[10] SS's uncle, J. A. Spender (1862–1942), the 'legendary "great man" of the family', was a famous Liberal journalist, and editor of *The Westminster Gazette* from 1896 to 1922. Dorothy Thompson (1894–1961) was also an ardent, crusading journalist, and her syndicated column 'On the Record' had made her an influential moulder of public opinion. At the time of this letter, she was married to Sinclair Lewis.

[11] WHA went to offer his services to the British Consulate in New York some time during the spring or early summer of 1940. He wrote to Mrs Dodds that he was 'told that only technically qualified people [were] wanted back'.

somewhere else). You are too old a hand to believe that History has a local habitation any more.[12]

As to Christopher, I can only tell you what I think, which may not be what he would say or even authorise.[13] What he is trying to do must seem meaningless unless one beleives, and I do, firstly that there is such a vocation as the mystical contemplative life, and secondly that of all vocations it is the highest, highest because the most difficult exhausting and dangerous.[14] Because of this, very few people are called to it, fewer even than are called to be artists. And one must be called; if one attempts it without being, in a sense, compelled, one is guilty of the most dreadful presumption and destroyed. But if one *is* called, then one has to live it, and on a plane where the ordinary sensual life of good cooking, fucking and war has no place.

I have absolutely no patience with Pacifism as a political movement, as if one could do all the things in ones personal life that create wars and then pretend that to refuse to fight is a sacrifice and not a luxury.[15] On the contrary it is perhaps the only material reward that the contemplative gets in this world. That is why I respect Gerald who really practises what he preaches, and have very little use for Huxley.[16] I know that I am not fit for such a vocation; Christopher feels that he is called, and is certainly taking it very seriously. I think his friends should have enough faith in him to trust his judgement for himself; He never, as far as I know, tells others that they ought to do the same thing. On our level we have to fight if required; on the level he is trying to reach (and I take the conventional Christian view about this) the life in time has no relevance.[17]

[12] *A Midsummer Night's Dream*, 5.1. 15–17 'the poet's pen / . . . gives to aery nothing / A local habitation and a name'.

[13] WHA had probably not seen Isherwood since early Aug. 1940 when he visited him in Los Angeles.

[14] Isherwood was in Hollywood writing film dialogue for MGM and immersing himself in the study of Vedanta. In the autumn of 1940, he became a disciple of Swami Prabhavananda, a local guru.   [15] See *PD* 56–7.

[16] Gerald Heard and Chris Wood had moved to the USA with Aldous and Maria Huxley in 1937. By Mar. 1941, although Heard continued to live in Los Angeles until Oct., he was building himself (in collaboration with Felix Greene (b. 1909), the British broadcaster and sinologist) a small institute, Trabuco College, near Laguna, about 100 miles south of Los Angeles. At the same time, he was trying to synthesize the results of his scientific and psychic research. (See also Letter 10, n. 7.) Aldous Huxley (1894–1963), who also lived in Los Angeles, was dividing his time between highly-paid film work and prolific advocacy of pacifism. On 7 Feb. 1942, he described Trabuco to Isherwood as 'a huge estate of three hundred and sixty acres, in a very beautiful, rather English country-side' (*The Letters of Aldous Huxley*, ed. Grover Smith (London, 1969), 475).

[17] Isherwood had been a pacifist since 1939. When his contract with MGM expired in May 1941, he planned to volunteer for a labour camp for conscientious objectors. He did

But enough of all this. Please treat this letter as entirely private and do not show it or quote it to any one. This house is very nice, a sort of co-op boarding house of George Davis, Benjamin Britten, Golo Mann, and some others.[18] I have an uneventful but happy life, writing a good deal, lecturing etc. My only amusement is the Opera—last night we had a wonderful performance of Don Giovanni.[19] Bengy and I have done an Operetta about an American mythical figure called Paul Bunyan which they are putting on at Columbia University for a week at the beginning of May.[20]

I have a lovely grey little cat called Sophie who sleeps on my bed at night. I see Jean Connolley quite often and like her very much.[21]

Reading through this letter I feel it sounds rather piggy, but you mustnt think that it means, even though I never write you, that we dont think of you and everyone else in London a lot, worry about your safety and miss you a great deal, Stephen dear. When this bloody business is over, it will be a great joy to see you again.[22]

Much Love
wystan

TL Berg. Cited in Osborne, 206–7, Finney, 182, and Carpenter, 292–3, 309 (all dated '13 March 1941').

not, in fact, enter the camp, but in Oct. of that year he went to work at a Quaker school in Pennsylvania (see Letter 9, n. 6).

[18] The Middagh St. brownstone was owned by George Davis (b. 1906), the literary editor of *Harper's Bazaar* and one of WHA's earliest contacts in New York. WHA paid $25 a month for a sitting-room and a bedroom on the top floor of the house.

[19] *Don Giovanni* was performed, to loud applause, on 13 Mar. 1941 at the Metropolitan Opera House in a production conducted by Bruno Walter and starring Ezio Pinza as Don Giovanni and Zinka Milanov as Donna Anna.

[20] *PB* was performed at Brander Matthews Hall, Columbia University, from 5 to 10 May 1941.

[21] In 1939, Jean Connolly (1910–50) separated from Cyril Connolly. She returned home to the United States in June 1940. In 'Some Memories' in SS's *Tribute*, Cyril Connolly wrote that his wife 'became one of Wystan's closest women friends, the first, I believe, to call him Uncle Wiz and whom he described in her copy of his *Epithalamium* as the only woman who could keep him up all night' (70).

[22] WHA next saw SS in late Apr. 1945 in London, when he stopped off on his way to Germany with the United States Strategic Bombing Survey. SS did not make his first visit to the US until 1947.

9. *16 January 1942*[1]

Jan 16th '42   1223 Pontiac Street | Ann Arbor | Michigan

Dearest Stephen,

It was lovely to get your letter. I can well imagine how dreary the Fire-Brigade must be, when you can neither go away nor have anything to do.[2] And I suppose they dont even let you wear one of those lovely brass helmets any more—You would look *such* a camp in one.

I have thought of you a lot during the past year, as I have been having a great personal crisis like you before me, of which I have reason to suspect that you have an inkling.[3] Things are going to work out alright, I think, but it takes more faith and patience than is natural to me.

My plans are a bit vague. I have asked for deferrment from the army until after the university year is over in May.[4] In the meantime there is just a possibility that I may get a job in Washington: of course my request for deferrment may be refused in which case I suppose I shall presently be a quartermaster's orderly or something. Meanwhile I go on with my writing—an enormous oratorio.[5]

Christopher is working in a refugee camp in Pennsylvania.[6] After

---

[1] WHA arrived in Ann Arbor at the end of Sept. 1941. Within a few days, he had moved into the house at 1223 Pontiac St., described in Farnan as an 'ultramodern affair of wood slats' (72). He lived there with a kind of houseboy/lodger, Charles Miller (see his *Auden: An American Friendship* (New York, 1983)), until 31 Jan. 1942.

[2] SS's works give several dates on which he joined the Auxiliary Fire Service for wartime duties. The most recent version (in his *Journals 1939–1983*, ed. John Goldsmith (London, 1985), 57) gives the autumn of 1941.

[3] In July 1939 Inez Spender had finally left her husband and gone to live with Charles Madge (see Letter 2, n. 2). They were later married. In mid-July 1941 Chester Kallman told WHA that he was having an affair with an English sailor, Jack Barker ('Jack Lansing' in Farnan), and thus precipitated what WHA referred to as 'The Crisis'. WHA wrote to Caroline Newton on 19 Jan 1942: 'Chester is in New York where there is an English sailor. They are both very happy, which makes me so.' By Feb. 1942 Kallman was back in Ann Arbor, living with WHA and working for his Master's degree (see Letter 10, n. 2).

[4] The University of Michigan authorities arranged this with the US Draft Board.

[5] WHA seems to have started *FTB* in Oct. 1941 and completed it in July 1942. Britten, Pears, and Elizabeth Mayer had visited him in Ann Arbor, partly to discuss the oratorio, during late Nov. 1941. At the time of this letter, WHA still believed that Britten would set the work to music.

[6] The Co-operative College Workshop in Haverford, Pennsylvania, a Quaker institution set up to help German refugees adapt to life in the United States. Isherwood told E. M. Forster that his job was 'social, menial, confessional, advisory, interpretative, consolatory, apologetic' (Finney, 181).

seeing him this summer, after a year, I feel quite happy that what he is doing is the right thing for *him* to do.[7] (it wouldnt be for me).

You mustnt judge him by rumours or even anything he writes to you, because in what is a period of complete re-organisation for him, he cant express himself properly. So please, Stephen dear, whether you write to him or not, do think of him warmly, because he needs it as we all do. In this period when we are all separated physically and all undergoing changes and doing different things, it is hard to write letters explaining what one is up to. Because of the lack of context words create more misunderstanding than otherwise, but deep down, I have a firm conviction that we are not apart but all engaged on the same thing; and I do hope you feel the same. That is why I so distrust public statements of one's position, or criticism of other people's.

There have been practically no books of interest coming out recently in America. Two good volumes of poetry, one by Marianne Moore and one by Louise Bogan, which I'll try to send you as soon as I am over the financial crisis of the moment.[8] The one really important book I read last year was published by the Oxford Press, so I expect you can get it over

[7] During his time at Haverford, Isherwood made occasional trips to New York, and he presumably saw WHA there during the summer of 1941. Their last meeting before that had been in early Aug. 1940, shortly before Isherwood moved back East, when WHA had visited him in Los Angeles.

[8] Both poets lived in New York and were friends of WHA. He seems to have encountered Marianne Moore (1887–1972) during 1939, not long after he arrived in the USA. The book which he refers to here is *What Are Years* (New York, 1941). In 1940, WHA told Theodore Roethke that he thought Louise Bogan (1897–1970), who wrote for the *New Yorker*, was the 'best critic of poetry' in America. They first met in mid-Jan. 1941 at the Manhattan apartment of Cyril Connolly's mother-in-law. Bogan reviewed *DM* enthusiastically in the *New Yorker*, 17 (12 Apr. 1941), 84–5, and in Oct. 1941 she was one of WHA's references when he applied for a Guggenheim Fellowship. Some of his letters to Bogan, and his praise of her work during 1942 reflect his thoughts as he contemplated the first major sifting and rewriting of his poems, the volume which was eventually issued by Random House on 5 Apr. 1945 as *The Collected Poetry of W. H. Auden.* (WHA had broached the idea of the book in a letter to Bennett Cerf a few days earlier on 8 Jan. 1942.) On 18 May 1942, he wrote to Bogan: 'Now and then I look through my books and is my face red. One of the troubles of our time is that we are all, I think, precocious as personalities and backward as characters. Looking at old work I keep finding ideas which one had no business to see already at that age, and a style of treatment which one ought to have outgrown years before. I sometimes toy with re-writing the whole lot when I'm senile, like George Moore.' WHA reviewed Bogan's *Poems and New Poems* (New York, 1941) in *Partisan Review*, 9. 4 (July–Aug. 1942). He praised her 'steady growth of wisdom and technical mastery, the persistent elimination of the consolations of stoicism and every other kind of poetic theatre, the achievement of an objectivity about personal experience which is sought by many but found only by the few who dare face the Furies', and he concluded that Bogan would be paid the respect she deserved when 'many, including myself, I fear, of those who now have a certain news value, are going to catch it' (339–40).

there, and if so, do read it. It is *Christianity and Classical Culture* by
C.N. Cochrane.[9] I have been reading St Augustine a lot lately who is
quite wonderful, only you must use Watt's translation not Pusey's.[10]
Also, as a new camp, Disraeli's novels which must have been the
inspiration for all of Harold Nicolson's books.[11]

Did you hear that my mother died last August?[12] It was a much greater
shock to me than I expected.

Much love and happiness to you
Wystan

TLS Berg. Cited in Osborne, 210–11.

10. *12 April* [*1942*][1]

12/4/32   1504 Brooklyn Avenue | Ann Arbor | Michigan

Dearest Stephen,

Thanks so much for your long letter and *Ruins and Visions* which is an
advance, I think on *The Still Centre*[2]. My favourites, *Song*, *The Ambitious
Son*, *The Drowned*, *The Fates* (especially part II, one of the best things
you've ever done), *In a Garden*, and *Dusk*.

You dont need praise from me, however, but a poet's warning. As I
see it, the next step you have to take, is to go beyond fashioning your
poetry from 'your opposite'. I'm sure you will, because in The Ambitious
Son, you seem to understand intuitively what the problem is, ie that the

[9] Cochrane's book was published in June 1940. WHA's review of the revised edn.
(1944) is repr. in *FA* 33–9, as 'Augustus to Augustine'.
[10] William Watts's translation of the *Confessions*, first published in 1631, was reprinted
by the Loeb Classical Library in 1912. E. B. Pusey's translation, first published in 1838,
was available from the Oxford University Press.
[11] Harold Nicolson (1886–1968) was a diplomat, critic, and biographer (notably of
Swinburne, Curzon, Verlaine, and Byron). WHA had known him and his wife Vita
Sackville-West (1892–1962) slightly since the summer of 1933 when Nicolson came to
talk at the Downs School.
[12] She died in Birmingham at the age of 72 on 21 Aug. 1941.

[1] WHA moved to this 'divinely Victorian' house, which he was renting from Prof.
Thomas Knott, the editor of the *Merriam-Webster Dictionary*, on 3 Feb. 1942. He and
Chester Kallman lived there until WHA left the University of Michigan at the end of May
1942. (See Farnan, 75–80 for details.) For the spring semester, WHA taught English
136—'The Analysis of Poetry'.
[2] *Ruins and Visions*, published in London in Feb. 1942, was SS's next collection after
The Still Centre, published in May 1939. (For 'Dusk', see Letter 8, n. 3.)

'pity for the weak and the poor', which you keep re-iterating (too often) is a 'camp'.[3]

I believe that you are a very strong, ruthless character. When you behave badly, it is due not to weakness of will but excess of will, unlike people such as, for example Cyril[4] or me, who, when we behave badly, do so out of fright and a fear of independence. (of course in the ultimate sense both evils are egotistical rebellion, but they are the two opposite forms it can take)

I know far too much about weakness, to have much 'poetic pity' for the poor, and the beggars. I have far too much death-wish to pity the drowned in a poem. (I suspect for instance that your *real* personal feelings about the deaths of others are; Goody. He's dead and I'm alive)

There are two kinds of people, the hypertense like you, and the hypotense like me.[5] I have learnt that as the second kind, one has to build up an elaborate system of habits, drugs, etc, in other words the regime of an *invalid*, or one is lost. That in its turn, of course, becomes a menace to ones character and one's work, because in time one forgets that one is weak.

You as the other kind, have the opposite danger, ie you escape from the guilt of having a destructive effect on those weaker than yourself, by imagining you are a sensitive sympathetic plant.

For the same reason, our forms of jealousy are different. You (at least I fancy so) can be jealous of someone else writing a good poem because it seems a rival strength. I'm not, because every good poem, of yours say, is a strength, which is put at my disposal. What *I* envy, are strengths which by their nature, I cannot make use of as support, eg. your prick.

In Chester's case, my mistake was demanding that he should be my Mother-Father, and one has no right to ask that of another, least of all someone fourteen years younger. I guess that in Inez' case, you were too much of a father, and not enough of a son.[6]

In consequence the next step for us as poets, lies in opposite

---

[3] The final stanza of 'The Ambitious Son' contains the lines: 'Yes! I could drown in lives of weakness, / For I pity and understand'.

[4] On 15 Nov. 1938, WHA had written to Cyril Connolly praising his book *Enemies of Promise* (London, 1938) and its careful dissection of his own fecklessness, saying, 'you really write about writing in the only way which is interesting to anyone except academics, as a real occupation like banking or fucking with all its attendant egotism, boredom, excitement and terror' (*Tribute*, 72).

[5] A hypertense person has abnormally high blood pressure and is emotionally volatile, whereas a hypotense individual has abnormally low blood pressure, and so is supposed to be emotionally unresponsive.

[6] See Letter 9, no. 3.

directions; You have to get over your camp of pity and accept your strength, I over my camp of tough aggressiveness, and accept my weakness, ie your poetry has to lose its whiff of the yearning school-girl, and mine its whiff of the hearty scoutmaster. Technically this probably means that I should deprive myself of the support of strict conventional verse forms, while you should impose them on yourself, in other words, we should both attempt the *difficult*. (for us each).

You take the whole Gerald Business too seriously; my criticism of him and his fellows is that they are too political; ie if you feel you have a calling to the contemplative life, that's OK with me, but you mustnt then go on to say that you should be kept by the Prime Minister, as a pet yogey-bogey adviser on political strategy.[7] Personally I believe that such people by their prayers and personal atonements *do* help the world, but not on the conscious level. Any help they can give unconsciously depends absolutely on their accepting the fact that consciously they help nobody, on their being regarded by the world as utterly selfish escapists. Above all they must *never* write books.

I finish here in May. The future is uncertain. I have been given a Guggenheim Fellowship to finish an Oratorio I have been working on for the past year, but I may be drafted.[8] If I am, I shall try to get them to let me join the Merchant Marine which sounds more amateurish.

If you get a chance read *Christianity and Classical Culture* by Cochrane, (O.U.P.) one of the most exciting books I have ever read.[9]

Much love, my dear
Wystan

ALS (Fountain Pen) King's College, Cambridge.

[7] As he built Trabuco College (see Letter 8, n. 16), Heard began to believe in the necessity for a spiritual élite to become more than merely passive critics of their society. For instance, in his book *Man the Master*, published in Nov. 1941, he called for a neo-Brahmin—like himself—to 'offer his services as the new missionary diplomatic agent of mankind' (330).

[8] WHA knew by the end of Mar. 1942 that he had been awarded a Guggenheim Fellowship. It was supposed to begin in Aug. 1942, but in the event it was postponed for a month when it seemed that WHA might be drafted. On 1 Sept. 1942, he was turned down, because of his homosexuality, by an Army psychiatrist, Dr Gross, after a 7.30 a.m. examination at Governor's Island, New York. On 2 Sept. he described Dr Gross to Caroline Newton as 'both unpleasant and grotesquely ignorant'. However, on 14 Sept. he told William Mayer, Elizabeth Mayer's husband and himself a psychiatrist, that Dr Gross was 'a bit Y.M.C.A. but very nice', and he added, 'he's lunching with me this week.' Immediately after his rejection, WHA claimed his Fellowship, and by 23 Sept. he had moved to Swarthmore in Pennsylvania.

[9] See Letter 9, n. 9.

11. 20 June [1951][1]

June 20th   Via Santa Lucia 14 | Forio d'Ischia | Prov. di Napoli.

(D[r] D[r] Sitwell's day, I believe)[2]

Dearest Stephen,
     Many thanks for your letter of June 18th. I feel exactly as you do about
the B–M business.[3] Whatever the real facts are, they are unintelligible;
even the word betrayal has become meaningless. I still refuse to say,
however, one can trust *no-one*; one may not know who they are, but I
believe passionately they do exist somewhere at this moment.
     If *Europeo's*[4] story is true—and it is the only plausible explanation of
their extraordinary route—that they were already under suspicion by
MI.5, then why did the Foreign Office a) do nothing for days after they
were missing b) insist on a totally preposterous story about the love that
dares not tell its name?
     Glad you liked *Nones*: I'm not sure I know what you mean by the
words 'trying to say too much', in respect of a poem. Do you mean that it
is obscure, ie that it should be longer?[5]
     Have read *World within World* several times with increasing respect.[6]
The only criticism I have is that, while confessing your sins of weakness
you pass over in silence your sins of strength, ie of calculation and
coldness of heart; and nobody, my dear, who is as successful or can be as

---

[1] WHA arrived back on Ischia around 30 May 1951 after spending three weeks in
England as the Spenders' guest.
[2] Edith Sitwell (1887–1964) already had two honorary doctorates (from the universities
of Leeds and Durham) and she would occasionally add these titles to her signature. On 20
June 1951 Oxford conferred a third on her.
[3] The scandal over the diplomats Guy Burgess (1911–63) and Donald Maclean
(1913–83), who had vanished from England on 25 May and whose whereabouts were still
a mystery. Shortly before he defected, Burgess twice tried to reach WHA by phone at the
Spenders' house. WHA did not get round to returning the calls, but a rumour sprang up in
the press that Burgess might be heading for Ischia. WHA's villa there was staked out by
police and reporters. On 14 June WHA had written to SS, 'I still believe Guy to be a
victim, but the horrible thing about our age is that one cannot be certain'.
[4] I have been unable to find a copy of this weekly news magazine, published in Milan.
[5] *Nones* was published in the USA on 21 Feb. 1951 and in England on 22 Feb. 1952.
(The publication dates were presumably arranged for WHA's birthday on 21 Feb.) SS
reviewed both edns., very favourably, in *Poetry*, 78 (Sept. 1951), 352–6, and in the
Spectator, 188 (29 Feb. 1952), 267.
[6] *WWW* appeared in Apr. 1951. The page numbers WHA gives are to the American
edn. of the book, and the footnotes here follow him.

funny as you, is without them.[7] The self you portray would never have
got invited to all those houses and conferences. We love people because
of their warmth and endearing weaknesses but we want to get to know
them because of their powers. Which reminds me of another point;
talking of your sister, you refer to her freedom from a sense of 'guilt or
sin' (p. 271) as if a sense of guilt and a sense of sin were identical.[8] That
is a confusion due, I think, to your decadent Puritan upbringing in which
there were rules without a philosophy to explain their rightness. If I am
relatively free from a sense of guilt, it is mainly because I was brought up
in a home which, however dotty and neurotic, was genuinely and not
conventionally christian in belief. Guilt feelings are exactly what the
psychologists say, products of the super ego, ie of self love. Guilt-feeling
A = Poppa will spank or Momma won't speak to me. If God exists, he is
certainly not like Poppa and Momma, ie if I sleep with my sister or burn
some Jews in an oven, I am no more likely to be struck by lightning than
if I have lived a saintly life. There is a punishment, of course—the loss of
authentic being in myself, but precisely because I have lost it, I am
unaware of anything wrong. Guilt-feeling B = Wystan doesn't do such
things, ie what I mind is not what I've actually done but the shock to my
self-esteem. A sense of sin is quite different. eg I have been having an
affair with X for some years, and suddenly I come to the realisation
through weaknesses which I begin to notice in his character that what I
had imagined was affection and good-will on my part was really a
devouring passion for possession, the wish to create another in my own
image. I certainly have'nt been punished in Guilt-A sense, eg. I have'nt
caught syphilis.[9] Nor is it an Ideal Self versus a Weak self in Guilt B
sense, for I have been carrying on all the time with a perfectly good
conscience. What has happened is that I have come, so to speak, to my
senses. How sinful I feel now will depend, not on my super ego, but on
the amount of real love for X that, despite my lust for possession, I may
have, or believe that I am capable of having. If I really have none, I shall

[7] After 'without them' WHA deleted 'You leave an unexplained gap between'.

[8] In *WWW*, SS wrote that 'As an Anglican, Auden had difficulties to overcome in
accepting the moral and ethical judgements of the Church. He was, as I have already
noted, peculiarly free from a sense of guilt or of sin, and now when he used these terms
they had a curiously theoretical air. With my Puritan upbringing convincing me of a guilt
from which I had spent years struggling to be free, it was curious to hear Auden discussing
sin as an intellectual position of which one could be convinced by the reasoning of
"Mother Church"' (271). Further on, he added, 'My brothers and sisters and I were
brought up in an atmosphere which I would describe as "Puritan decadence"' (285).

[9] After 'syphilis.' WHA deleted 'Nor have any of my actions contradicted what an ideal
self might'.

feel, neither guilty nor sinful, but proud of my power over others, ie I shall remain *in* a state of sin.

That is why it is necessary to have an authority (in whom, of course, one has to believe and trust) to say what is sinful and what isnt, because A) Guilt-feelings are no guide. One can feel guilty about perfectly innocent matters like accidentally seeing somebody nude. Guilt may even be a product of physiological disturbances. B) In the case of those sins which are one's greatest temptation (they vary from person to person), ie where the emotional drive behind them is very strong, it is almost impossible not to have a good conscience at the moment when one commits them, not to believe one is doing right.

To change from the serious to the literary, I find your discussion of poetic form on p. 284 questionable.[10] You are quite right in saying that the sonnets of Bridges are lifeless, and the sonnets of Hopkins are alive, but the latter are no 'freer' than the former. Hopkins has changed the prosodic rules, but the rules he adopts he obeys just as strictly as Bridges obeys the traditional rules, ie both of them are formally 'correct', for correctness only has meaning in relation to the particular law which defines it. In England it is correct to drive on the left, in U.S. it is correct to drive on the right. My objection to most free verse is that I cannot feel any necessity behind it, for me to judge whether it is correct or not. In Eliot's verse, even if I cant formally analyse it, I feel there is such a law, just as if I look at an unfamiliar geographical projection, I feel there is a uniting principle behind what appear to my eyes as arbitrary distortions. The trouble to-day with so many would-be artists is that they see, quite correctly, that many of the greatest works, eg the last plays of Shakespeare, the last quartets of Beethoven, Samson Agonistes etc are extraordinary free and easy (the same can be seen in the moral freedom of some saints) and think that they can start off writing like that. But that sort of grace is the end point of a long process, first of learning technique (every technique is a convention and therefore dangerous) and then unlearning. It is much easier to learn than to unlearn, and most of us will not get further than the learning, but there is no other route to greatness, even if we get stuck half-way. To know that it is duty not wilfullness that is telling one to break the law, one must first have learnt to love the law.

Thanks ever so much for putting yourself to all the bother of packing

---

[10] In *WWW*, SS noted in passing that 'the tormented statements of Gerard Manley Hopkins, in which living material endeavors to force itself into the mold of the sonnet, suggests the sonnet far more powerfully than the correct sonnets of his friend Robert Bridges' (284).

my camera.[11] As to the books, I don't think any of them sound my perfect dish. I didnt think much of Valery's Dance piece either. I dont, actually, care so much as you seem to for Regards sur le monde actuel. For me his great prose works are Mélange and Mauvaises Pensées.[12]

lots and lots of love to Natasha, Matthew, Elizabeth[13] and you.

Wystan.

P.S. O Yes, about my alphabetical arrangement in the *Collected Poems*.[14] My reason for doing that was not to pretend that I have gone through no historical change, but because there are so very few readers who can be trusted to approach one's poems without a preconceived notion of what that development has been, I wanted to[15] test the reader who believes that my earliest poems are the best; eg make him read a poem and then guess its date.

ALS (Fountain Pen) Berg. Cited in Carpenter, 340.

[11] In his letter of 14 June, WHA asked SS to have one of the servants forward the camera that he had left at the Spenders' house.
[12] *Dance and the Soul* (London, 1951), a dialogue, was described by SS in *The Spectator*, 6419 (6 July 1951), 26, as a 'work of transcendent beauty and truth'. In the same issue, SS also reviewed *Reflections on the World Today* (London, 1951). The other Valéry books mentioned by WHA are *Mélange* (Paris, 1939) and *Mauvaises Pensées* (Paris, 1943). WHA seems to have been writing 'pensées' of his own during early June 1951. These may have been the observations published as 'Notes on the comic' in *Thought*, 27. 104 (Spring 1952), 57–71. His contributor's note in this issue of *Thought* announces that he is working on a book 'about many things' to be called *Thinks*.
[13] SS's wife, the pianist Natasha Litvin (whom he had married in Apr. 1941), and their children Matthew (b. 1945) and Elizabeth (b. 1950).
[14] In *CP45*, WHA's poems are, in a decision probably inspired by I. A. Richards, arranged by the alphabetical order of the first lines. He had first used this method of organization in *The Poet's Tongue* (London, 1935), an anthology he edited with John Garrett.
[15] After 'wanted to' WHA deleted 'catch out'.

Appendix

AUDEN AND SPAIN

AUDEN'S time in the Republican part of Spain from 13 January to around 2 March 1937 is the most intensively mythologized blank-spot of his career.[1] Of the three major journeys which he made between 1936 and 1938—to Iceland, Spain, and China—the Spanish experience seems to have had the heaviest impact on his thought, although, perhaps because he travelled alone, it is the most sparsely documented of the three visits. By the time that Auden or his friends were prepared to say anything, however brief, about what he had seen there, the facts of the trip had been modified by hindsight, demand for a good easy-to-follow story, and simple forgetfulness. There are three direct literary results of the journey: 'Spain',[2] which Auden presumably completed in March after he had returned to England, the journalistic sketch 'Impressions of Valencia',[3] and a note (Letter 4 above), apparently the only surviving piece of correspondence from his stay there, which was probably left at Spender's hotel in Barcelona on 30 January, the day when Auden set off for the Aragon Front.[4] In this Appendix, I try to establish for the record roughly where Auden went in Spain and when, approximately, he did so. However, it is important to bear in mind that any traveller's actual experience of the country during the Civil War was shaped as much by Spain's political situation and by the practical difficulties of moving around—the mandatory visas and passes, border-controls, petrol rationing, and territorial conflicts within the Republican armies—as by distances and terrain.

Auden was in London in early January, waiting to leave for Spain with a Medical Unit, one of the few officially approved ways of entering the country. At this stage, he seems to have intended to drive an ambulance in the heavy fighting around Madrid. The morning of 8 January was spent with Britten, drinking coffee in Tottenham Court Road, where he

---

[1] The details of Auden's journey will be easier to follow with a map of northern Spain to hand. The year 1937 should be assumed with any date, unless otherwise stated.

[2] SP 51–5.

[3] Repr. in EA 360–1.

[4] Carpenter, 214, suggests that this note was written sometime after 21 Feb. (i.e. 27 Feb., the next 'Saturday' after 21 Feb.) in Valencia. However, correlation of Auden's visit with the journeys to Spain made by Spender, who just missed him, and Cyril Connolly, who saw him twice, make this date and place improbable.

gave the composer two recently completed poems, 'Lullaby' and 'Danse Macabre'.[5] Britten noted in his diary that Auden expected to leave the next day, but in the event, his departure was postponed until 11 January.[6] Isherwood met him in Paris on the morning of 12 January and they spent the afternoon getting drunk with Brian Howard and the night in bed together. The next day, 13 January, after a 'solemn parting', Isherwood saw Auden off to Spain.[7]

From this point on, little went according to plan. Auden's mother, for instance, told enquirers that she expected him to be away until May.[8] Actually, he was back in London by 4 March. Moreover, having told friends that he was going to Madrid to work as an ambulance driver, soon after he arrived in Spain he surfaced in Valencia, writing journalism and perhaps also broadcasting propaganda from the tiny socialist radio station there. Given this confusion, Auden's movements can only be reconstructed now from the accounts of people who either saw, or in Spender's case, just missed him as he spiralled around the country. Two widely canvassed—and obviously related—'sightings' must be discounted as, at best, hearsay. Robert Graves reports that Auden spent some time playing table tennis at Sitges (just below Barcelona), and Roy Campbell finds Auden guilty of the same thing, though this time at 'Tossa del [sic] Mar'. Both Graves and Campbell, although they were Nationalist sympathisers, had left Spain before Auden arrived.[9] Still, Campbell is right to pick out the seaside village of Tossá de Mar. On what was probably the night of 14 January, Auden stayed at the Casa Johnstone hotel there, owned by Archie and Nancy Johnstone (Mrs Johnstone was a Faber author), when he was on his way down to Barcelona. According to Mrs Johnstone, he was still hoping to find medical work, though now as a stretcher-bearer.[10]

Soon after this, Auden was in Valencia, the main centre of Republican administration at the time. To get there, he must have passed through Barcelona, though it seems likely that he did not stop in the city for long.

[5] *EA* 207 and 208–9.

[6] Donald Mitchell, *Britten and Auden In the Thirties: The Year 1936* (London, 1981), 141.

[7] *CHK* 263–4.

[8] Carpenter, 215.

[9] Graves's remark comes in 'These Be Your Gods, O Israel!' in *The Crowning Privilege* (Garden City, NY, 1956), 137. But see Martin Seymour-Smith, *Robert Graves: His Life and Work* (London, 1982), 278–80. For Campbell, see 'Epitaph On the Thirties' in *Nine*, 2. 4 (Nov. 1950), 345, and Peter Alexander, *Roy Campbell: A Critical Biography* (Oxford, 1982), 165, 172.

[10] Nancy Johnstone, *Hotel In Flight* (London, 1939), 84–5.

Cyril Connolly, who was on a three-week trip to Spain with his wife, Jean, and Lord Antrim, had reached Valencia some time before 12 January and was planning to travel deeper into the country before turning for home towards the end of the month. The Connolly party, with a letter of introduction from Isherwood, first met Auden in Valencia.[11] Since they were only there for a few days in mid-January, Auden must have arrived in Valencia by 17 or, at the latest, 18 January. Many years afterwards, Connolly reported that, when they met, Auden was working for the government radio, but this may well be an instance of him converting something he had read into a piece of his own experience.[12] In any case, after the Connollys and Antrim had moved on, Auden stayed in Valencia until at least 25 January, when he took part in a doom-laden evening of drink at the Hotel Victoria with, amongst others, Arthur Koestler.[13] (He must have written 'Impressions of Valencia' by now, because it appeared in *The New Statesman & Nation* on 30 January.[14])

Some time during the next week, he seems to have travelled back to Barcelona on his way up to the Aragon Front. On 30 January, a 'Saturday', having seen the now homeward-bound Connollys again, this time in Barcelona,[15] he left the note at the hotel where Spender was expected. Spender had been in Spain with T. C. Worsley since early in January under orders from the Communist Party, which he had recently joined. Their brief was to investigate the fate of the crew of the Soviet supply ship *Komsomol*, sunk in the Mediterranean by the Nationalists on 14 December 1936. On 5 January Spender wrote to Isherwood saying that he was going on 'rather an important job to the rebel part of Spain'.[16] (Even if Spender had not told Auden directly, because Isherwood had seen him in Paris on 12 January, Auden would have known that Spender was also in the country. This is the point of the phrase 'I did so want to see you'.[17]) Spender and Worsley were in the southernmost part of Spain and in north Africa for almost the whole of their trip, but on their way home at the end of January both confirm, in separate accounts, that they stayed in Barcelona; for 'two or three nights' by Spender's reckoning.[18]

[11]   Cyril Connolly, 'Some Memories' in *Tribute*, 69.
[12]   Ibid. 69.
[13]   Arthur Koestler, *The Invisible Writing* (New York, 1954), 336–7.
[14]   NS 13. 310, 159.
[15]   Connolly in *Tribute*, 70.   [16] *LTC* 130.
[17]   See Letter 4.
[18]   *WWW* 197. For Worsley's account, see T. C. Worsley, *Behind the Battle* (London, 1939), 77–115.

They just missed Auden, who, as I have said, had doubled back to the city in order to reach the Aragon Front.

Both the line between the Republicans and Nationalists, and the lines of political demarcation within the fragmented Republican ranks, would have made a journey from Valencia directly to Sariñena (the little town which Auden told Spender he was aiming for) impossible. The main fighting was concentrated further west around Madrid, but the railway line from Valencia to Saragossa, the nearest big town to Sariñena, ran through territory already held by the Nationalists. Moreover, it was extremely difficult for journalists, especially those like (apparently) Auden who were without Communist Party accreditation, to travel freely. A state of profound tension, which a few months later erupted into armed struggle, existed between the Socialist-Communist Government in Valencia, backed by the USSR, and the anarchist and 'Trotskyite' POUM (Partido Obrero de Unificación Marxista) militias who controlled Barcelona and who provided almost all the troops for the Aragon Front. The government was focussing its propaganda efforts on the defence of Madrid (a fact which is reflected in the declaration in 'Spain' that 'Madrid is the heart' over which Fascism and Democracy are fighting) and it was labouring to establish itself as the single authority on the Republican side. Part of this effort involved trying to corral the diverse militias into a single army, the Ejército Popular, or as Auden calls it in 'Spain', the 'people's army'.[19] To this end, it was quietly depriving the still independent anarchists in Barcelona and at the Aragon Front of weapons and publicity. As a result, the Front was relatively peaceful during the period of Auden's visit. I have not, though, found a single report of anyone being able to travel by car or train to the Aragon Front without first passing through anarchist-run Barcelona.

Auden did manage to get there; twenty-six years later he told an interviewer that he had gone to the Front between Saragossa and Barbastro (an exact description of the location of Sariñena).[20] Some remarks by Claud Cockburn, who was then working in Valencia for the Communist Party, support the hypothesis that Auden reached Valencia, turned round and left for the Aragon Front, and then came back again to Valencia. Cockburn maintained that 'the bloody man went off and got a donkey, a mule really, and announced that he was going to walk through Spain with this creature. From Valencia to the Front. He got six miles from Valencia before the mule kicked him or something and only then

---

[19] *SP* 54.   [20] Unpublished 1963 interview with T. G. Foote for *Time*.

did he return and get in the car and do his proper job.'[21] If we bleach out Cockburn's picaresque details, his basic story fits with the facts scraped together from other sources.

How long Auden was up in the mountains north-west of Barcelona is impossible even to guess at, but once more events did not work out as he had expected them to. Instead of staying at the Front for 'about 1 month', Auden appears to have been back in Valencia by 21 February, his thirtieth birthday, which Carpenter says (though he gives no source) was spent in the Republican capital.[22] He may also have become involved—again or for the first time—with the radio station in the city. Whatever the case, by the time that Spender, making a second journey, reached Valencia around 23 February, the radio station had closed down. This further frustration, compounding Auden's distress at the brutalities he had witnessed, may have convinced him that it was time to leave. At some point after 21 February, then, he travelled back up the now bombarded railway line between Valencia and Barcelona, and from there, probably on 2 March, caught an express for Paris. On the evening of 4 March, he was sitting next to Isherwood in the Mercury Theatre, London, watching *The Ascent of F6*.

To retrace Auden's journey is also, incidentally, to taste again some of his poem's original flavour. The imperatives of 'Spain' are not just based on some loose notion of a Marxist analysis of history, or on a simple rallying call to the fight against Fascism, although both these factors are present. The poem also, unambiguously—and from the elder Auden's point of view disastrously—takes sides in a factional struggle within the Republican forces: the one between the Soviet-influenced Government and the independent revolutionary militias. Orwell, who was at the Aragon Front at the same time as Auden, described this struggle in *Homage to Catalonia* (London, 1938), and when Connolly got back to England—a month or so before Auden—he too discussed the Republican divisions, in the piece 'A Spanish Diary' which he published in the *New Statesman & Nation*.[23] Connolly sets out two opposing positions: 'The Communists and Socialists say "First win the war, then attend to the revolution"'. The poem's main assertion is, of course, a perfect encapsulation of this argument: 'To-morrow . . . / all the fun under / Liberty's masterful shadow . . . / To-morrow . . . / The eager election of chairmen / By the sudden forest of hands. But to-day the struggle.'[24]

---

[21] 'A Conversation with Claud Cockburn' in *The Review*, 11–12 (1964), 51.
[22] Carpenter, 214.
[23] NS 13. 313 (20 Feb.), 278.   [24] *SP* 54.

And, Connolly continued, 'The younger Anarchists and the P.O.U.M. say, "The war and the revolution are indivisible and we must go on with both of them simultaneously." ' Sure enough, 'Spain' pointedly counters this revolutionary impulse.

The sheer sense of will, the sense of great literary powers placed, decisively but without full conviction, in the service of a just cause, is essential to the effect of Auden's poem. But in the context of Spain in 1937, that cause is quite specifically and narrowly defined. Auden's most hortatory ode relies on a line of propaganda which was rapidly discredited. As the war dragged on, the language and structure of 'Spain' became increasingly compromised by their links to a Government which was more and more clearly the tool of a repressive Soviet foreign policy. In the end, having broken down so comprehensively the barriers between public imperatives and the private moral conscience, the poem had no defences against the tide of History, and it was swamped. It was against this wholesale debasement, not against a particular line or phrase, that Auden, later on, took such drastic measures.

A Change of Heart

Six Letters from Auden to Professor and Mrs E. R. Dodds
Written at the Beginning of World War II

EDITED BY KATHLEEN BELL

THESE six letters written between September 1939 and March 1940 belong to a period known in Britain as 'the phoney war'. There was a popular expectation that a declaration of war would be followed by the immediate aerial bombardment of civilians, and memories of the immense slaughter of soldiers in World War I led people to anticipate a comparable level of military casualties.

In fact it was not until spring 1940 that the war gained momentum. Norway was invaded in April, British troops were evacuated from Dunkirk in May, and Paris was surrendered to the Germans in June. Under the pressure of these events, Auden visited the British Embassy in Washington to ask if he should return to England. He was advised to remain in the States.[1] After the initial panic, it was still possible to believe that this war would not be entirely catastrophic and that everyday life could continue much as usual.

When he wrote these letters Auden had found a happy personal life with Chester Kallman and wished to settle in New York, where Kallman lived. They had made a 'honeymoon' trip to New Mexico and California from June to August 1939. During their travels news broke of the non-aggression treaty signed by Germany and Russia; Auden wrote to Mrs Dodds of bursting into tears on hearing a news broadcast and suffering a violent pain in his stomach when the hourly bulletins began. The Nazi–Soviet Pact was signed on 23 August 1939. On 1 September German troops marched into Poland. The British Government issued an ultimatum; either the troops should be recalled within 48 hours or war would be declared. There was no retreat, and on 3 September 1939 Britain's war with Germany began.

---

[1] According to a letter he wrote to Mrs Dodds in June 1940.

Auden met Professor and Mrs Dodds in the late 1920s, being introduced by his father who was involved in the local classical association. At this time Dodds was Professor of Greek at Birmingham University while Mrs Dodds taught part time in the English Department. A warm friendship had quickly grown up between them and the Doddses used to provide accommodation for Auden's friends when it was difficult for them to stay with his parents.

In 1936 Dodds was appointed Regius Professor of Greek at Oxford University—a controversial appointment both because of Dodds's left-wing views (such as opposition to Word War I and support for Irish nationalism) and because his chief academic work had been in the field of neo-Platonism rather than classical literature. He and Mrs Dodds were at first acutely unhappy in Oxford and, had war not intervened, Dodds might well have resigned his professorship.[2]

Mrs Dodds had given up her own work as a university teacher so that her husband could accept the Oxford appointment. Although she was a scholar of considerable ability, having written a much-praised doctoral thesis on Croce and the Romantics,[3] her ill health made it impossible for her to undertake full-time teaching. Her loneliness was increased by her inability to bear children, although she compensated as best she could with a series of much-loved pets.

The Doddses did not belong in the conventional mode of Oxford academics. Their friends and acquaintances recall their strong accents—Dodds's Irish and Mrs Dodds's Cumberland. They loved the countryside, gardening, and animals but had little small-talk. Both could seem intimidating. A friend of Mrs Dodds has compared her with Gladys Mitchell's alarming detective, Mrs Beatrice Lestrange Bradley, while she has also been described more simply as 'witch-like'. Their friends and students, though, recall numerous acts of kindness.

They shared an interest in modern poetry. Dodds had met Yeats and Eliot, was instrumental in appointing Louis MacNeice to a Birmingham lectureship, and greatly valued his friendship with Auden. Mrs Dodds appointed herself Auden's proof-reader (he was incapable of checking his own proofs with any accuracy), was a valued collaborator on *The Oxford Book of Light Verse*, and took responsibility for placing his poems with magazines during the first years of his absence in America.

---

[2] For Dodds's account of his life and his friendship with Auden see E. R. Dodds, *Missing Persons* (Oxford, 1977), *passim*.

[3] Published as A. E. Powell (Mrs E. R. Dodds), *The Romantic Theory of Poetry: An Examination in the Light of Croce's Aesthetic* (London, 1926).

Auden had separate correspondences with Professor and Mrs Dodds. While he told both about his reading, writing, and teaching, he tended to tell Mrs Dodds more about his private life and his personal impressions of America and the war. It was to her that he confided his love for Chester Kallman (in a postscript since destroyed).[4] Rightly or wrongly he seems to have thought that she would be more sympathetic to what he called his 'change of heart' which limited his political activities to those he felt were within his nature (i.e. teaching but not propagandizing).[5]

To Dodds (whom he and Mrs Dodds referred to as 'the Master'[6]) he was more respectful. The tone he adopted to Dodds in his letters was that of a favoured pupil. When war started, Dodds's immediate commitment to the Allied cause and belief that Auden should return to England might have created a gulf between them. However, effort and honesty on both sides sustained the friendship.

Auden's departure for the United States in January 1939 and his decision not to return to England at the outbreak of war were controversial at the time and have remained so. The arguments for his return were varied and often confused but can be summarized under three main headings.

The first of these is patriotism. Questions asked in the House of Commons and the press concentrated on Auden's eligibility for national service and his duty, as an Englishman, to defend his country in time of need.[7] This could become, as in the writings of Evelyn Waugh,[8] part of an implied attack on a group roughly classed as left-wing intellectuals. However, adherents of the left were themselves not without sympathy for this view. Auden had already tried to deal with this argument, so far as it touched on his responsibility as a citizen, in *The Prolific and the Devourer*.[9]

The second theme of attack hinged on what might be termed the 'Lost Leader' argument. It declared that Auden, as leader of a significant

---

[4] The postscript was written to a letter dating from May 1939, when Auden was teaching at St Mark's School, Southborough, Mass. Dodds destroyed the postcript when he decided to bequeath all the letters to the Bodleian because Auden had marked it 'Personal and Confidential'. But Auden's next letter to Mrs Dodds makes it clear that he had written at length about Chester Kallman.

[5] In another letter to Mrs Dodds, undated, from Taos, presumably July 1939, also in the Bodleian.

[6] The title given to Plato by the followers of Plotinus.

[7] Detailed in Carpenter, 290–3.

[8] In *Put Out More Flags* (London, 1942), 47–9. References to a pair called Parsnip and Pimpernell are generally taken as allusions to Auden and Isherwood.

[9] This 1939 work was unpublished in Auden's lifetime, see *PD* in List of Abbreviations.

poetic movement, had a duty to remain in England with his followers and continue to lead them. In a *Horizon* editorial Auden and Isherwood were accused not only of having 'a strong instinct for self-preservation, and an eye on the main chance' but also of abandoning 'the sinking ship of European democracy, and by implication the aesthetic doctrine of social realism that has been prevailing there'.[10] Since Auden's political and aesthetic beliefs had been undergoing a long and gradual process of modification, so that he should be seen rather as the forerunner of a movement than its leader, it is hardly surprising that he regarded his change of heart as springing from more than a simple geographical transition.

The third ground of attack relates to a belief which Auden had himself held in 1936 when he decided to join the International Brigade. He wrote to E. R. Dodds at the time, 'I am not one of those who believe that poetry need or even should be directly political, but in a critical period such as ours, I do believe that the poet must have direct knowledge of the major political events'.[11] While Auden felt there was no onus on him to defend himself against the first or second charges, the third charge did concern him as his letters to the Doddses, his reviews from 1939 to 1941 in *The New Republic*, and, indirectly, *The Double Man*[12] make clear.

Auden's changed view of the responsibilities of the poet is not an isolated development in his thought but part of a larger-scale readjustment. As these letters suggest, he had spent much of the 1930s trying to link himself as a poet both to the community and to a process of political change. He began a programme note for the Group Theatre with the words 'DRAMA BEGAN AS THE ACT OF A WHOLE COMMUNITY,[13] and it is significant that even his first play, *Paid On Both Sides*, was subtitled *A Charade* and intended as part of a communal effort at entertainment during a country-house weekend.[14] Auden's work in film, on anthologies, and as an educator all demonstrate a desire to be involved with a community.

However, while a communally-based role for the artist seemed to be

---

[10] *Horizon*, 1. 2 (Feb. 1940), 69. The editorial was written by Cyril Connolly.

[11] Letter to E. R. Dodds written between 8 and 24 Dec. 1936 (Bodleian).

[12] (New York, 1941); *NYL* in England.

[13] Group Theatre programme for *Sweeney Agonistes* and *The Dance of Death*, 1 Oct. 1935, repr. in *PDW* 497.

[14] For performance in Aug. 1928 at the Somerset home of W. M. McElwee, an Oxford friend. See Carpenter, 79.

sanctioned by socialism with its vision of a state in which all members would be valued equally, it had always been in conflict with another role, that of the agent for socialist change. The agent was, admittedly, to subordinate himself to the community ('To think no thought but ours') but he was also 'To hunger, work illegally, / And be anonymous'.[15] Behind many of Auden's statements about poetry there lies a double vision—that of the poet speaking for the community and that of the poet working secretly as an agent of change within it.

Towards the end of the 1930s Auden began to question the basis of both roles and to question whether natural community, on which both depended, could still be deemed to exist. At the root of this questioning was the rise of Fascism with its dependence on identity of feeling as a substitute for the quest for truth.

Auden found it impossible to deny Fascism's socialist roots. At the same time he was unwilling to reject socialism simply because it had, like any political philosophy, a potential for distortion. Instead he laid the blame firmly on something he had always mistrusted—the imprecision of romanticism. He traced this back to Rousseau's desire for a return to nature and original community.[16] While he recognized the earlier value of community, Auden now believed that society was progressing from Catholic community to Protestant individualism. In a book review for *The New Republic* Auden proclaimed his new beliefs:

I welcome the atomization of society and I look forward to a socialism based on it, to the day when the disintegration of tradition will be as final and universal for the masses as it already is for the artist, because it will be only when they fully realize their 'aloneness' and accept it, that men will be able to achieve a real unity through a common recognition of their diversity . . .[17]

It is important to emphasize that Auden was still calling himself a socialist, even though his view of the roles of both society and artist had altered. What has entered Auden's thinking is a bundle of concepts which he describes as 'The Machine'. In *The Double Man* he writes:

> For the machine has cried aloud
> And publicized among the crowd
> The secret that was always true
> But known once only to the few,

[15] 'Our Hunting Fathers' (1934), repr. in *EA* 151.
[16] At Swarthmore College, where Auden taught from 1942 to 1945, one of his lecture courses took the theme 'Romanticism from Rousseau to Hitler'.
[17] 'Tradition and Value', *The New Republic*, 102. 1311 (15 Jan. 1940), 90–1.

> Compelling all to the admission,
> Aloneness is man's real condition . . .[18]

The Machine is not merely mechanization but also its effects. People are no longer compelled to live interdependent lives; instead, as countries become interdependent through their development and use of resources, their citizens gain independence. They cease to be bound by necessity to a way of life which is shaped by the work which supports it. Mobility is possible and the community of shared interests is made available to the many. The quest, instead of being carried on symbolically by its representative on behalf of a community, has become the responsibility of each newly-freed individual.

A further result of the advent of the Machine has been the requirement for greater specialization. Earlier, Auden had made a simple distinction between the active and the contemplative (or, in educational terms, the technicals and the academics).[19] Now he saw the role of the active being superseded by the machine as factory work required more machine-tending than efficient bodily exertion. Because such work was repetitive and routine it did, to a certain extent, free the contemplative faculties. Moreover as shorter working hours were introduced the concept of spare time arose, to be filled according to inclination. Effectively, work became for many people the means of supporting a vocation.

The idea of a vocation changed the responsibility of the poet. Since there was no longer a primary community of involvement but only a series of secondary communities of interest, the basic duty to be directly involved in the political process had evolved into a more complex civic role. Auden asked himself whether a poet could properly be a political leader and concluded that he could not.

This was in part directly attributable to his own experiences of political involvement. He had been appalled by his ability to make a tub-thumping speech ('it is so exiciting but so absolutely degrading', he wrote to Mrs Dodds)[20] and began to perceive himself as an 'anti-political'[21] whose interests, were he to immerse himself in politics, would come into conflict with the general good. Although he continued to take his social responsibilities seriously, he refused to be a politician in the narrow sense of the word. Instead he took on a responsibility for

---

[18] *DM* 65, repr. in *CP76* 190.
[19] Terms used in *Education Today and Tomorrow* (London, 1939), written jointly with T. C. Worsley.
[20] In a letter postmarked 11 July 1939 (Bodleian).
[21] Auden used this term in *PD* 14.

language, determined to combat its debasement and corruption in propaganda for left or right.

A vital influence on Auden's thought and writing at this time was Rilke, then being translated into English by Stephen Spender among others.[22] While his poetic influence may not have been a good one for Auden, too often leading him into imprecision, Rilke's view of the artist's role in times of conflict undoubtedly helped Auden to articulate his own beliefs at the time. Despite his decision to stay in New York with Kallman, earning his living by writing and teaching, Auden did feel considerable grief at events in Europe as well as an inevitable guilt at not being directly involved. He made no public defence of his own position, probably suspecting that he was influenced in his views by both the responsibilities and the happiness of his personal life. However, he did defend Rilke's doctrine of non-involvement in World War I in terms that seem partly applicable to his own situation.

In his review 'Poet in Wartime', Auden wrote that for Rilke the years of World War I had been 'a negative and numbing horror' in the face of which all he could do was wait until it came to an end, not understanding. Auden had previously condemned poets for refusing to participate in political processes; now he wrote:

To call this an ivory-tower attitude would be a cheap and wicked lie. To resist compensating for the sense of guilt that every noncombatant feels at not sharing the physical sufferings of those at the front, by indulging in an orgy of patriotic hatred all the more violent because it is ineffective; to be conscious but to refuse to understand, is a positive act that calls for courage of a high order. To distinguish it from selfish or cowardly indifference may at the time be difficult for the outsider, but Rilke's poetry and these letters are proof enough of his integrity and real suffering . . .[23]

While this passage is not to be interpreted as a simple statement of Auden's own position, since Auden never cut himself off from the war to this degree, it must be significant that Auden uses such words as 'guilt' and 'suffering' in relation to the position of the non-combatant. It seems evident that Auden felt these emotions; what is remarkable is that he

[22] Auden's review of *The Duino Elegies*, trans. J. B. Leishman and Stephen Spender (New York, 1939), appeared in *The New Republic*, 100. 1292 (6 Sept. 1939), 135–6. He also reviewed *The Wartime Letters of Rainer Maria Rilke 1914–1921*, trans. M. D. Herter Norton (New York, 1940), and *Fifty Selected Poems*, trans. C. F. MacIntyre (Berkeley, 1940), in *The New Republic*, 103. 1336 (8 July 1940), 59–60, under the title 'Poet in Wartime'.
[23] 'Poet in Wartime', see n. 22 above.

refused to parade them in response to attacks from his friends. Even when writing to Dodds he refers simply to 'embarrassment' at being happy when his friends are not.

At this time Auden might have been described as a pacifist, although he was not absolute in his stand. In *The Prolific and the Devourer* he stated that his position forbad him to act as a combatant in any war because he did not believe that violence could be effective. None the less this did not exclude him from political action but merely limited the actions available to him. Simply refusing to fight and instead doing as one pleased as a private citizen was 'to be quite willing to cause a war but only unwilling to suffer the consequences'. When war came he would choose actions that were 'both non-violent and necessary'.[24] Eventually the inevitable movement of historical progress would cause wars to cease.

It is unclear how long these remained Auden's views. Soon after the war began he became concerned to inform Americans about the true situation in Europe, and *Decision* magazine, which published its first issue in January 1941 and with which Auden had been concerned from the early planning stages, was clearly intended to promote American support for the Allies.[25] His later decision to join the American army, though in a non-combatant role, suggests a further change of views. He may have been influenced by his friend Reinhold Niebuhr's argument that it is sometimes necessary to choose the lesser evil in the fallen world.

At this stage, however, although attracted back towards the Church, Auden could not be described as a Christian; instead he was attempting to fit Christian teachings into a progressive-socialist world-view. Two further stages were necessary to propel Auden into Christianity: the need for an absolute by whose standards Hitler could be unconditionally condemned and the realization that he himself was capable of actions which he believed to be wrong.

Editorial Note

These letters form part of a correspondence between Auden and Professor and Mrs Dodds which began in the early 1930s and ended with Auden's death. There are 90 letters and postcards in the Bodleian Library (MS Eng. lett. c. 464)—all of the correspondence which has survived. The six letters chosen for inclusion in this volume are the first

---

[24] *PD* 56–7.   [25] See Letter 2.

six Auden wrote after the outbreak of World War II in Europe. They conclude with the self-interrogation enclosed in the sixth letter. None of the letters from Professor or Mrs Dodds has survived.

While obvious typographic errors have been silently emended, Auden's spelling in the handwritten letters has been reproduced. However, where Auden's handwriting leaves doubt about the spelling, the correct version has been adopted. Underlinings have been rendered as italics. Directions such as P.T.O. and deleted false starts have been omitted as well as other deletions and interlineations. Auden's punctuation has been retained.

The format of the letters (date, address, greeting, valediction, signature) has been standardized with regular margins and all paragraphs indented.

Comments and markings in another hand (usually identifiable as Dodds's and relating to his autobiography *Missing Persons*) have been omitted.

Each letter is headed by a conjectural date if not included in the letter, and a brief description in the form ALS, TLS, and, in one instance, TL, follows the letter.

Letter 1: after 3 Sept. 1939 but within first three weeks of that month.

> GRAMERCY 5—1920
> George Washington Hotel
> Twenty-third Street and Lexington Avenue
> New York City, N.Y.

Dear Mrs Dodds,

How are you? Where are you? Do write and tell me if you alright. I understand the censorship in England is frightful now; we are fairly well informed here as to the war, but nobody I know has had any private letters from England, since it began.

My own plans v. uncertain. Am getting an introduction to Lothian.[1]

I enclose two poems; if they are any use, and anyone reads poetry now, do what you like with them. The second one I fear is not militant enough or helpful enough[2]

Sympathy here pretty strong but also isolation; and the lack of concrete western activity is beginning to bore people.

Believe that if the powers would publish peace terms, it would be easier to lift the embargo

Read Thucydides everyday, and wish you were all here.

> Much love
> Wystan

ALS; printed address and telephone number (hotel notepaper).

---

[1] Philip Henry Kerr, 11th Marquess of Lothian, was appointed British Ambassador to Washington in 1939. He was advising actors to return home only if they were eligible for military service (i.e. male and under 32); doubtless the same applied to poets. See Michael Sanderson, *From Irving to Olivier: A Social History of the Acting Profession in England 1890–1980* (London, 1984), 266.

[2] One of these poems may have been 'September 1, 1939' repr. in *EA* 245–7. Auden at some time sent Mrs Dodds a copy (with the title 'September 1939') which is now in the library of the University of Tulsa, Oklahoma. However, it may have been sent later (possibly with Letter 2).

Letter 2

27/10/39   1 Montague Terrace
                                            Brooklyn Heights
                                            N.Y.

Dear Mrs Dodds,

You cant imagine what a delight it was to get your letter, the first news other than domestic that I have had since the war began. How horrid about the op: I hope you are healing and that the results have been worth it; I wish you werent always so reticent and had said exactly what it was; you make it sound like something vaguely disgraceful, Venereal disease or something.

Here we are very isolationalist; and some think it a shame that so few people have been killed yet and say its not a proper war at all. But for me it is a great relief every morning to find that Hitler hasnt started trying that day.

We get pretty good reporting, better I fancy than you, but as I dont know what the censorship is like, I wont say much. The effect of the Nazi–Soviet Pact has been of course to give the red-baiters a field-day; while the reds do dialectical acrobatics like Oxford philosophers. They are very cross with France for jailing the communists and equally cross with England for not jailing them, which they say is Machievellian.

I am trying to organise the German Exiles and others here to produce some material which we might distribute, but it is a difficult job. The efforts I have seen so far are either so statistical that no one would read them, or so bitter that they would only have the opposite effect from what they intend. Duff-Cooper[1] has been here prophesying a revolution in Germany from the Right with a possible restoration of the Monarchy.

I am taking an Evening class in poetry which is very odd; we range from the 17 year old son of Ernest Jones[2] to a 58 year old suffragette. I am also working on the libretto of an opera[3] with Britten who is here, and

[1] Alfred Duff Cooper, husband of Lady Diana Cooper and a Conservative MP, had resigned ministerial office in opposition to the Munich agreement of 1938. He was on a lecture tour of America, frequently speaking on 'The Survival of Liberty'.

[2] Ernest Jones was the colleague and biographer of Freud. His son, the novelist Mervyn Jones, has described the class he took with Auden. See his *Chances* (London, 1987), 51.

[3] *Paul Bunyan*, produced at Columbia University in May 1941.

an elegy on Freud.[4] Dont bother about trying to sell my poems. Judging by the Listener which my mother sent me, this is no time in England for the sort of thing I do.[5] I've been writing a lot, and enclose one for your interest.

Glad to hear Bill and Louis are both safe pro tem: what is Stephen doing?[6] When this bloody war is over you are *all* to come here and live in this house which has the most beautiful view in New York: looking out over water at the towers of Manhattan. The skyscrapers with the exception of Radio City which is one of the architectural wonders of the world, are ugly close to but lovely from a distance. You shall run the house with the help of a black Mammy, and the Master shall teach Greek at Columbia: Bill of course will support us all by painting the inhabitants of Park Avenue, while Louis teaches the New Yorker how to dress. But you'll have to learn to call biscuits cookies and scones biscuits.

Love is in excellent health.

Much love
Wystan

TLS

Letter 3: 26 Nov. 1939. Auden typed two lower case *i*s for the eleventh month.

26.ii.39
1 Montague Terrace
Brooklyn Heights
N.Y.C.

Dear Mrs Dodds,

Your letter of Nov 7th just arrived. I feel as if writing letters to England ought to be my war work; it is certainly, as you know, a task to me. Just got back from Canada where I had to go in order to start becoming

---

[4] 'In Memory of Sigmund Freud' (1940), repr. in *CP76* 215–18.

[5] A debate on the ethics of war was taking place in the letters page of *The Listener*. A letter from Auden's father, attacking the biblical justification for Christian pacifism, appeared 2 Nov. 1939, 876–7. Perhaps this is the source of the lines in *PB*: 'From the theology of plumbers or the medical profession, . . . / Save animals and men', 72. (Auden's father was a doctor.)

[6] William Coldstream, Louis MacNeice, and Stephen Spender.

American.[1] American Burocrats are the nicest of their kind in the world—so polite and helpful—an example to our insolent busybodies at Harwich and Elsewhere.[2] In the course of my medical examination I had to take down my trousers to show that I hadnt any sociable disease: the doctor was very surprised because I dont wear underclothing and the following dialogue took place:

> Doc. What's your job?
> Me. I'm an author.
> Doc. O I see: nudist, eh?

Montreal is rather frightful; compared with it, Birmingham is an Athens. There were a few of the expected horrors about, like childrens game called Hit Hitler, and a magazine with a roaring lion on the front called Offence, but it was encouraging to find that they were being displayed rather furtively in second-class stationers as if they were pornographic.

Yes, I gathered our aeroplanes are better, but am rather alarmed by these mines; I suppose an engineering don from Sheffield University or somewhere will invent an antidote, though.

Do call Crisis[3] anything that seems suitable; I sent an elegy on Freud to the Lord Mayor for his Red Cross fund,[4] but dont know whether or not he got it. At the moment I am hard at work on my Operetta which is rather fun; Gilbertian rhymes etc; apart from Henry Adams,[5] I've been reading mostly science. I havent started Yogi[6] yet (The reason why they are so hard to find in India is that the best ones are here) but am doing a

[1] Having broken the terms of his visa by working, Auden had that day re-entered the US at Rouse's Point in upstate New York. Canada, like Britain, was at war with Germany. This was Auden's first visit to a belligerent nation in World War II.

[2] An oblique reference to Christopher Isherwood's failure to get a British visa for his German boyfriend, Heinz. Heinz was refused entry to the country at Harwich. See CHK (L) 122–5.

[3] Mrs Dodds was trying to place this poem, later called 'They', in an English magazine. It appeared in Horizon, 1. 1 (Jan. 1940), 10–11, repr. in EA 243–4. See Letter 4 n. 1.

[4] The Lord Mayor of London had declared a British Red Cross Week to run from 7 to 14 Jan. 1940. It is not clear what use, if any, was made of the Freud elegy which appeared in Horizon, 1. 3 (Mar. 1940), 151–4.

[5] The Education of Henry Adams (Boston, 1918). Auden used Adams's concept of the Virgin and the Dynamo in DM, 63 (repr. CP76 189) and he mentioned Adams in the footnotes to DM 146. He probably used the Modern Library edn. of Adams's book (New York, 1931), see 380–3.

[6] In an earlier letter (Aug. 1939, Bodleian) Auden had announced his intention to take up 'Yogi' in order to learn some spiritual exercises and combat the separation between the active and the contemplative.

preparatory course of physical exercises with a german girl;[7] *most* painful, but illuminating. Apparently my solar-plexus and my head are very much alive, but not the chest centres; I suppose because I'm a thinking-intuitive.[8] Have you seen the French Film End of a Day;[9] I think it is probably the best movie I've ever seen. Hope to see the new Marx Brothers[10] picture next week, though I', told as good as some of the others[11]

O yes, I forgot to say that I have a new book of Poems coming out here in the Spring[12]—I've just done the proofs and *How* I wished you were here to do them for me. I Have'nt sent Faber the manuscript yet. Do you think I ought to give my English royalties to the Red cross for the duration? At the moment there dont seem to be many wounded, but one never knows when it will start. (I cant justify it, but somehow I feel optimistic that the slaughter isnt going to be so frightful)

The Evening class is fun, though I wish I hadnt so many (26). Compared with children, they need so much more coaxing to get anything out of them, I never realised before how shy and nervy adults are.

I heard a rumour that Louis is already on his way;[13] I do hope this is true. Goodness how I wish you were here; its a lovely cold Sunday afternoon. Chester is reading Measure for Measure; the radio is playing the St Matthew Passion, and the tugs go backwards and forwards in the bay.

I Enclose a Christmas poem I was ordered to do for Harpers Bazaar.[14] I did send a copy of my aphorisms[15] home but I fear they have got lost on the way.

Love to all
Wystan

TL

[7] Tania Stern, a friend since 1936.

[8] Jung's term which Auden frequently applied to himself.

[9] *La fin du jour*, Julien Duvivier, dir. (1939).

[10] Presumably *At the Circus* (1939).

[11] This was probably intended to read: 'though I'm told it's not as good as some of the others.'

[12] *AT* (NY).

[13] Louis MacNeice had accepted a post lecturing at Cornell University for three months from Jan. 1940.

[14] 'Blessed Event', first published as 'The Nativity' in *Harper's Bazaar*, 73. 14 (Dec. 1939), 48, repr. in *CP76* 238.

[15] *PD*.

Letter 4

16.1.40   1 Montague Terrace
                                                   Brooklyn Heights
                                                   N. Y. C.

Dear Prof Dodds,

Many thanks for your letter. Before I forget will you tell Mrs Dodds how
sorry I am about the *Crisis* affair. I dont understand it. Stephen wrote
and asked me for a poem and I sent him one, but not that one. He must
just of taken it out of the *Atlantic Monthly* as Mrs Dodds has the only
typed copy.[1]

Delighted to hear about Louis and shall much look forward to his
coming.

Now as to your letter.

For the past ten years we have all been talking about the isolation of
the artist from the community, the dangers of ivory-towerism, the
importance of roots. I am now quite certain that 90% of what we said
was bosh.

As I see it at the moment, writers were the first people to enter the
Machine Age which they did with the invention of mechanical printing,
which destroyed the personal nexus of artist and audience.

The romantics who talked about their isolation spoke correctly but
what they said was prophetic of the rest of human occupation. Owing to
its newness one can see clearly in America what is true for Europe too
but obscured there by the dying but still vigorous past ie one can see
what pattern of life the Machine permits, a pattern which au fond is valid
whatever the political system.

---

[1] The poem 'Crisis', which Mrs Dodds had been trying to place for some time,
appeared in the first issue of *Horizon* without her prior knowledge. In an Aug. 1986 letter
to me, Stephen Spender explained: 'I am afraid I have no recollection of the poem
"Crisis". I note that this poem appeared in the first number of *Horizon*. I am sceptical
about Auden's explanation of what happened. Cyril Connolly and I were just starting
Horizon and I am sure I must have asked Auden for a poem. It seems extremely unlikely
that I should have passed over the one he sent (a poem other than 'Crisis' I suppose) and
taken one out of *The Atlantic Monthly* without consulting Auden. I doubt if we ever saw the
Atlantic at the outbreak of war. If Cyril Connolly did this it would mean that he did so
without consulting me, his co-editor, or Auden or *The Atlantic Monthly*. What I am bound
to think is that Auden sent us the poem "Crisis" he had already sent to the *A. M.*, perhaps
meaning to send us a different poem, and then improvised this somewhat gauche
explanation. However, this is my guess only.'

(1) The Machine has destroyed Community. ie the association of people to place, regulated by the disciplines of nature. The village was a community. The Factory isnt. No one thought of how to cut down the number of hours spent in the village.

(2) The Machine has destroyed the Neighbour, the companion of chance and left only Personal relationships of choice united by the automobile and the telephone.

(3) Before the machine there were two ways of living which both promised a full life, the active and the contemplative. Now only the latter is fruitful. Unless one is a ballet dancer or an explorer or something, the externalised life is only a duty or a source of income. The type who is best adapted to the Machine age is the introvert (using introversion in the Jung sense).

(4) At the same time however the machine has made the world so much a single interdependant economic unit, that in fact, (though not in most peoples thinking) our economic interests are becoming increasingly identical, ie it is becoming more and more obvious that there are not rival *class* economic interests, but only rival personal (and therefore very short term) economic interests. The greatest class-struggle now is not between the *owners* of the means of production and the ownerless; but between the *managers* (where in business or politics) and the managed.

(5) The Machine by its communications and by making all history available to the present, though the impersonal traditional community has gone, has increased the possibility of the personal relationship to include both the absent and the dead.

You speak of England as roots, but after all what is my England. My childhood and my English friends. The England of 13 Court Oak Rd Harborne[2] is a completely foreign country to the England of 12 Court Oak Rd and vice versa. The ice-cream-soda jerker is every bit as isolated as the highbrow artist.

What is going on now on a mass political scale seems to me to be a parallel to Rimbaud's abandonment of poetry for Abyssinian business, and the mess he made of the latter is significant. People darent face the truth that tradition, community, roots and what have you have gone for ever, and in their terror are trying to make it artificially. Both Russia and Germany are political romantics, trying to go back to the tribe where tradition was binding.

---

[2] The home of Auden's parents.

In fact they are trying to base Society on the General Will, at the very moment when, for the first time, society is governed solely by Social Contract. Burke was talking about something which still existed in the 18th century. In the Twentieth to talk of roots is as meaningless as to talk of race.

As an artist, I believe America to be the best place to live, because here it is impossible to deceive oneself. All you say about its destructive power on writers is perfectly true. Its a terrifying place and I daresay I'm no tougher than the rest, but to attempt the most difficult seems to me the only thing worth while. At least I know what I am trying to do, which most American writers dont, which is to live deliberately without roots. I would put it like this. America may break one completely, but the best of which one is capable is more likely to be drawn out of one here than anywhere else.

Much love to all
Wystan

ALS

Letter 5

26.2.40

1 Montague Terrace
Brooklyn Heights
New York.

Dear Mrs Dodds,

Thanks so much for your letter. I expect you will have heard from Louis. He arrived while I was away in Baltimore. When I saw him he had just set fire to himself in bed and burn his arm badly without waking up.

I suppose the $\phi\omega\nu\eta\chi\rho\iota\epsilon\gamma$[1] is now a routine Awful stories here about the traffic breakdown during the cold spell.

Life is very quiet here. I'm giving a course of lectures at the New School for Social Research and writing a longish philosophical poem in octosyllabic couplets.[2] So far I've done about 1100 lines. Will send as soon as finished. At the moment it seems quite good but I dont know if

---

[1] Code for 'phoney war' using the German *Krieg* for 'war' and transliterating the whole into Greek script, presumably to avoid censorship.
[2] 'New Year Letter', included in *DM* and repr. in *CP76* 161–93.

anyone will have the patience to read it. Have been reading rather stodgy books. Sandburg's Lincoln (four vols) Parrington's Main Currents in American Thought, Meade on her south sea island cultures (a wonderful book) and a book by Jaeger about the Greeks.[3] My poems are out and I hope you will get the copy I sent you soon. Huxley's new novel about Hearst is *awful*.[4] Everyone is reading something called "How Green is my valley".[5]

My chief luxury is the opera but that wouldnt interest you, I think.[6] I saw the Horizon article.[7] I think it meant to be friendly.

> Much love
> Wystan

ALS; date confirmed by postmark.

Letter 6: *c.* 11 March 1940.

> 1 Montagu Terrace
> Brooklyn Heights
> N.Y.C.

Dear Dodds,

Thanks so much for your letter. Of course one can deceive oneself in America. One can do that anywhere. Only the deceptions vary. I did plenty in England. Anyway I enclose a little dossier.

Louis is safe at Cornell and seems to be enjoying himself. Are you short of anything. Would you like me to send a ham? I cant make out from the papers how severe the rationing is.[1]

---

[3] Auden reviewed Carl Sandburg's *Abraham Lincoln: The War Years* for *Common Sense*, 9. 3 (Mar. 1940), 25–6. Other books mentioned are Vernon Louis Parrington, *Main Currents in American Thought* (New York, 1927–30); Margaret Mead, *From the South Seas* (New York, 1939), a compilation of her three major anthropological volumes; and Werner Wilhelm Jaeger, *Paideia: The Ideals of Greek Culture*, vol. 1, trans. Gilbert Highet (Oxford, 1939).

[4] *After Many a Summer* (New York, 1939).

[5] Richard Llewellyn, *How Green Was My Valley* (London, 1939). John Ford soon made this popular book into an Oscar-winning film.

[6] Neither Professor nor Mrs Dodds appreciated music.

[7] See my 'Introduction', p. 96 and n. 10.

[1] The Emergency Powers Act, passed soon after war broke out, enabled the British government to impose rationing, but in fact this did not begin on a large scale until June 1940.

I do hope Mrs Dodds is better. I'm getting on with my poem and will send it when finished.

Am reading Kierkegaard's Journal at the moment which is fascinating. Have you read Dr Meade's studies of South Sea cultures? They're wonderful. The lectures at the New School are going alright but I have learned not to let them have discussions but talk all the time. Democracy in education *method* doesnt seem to work, at least not with a large class.

Hope you are getting up to Ullswater for Easter.

love to all
Wystan

ALS; envelope has two postmarks, one unclear, one 11 March 1940.

[These hand-written questions and answers were enclosed with Letter 6.]

War or No war, do you want to stay in America.

Yes.

Why?

First and foremost because, for the first time I have a happy personal life. Secondly or because of the firstly, I find I can write here.

But you have no guarantee that this state of things will continue.

No.

If it were'nt for your private life, would you go back to England?

I dont know. Judging by my past behaviour I probably should. Trouble is attractive when one is not tied.

Do you feel perfectly happy about staying here?

No.

Why?

Because Dodds thinks I should go back, and because I am embarrassed at being so happy when many of my greatest friends are having an unpleasant time.

Do you care what happens to England?

Qua England, not in the least. To me England is bits of the country like the Pennine Moors and my english friends. If they were all safely out of the country, I should feel about the English as I feel about the Spanish or the Chinese or the Germans. It matters what happens to them as it matters what happens to all members of the human race, but my concern is as a fellow human being not as a fellow countryman.

What do think of Dodds argument against your absence-of-roots theory?

Weak. Of course Little Mudford still exists but it is dying, and unless it realises this it will try to keep itself going artificially and more 'tribally' with police and brass-bands. History is being determined not by Little Mudford but by Birmingham (trying to be Little Mudford again). The fellow travellers on ships and trains that he speaks illustrate my point exactly. They may be chance *meetings* but they are not chance *relationships*. One can get away from them if one doesnt like them. To continue the relationship is a matter of choice and will. If he believes so strongly in roots why doesnt he live in Southern Ireland?

Well, what about his remark 'An author writing about the war in America doesnt have a special nexus with readers experiencing the war in this country. Radio can put him in sight and in earshot but it cant put him in touch—and touch is what matters'?

If you push this argument to its logical conclusion it makes nonsense of any literature as It makes communication of experience depend upon identity. Of course no one in America can write about the *war* in the sense of what the trenches or the black outs are like, but I suppose Dodds will hardly deny that America is just as involved in the historical process as anywhere else What experiences are most vital for a writer and where as a writer he should be are certainly real questions but I dont know that anyone can give a readymade answer. As for the 'contemplative life', I never said that action was unnecessary, only that most of it is *personally* unfruitful. Of course without the proper actions, no life at all is possible. There are actions which are fruitful for some people e.g. gardening, skilled sports and techniques etc, (even politics for those— there are few of them—who are specially gifted), but most people in an industrial society cannot derive much from their physical life alone. It is a wilful misunderstanding to drag in Ghandi[2] as if contemplation only meant gazing at one's navel. A scientist in a laboratory is leading a contemplative life.

On what conditions would you come back to England?

If anyone can convince me that there is something that has to be done, by a writer with my kind of gifts that can only be done in England and is so

[2] At this time Gandhi tended to be regarded in the West as a quietist and not as a political activist.

important that it justifies smashing his private life. (which also has certain responsibilities). I am neither a politician nor a novelist, rapportage is not my business. If I came back, as far as I can see the chances are I should lead much the same life as I do here, ie reading, writing and teaching. I came here with the intention of settling here I am sceptical about the value of writers to a belligerent country, but of course I may be deceiving myself. I am afraid as I suppose most people are of what may happen.

Frank McEachran (1900–1975)
An Unrecognized Influence on W. H. Auden

JOHN BRIDGEN

I

EXISTING accounts of Auden's education mention many people who fostered his enthusiasms, introduced him to certain authors, and influenced him in various other ways. These accounts suggest that Auden's most abiding literary and philosophical concerns either began at Oxford or were largely self-engendered before this. However, they have overlooked the fact that in his last year at Gresham's Auden came under the influence of a man of broad and varied cultural interests. Frank McEachran arrived at Gresham's at Michaelmas 1924 (Auden was in the Sixth Form), and he had a direct influence on Auden until Auden went up to Oxford after the summer term in 1925. I believe that, stimulated by McEachran, Auden arived at the basic literary and philosophical framework of his lifetime's intellectual enquiry while he was still at Gresham's.

Although out of natural reticence McEachran kept a studied silence where his influence on brilliant boys was concerned, he told me of his friendship with Auden at Gresham's and after. In fact, the friendship was well known to his colleagues and friends at Gresham's. (I myself first met McEachran in 1955 when he came to give a talk at Clayesmore School where I was a pupil, and I corresponded with him in later years.)

With a boy so precociously brilliant as Auden, the influence of course went two ways. But McEachran was a remarkable man and a teacher of genius, and we do find, to use one of McEachran's favourite words from Herder, *Wirkung*. Auden identified peculiarly closely with McEachran's life, and, in his turn, he certainly became a main bearing for McEachran. Their friendship was romantic and platonic. McEachran realized that Auden was an especially talented pupil, and he wished to impart to Auden the very best that was in him. Auden probably felt on equal intellectual terms with the older man, but he also looked up to him, at least in the early stages of their friendship, as a father figure. McEachran was from a similar middle-class background to Auden, only seven years older, one of three brothers, and, born in Wolverhampton, he even came from the same part of England.

Auden's main friend in his last year at Gresham's was John Pudney. Pudney has left ample record of the fact that at Gresham's he fell strongly under the influence of McEachran.[1] In his later years, Pudney told friends of McEachran's effect both on himself and on Auden. Auden, Pudney, and McEachran all contributed to the 1955 Howson Memorial edition of the *Grasshopper*, a Gresham's literary periodical that McEachran founded and edited. G. W. Howson was the Headmaster to whom the school largely owed its renown and who had instituted the honour system of which Auden expressed such detestation in his essay, 'Honour', for *The Old School: Essays by Divers Hands*.[2] Auden's contribution to the *Grasshopper*, 'Qui e l'uom' felice: or Everyman in his Eden'[3] indirectly attests to the psychological self-questioning that the honours system engendered in him. Pudney's article talks a great deal of both Auden and McEachran, while McEachran's article, 'The Unspoken Word', tells the story of the young Auden throwing his poems in the Gresham's pond (from where they were later retrieved). The article, as a whole, is a clarion peal of praise for Auden.

In the little that he himself recorded about his time at Gresham's, Auden never mentioned McEachran. Nor did Robert Medley in his 'Auden at the Gresham's School, Holt'.[4] But Medley has told me this is because he wrote only of the time when he himself was at Gresham's, and McEachran arrived just after he left. Moreover Medley does recall Auden mentioning McEachran, and he also recalls his own younger brother speaking enthusiastically about him. (Medley also told me that the teacher with 'the magnificent reading voice' to whom Auden refers in *The Old School* was the Senior Classics Master, 'Tock' Tyler, a friend of McEachran's.)

Written evidence of McEachran's importance for Auden may be found in Auden's 1929 Berlin journal:

McEachran is right in his article on Dante. The real tragedy is not the fate of a man in power, nor even the conflict between two alternatives both bad. For instance the teutonic conflict between loyalty to the family or to ones husband is

---

[1] *Home and Away: An Autobiography* (London, 1960).
[2] Graham Greene, ed. (London, 1934).
[3] *Grasshopper*, Gresham's School, Holt (1955), 35–7.
[4] *Tribute*, 37–43.

only tragic if one accepts the teutonic ethic. Or rather it is tragic to me because I see the hero fail through being in the power of a false ethic.[5]

Here in Auden's own hand is a reference to McEachran, whose work he is apparently reading four years after leaving Gresham's and at a key point in his creative life. The article to which Auden refers is 'The Tragic Element in Dante's *Commedia*', published in *The Criterion* in December 1928. In it, McEachran argues that for Dante only one condition is ultimately tragic: 'to be for ever cut off from the sight and the intercourse of God'.[6]

At the time of his most direct influence on Auden, McEachran was already disseminating at Gresham's the central themes and ideas of a series of articles he published from 1927 onwards[7] and of his three major works which appeared at the start of the thirties, *The Civilized Man*, 'The Search for the More Precise *Humanitätsideal* in the Works of Johann Gottfried Herder', and *The Destiny of Europe*. The essay on Herder, McEachran's Oxford B. Litt. thesis, was begun in Germany in the early twenties when McEachran was English Lecturer at the University of Leipzig, and was eventually expanded into a book, *The Life and Philosophy of Johann Gottfried Herder*. McEachran took a first in German at Oxford in 1924, having switched from French after his first year. He was a classicist, as Auden's father was, and was also expert in English, German, French, and Italian culture. His approach combined the literary, the philosphical, and the historical. His first two books, *The Civilized Man* and *The Destiny of Europe*, are broadly critical surveys of European civilization. Auden found in McEachran a catalyst to his own quest into the cultural tradition of Europe. *The Civilized Man* in particular suggests that the fundamental dualities in Auden's thinking— freedom and determinism, the individual and society, nature and mind—were shaped by McEachran's teaching.

Perhaps what intrigued Auden most when he first met McEachran was McEachran's ambiguous position. Here was a kindred spirit who stood within the middle-class public-school world and, even as a master, was subject to some of its limitations, and yet who could be aloof and see beyond it. As most of his writings show, McEachran was more

[5] Berg; unnumbered pages. I am grateful to John Fuller for this reference.
[6] 8. 31, 224.
[7] Many of these articles were published in *The Criterion*. By 1928, both Auden and McEachran knew Eliot. McEachran was first published in *The Criterion* that year, and Auden in 1930. Eliot accepted both of their first books for Faber & Faber in 1930.

attached than Auden to traditional British liberalism, the middle classes, and the public schools, yet he, too, could be radically critical of them.

There is no doubt that Auden's early experience of the private/public dichtomy at Gresham's—or the 'tension' as Edward Mendelson has called it 'between personal wishes or fantasies . . . and the claims and obligations of the social realm'[8]—was important. In McEachran the young rebel found an insider ally who recognized the honours system for what it was. R. J. Eccles, Howson's trusted lieutenant who followed him as headmaster, continued the honours system, and the school tended, after Howson, to split into a pro-Eccles and an anti-Eccles camp. Auden and McEachran were decidedly in the latter. Morale was not good. However, Auden paid little attention to Gresham's rules and went his own way. McEachran was aware of the tensions set up in Auden by the honours system. Indeed, their shared uneasiness within that system was fundamental to their friendship. Both McEachran and Humphrey Moore (a colleague of McEachran's) have told me that McEachran gave Auden greater confidence in his private life while at the same time helping him to overcome his sense of isolation. He understood Auden's feelings of aloofness, his desire for privacy and independence, and his need to write. But he knew, too, the dangerous temptation in a society like Gresham's of trying to live the private life cut off from the public— to escape to 'islands'. He encouraged the young poet to connect the difficult pressures of school life with wider social pressures and to deal with these pressures creatively and from a critical distance.

II

Auden and McEachran both believed in what Auden was later to call 'the social nature of personality'.[9] They were convinced that man is naturally a social animal and that he seeks through co-operation to live in a just and free society. Neither Auden nor McEachran ever countenanced any theories of social contract nor any theories of social salvation based on 'the general will'.[10] They discovered in one another a fundamentally anti-political individualism forced by the pressure of an unhealthy public environment to take a radical political stance. They

[8] 'Preface', *SP*, p. x.

[9] See 'The Public v. the Late Mr. William Butler Yeats' (1939), repr. in *EA* 389–93.

[10] See McEachran's 'Henry George and Karl Marx or Economics and the General Will', one of eight unpublished papers written during the 1970s now in The Brotherton Library, Leeds (Leeds University Manuscript 594). The phrase originally comes from Jean Jacques Rousseau, *Du contrat social* (1762).

both viewed Gresham's as, in certain ways, a Fascist state. They observed how it operated: playing on the emotions of the immature and vulnerable; basing the 'moral life . . . on fear of the community';[11] repressing freedom through the censor. They saw its conformist and sometimes self-destructive effects. From that time they shared a radically anti-Fascist, anti-authoritarian, and anti-totalitarian conviction which was to be unchanged throughout their lives.

Auden and McEachran combated the 'Fascism' of Gresham's by adopting a position Auden was later to describe as 'anarchist individualist'.[12] Auden had the young artist's natural anarchism, but it was McEachran who helped to develop this into a philosophical position. For Auden this marked the beginning of a dialectic between self and society that he was to explore creatively throughout his life. It gave him the ability to identify in any society the underlying power structure to which the individual is subject. And it enabled him to place the enemy, both intellectually and through comedy (for which he and McEachran shared a gift). His developing sense of independence, the time he was able to spend alone, and his friendship with McEachran enabled Auden to be 'extremely happy' in his last year at Gresham's.[13]

During this period, Auden was influenced by McEachran's old-style liberalism—the philosophy from which both political and economic liberalism were to develop in the thirties. McEachran's liberalism saw the individual as the basic unit of a society which is part of a natural order, in the economic, social, and widest sense. This natural order is both orderly and anarchic. The natural law of an impersonal market organizes economic power, keeping political power in check and bringing about a harmony of private and public interests. The tendency of the whole is anti-collectivist. This philosophy of liberalism had its fullest expression in what McEachran called 'the third great era of civilized freedom' which lasted from 1832 to 1932. This was an era of free trade, 'the epoch of liberal politics and of toleration' which, for all is defects, McEachran said was 'the one great era in history when the world lived in immense hope'.[14] There were two further ingredients in McEachran's liberalism that made it amenable to Auden: firstly, Henry George's economic philosophy of the social value of rent from land (of which

[11] Auden, 'Honour', 17.
[12] In a 1940 book review, Auden said he left school 'a confirmed anarchist individualist'. 'Poet and Politician' quoted in Carpenter, 41.
[13] Auden, 'As It Seemed to Us' (1965), repr. in *FA* 508.
[14] *Henry George and Karl Marx*, pamphlet published by the Robert Schalkenback Foundation (New York, 1936), 5.

philosophy McEachran was to become a leading English exponent), and secondly, Irving Babbitt's 'inner check' which permits the individual to be free in society because the 'higher will' implements the necessary restraint.

This vision of a liberal natural order—originating from ancient Greece, formulated in the Enlightenment, and influenced strongly by Herder as I will show—was a more powerful influence on Auden at Gresham's than socialism. But there is a connection between the two. Auden probably espoused socialism in defiance of his own moneyed class as he knew it at Gresham's. But it is significant that he began to embrace socialism at the same time as McEachran began to embrace Georgism. Georgism and socialism do have features in common. Marx called Georgism 'the capitalists' last ditch', but Georgism, like socialism, wished to break the state's monopoly power. Moreover, George considerably influenced the early rise of socialism (e.g. the beginnings of Fabianism and the rise of the Social Democrat Federation), although his teaching remains distinct from socialism. His insistence on society's economic basis, the Christian inspiration behind his economics, and his advocacy of the single tax were influential at the turn of the century.

For McEachran, George was an historical aspect of the encounter with Marx. His evolutionary philosophy contrasted tellingly with Marx's revolutionary one. George is the natural counterbalance to Auden's usually constrictive mythology of the frontier, and he is probably a distant influence on some of Auden's panoramic choruses in the plays and on the all-embracing town and country vision in some of Auden's poems, such as 'The Capital'.[15]

McEachran believed that the attempt of many intellectuals in the thirties to go beyond liberalism, usually to Marx, was unjustified because liberalism on a proper basis had never been achieved. He was to give a full account of his libertarian social ideal in his later book *Freedom—The Only End*. This book offers the best description of the anarchic individualism that he and Auden shared as young men. Here, for example, is McEachran on the state:

The state, which is simply a body of men preserving an unnatural monopoly, must of necessity be amoral. The men who constitute it do not think and will as individuals—which is the only real moral activity—but as a corporation, and the action that results is more like that of a blind force than that of human beings— an absolute, omnipotent and arbitrary blind force.[16]

[15] *EA* 235–6.   [16] (London, 1966), 70–1.

For McEachran, the modern state dislocates beneficent natural economic laws, causing that widespread almost indefinable general malaise that Auden frequently terms (e.g. in 'Paysage Moralisé') 'sorrow'. The early influence of McEachran's liberalism helps to explain why Auden was to be so ill at ease in the thirties with the role of court poet of the Left.

In many ways McEachran was an unashamed but caring apologist for the middle classes of his time. His conscience, like Auden's, was deeply stirred at Gresham's and after by public-school privilege. Both he and Auden shared a passionate social concern for education as well as an emotional attachment to the public schools, a kind of public-school idealism which included a certain kind of puritanism. (McEachran frequently pointed out that the public schools are really the private schools.) In several articles—'The Rift', 'The Gentleman Ideal', and later 'The Public Schools'—McEachran championed the public schools as bastions of middle-class freedom, paradigms of the proper co-operative relation between the public and private spheres, and vehicles of a precious aristocratic cultural ideal. But he also insisted on the overriding need to strive for one nation in which the exclusiveness of the public schools would be lessened and their inheritance made available to all who could profit from it. In 'The Rift' McEachran argued that the 'State' is 'becoming more and more democratic at the seat of government while its commercial and professional classes are becoming, if anything, less democratic in outlook'.[17] All the more reason, he urged, why there should be *one class of cultured Englishmen* drawn from all walks of life and centred in the public schools.[18] This would be an important step towards overcoming the snobbery which, McEachran insisted, 'is not inculcated by the public schools themselves . . . but by the actual social structure of English life as it is to-day'.[19]

McEachran saw English cultural unity as one aspect of a larger European cultural unity. He emphasized that only cultural unity among the nations could guarantee the civilized freedom and political order that must above all be valued and preserved. In *The Destiny of Europe* he points out that Europe inherits the classical heritage and its human ideal from the Roman Empire. This is its 'public' and unifying feature. Europe's nationalistic romantic heritage, on the other hand, is both

[17] *The Nineteenth Century and After*, 101. 601 (Mar. 1927), 381. As Fion McEachran.
[18] Ibid. 382.
[19] 'The Public Schools', *The Nineteenth Century and After*, 129. 768 (Feb. 1941), 194.

more recent and more private and divisive.[20] In *The Destiny of Europe* McEachran looked for the renaissance of a united Europe moving towards the *Humanitätsideal* and the inauguration of a 'fourth great era of civilized freedom', a phrase he sometimes used to express his hope for a further European renaissance which would continue and fulfill the previous eras of civilized freedom, however far in the future this might be.

III

During the period when he and Auden were at Gresham's and throughout most of the thirties, McEachran was seeking to integrate the old liberal Christian humanist world-view (in which Babbitt's teaching on the 'higher will' was influential) with a more romantic late Enlightenment world-view. The humanist world-view had a classical, dualistic, aristocratic framework and an essentially non-progressive, tragic emphasis; the late Enlightenment world-view had a Christian, organic, democratic framework and a more progressive, evolutionary outlook (in which the influence of Herder predominated). Both world-views influenced Auden. But neither McEachran nor Auden succeeded in integrating them until years after leaving Gresham's. Eventually, McEachran came to see an organic Christian viewpoint as the most relevant and true means to freedom for twentieth-century democratic man, although he did not abandon the classical human ideal. Auden's Berlin journal records his own effort to overcome humanist dualism in a Christian integration. In this he was influenced by the Christian monism of Herder: 'Humanism will never do', Auden wrote 'since it believes that the duality of the higher and lower will is inevitable and desirable. This dualism is the result of the Fall i.e. the dissociated consciousness in man.' The humanism Auden refers to is Babbitt's. His comment was to be paralleled by McEachran in his book on Herder:

The fall for Herder is, if anything, a fall from the natural state of original man into an unnatural state, from the state of *Anschauung* into the state of bloodless speculation, and the path to the lost perfection lies in the restoration of the original *Anschauung*, whether through God-Nature, through history, or through poetry.[21]

Auden's poetry of this time, especially the poem beginning 'It was Easter as I walked in the public gardens', reflects this dialectical debate.

[20] (London, 1932), 185.
[21] *The Life and Philosophy of Johann Gottfried Herder* (Oxford, 1939), 43.

'It was Easter . . .' is about the divided consciousness of the poet as a
representative individual at a particular time. It records his quest for
spiritual renewal and freedom in a decadent phase of society. Reason
and instinct, mind and matter, as Herder argued, must be reunited in
order for the mind to enjoy truly integrated perception. The poem
suggests that this integration will come about in a Christian way. The
dialectic at work is not Marxist (although in a sense it both includes and
transcends the Marxist one); rather it is an organic, Christian dialectic
which discovers a binding nexus in all things. The psychic and the
economic and the seasonal are all woven into a single dialectical pattern.
Auden's crisis of identity parallels the economic crisis of the time.
Collapse (winter) puts an end to 'the summer talk' of the mind's
'independent delight', and calls instead for 'the destruction of error' and
the 'death of the old gang' responsible for the economic and spiritual
dislocation.[22] A new beginning, leading to the possibility of a new unity
and wholeness of being, comes about through the death of pride. This
makes possible a new love, prelude to a new Easter.

From the early thirties, Herder was central to McEachran's thinking,
and McEachran's 1939 book about him marked an important stage in
the rediscovery of Herder in this country. McEachran was introduced to
the German thinker by Babbitt's early works, and during the twenties
McEachran and Babbitt corresponded a good deal. McEachran came to
see Herder as offering the most satisfactory answer to what he felt was
lacking in Babbitt's own diagnosis of twentieth-century civilization and
culture. For McEachran, Herder healed the impoverishing Cartesian
rift between mind and matter. McEachran's later Christian humanist
emphasis on liberating natural law is a consistent development from,
albeit a transformation of, his earlier emphasis on classical restraint
and limitation. Instead of the fundamentally tragic and aristocratic
dualism of nature/mind, McEachran was to affirm a new healing
integration, through belief in the divine pattern of the immanent and
evolving natural law. Moreover, Herder demonstrated philosophically
how a natural order could be combined with individualism; this was a
significant factor in the development of McEachran's and Auden's
anarchic individualism.

I believe it was his early introduction through McEachran to the neo-
classical ambience of Babbitt, Herder, Lessing, Leibniz, and their English
Augustan counterparts that gave Auden, while he was still at Gresham's,

[22] *EA* 39–40.

his first glimpse of his eventual artistic goals. What McEachran called Herder's 'true' classicism—a classicism which can include the elements of romantic and spontaneous feeling within it and which is above all characterized by a unified poetic blending of thought and expression—demonstrated to Auden the relation (especially as exemplified in Herder's *Volkslieder* (1778–9)) between a national tribal genius and a spontaneous popular poetry. Herder's part in the resurgence of a national poetic consciousness in Germany may thus have had a remote connection with Auden's later desire to revitalize popular or 'light' poetry in an English context. At the same time, it seems likely, bearing in mind its seminal influence on so many of the ideas that McEachran was promulgating at Gresham's, that Auden may have read Babbitt's *The New Laokoon* (1910). McEachran would have put him on to it.

Auden's early insistance, for example while he was at Oxford, on the primary significance of 'form' in art was probably influenced by *The Civilized Man* and *The New Laokoon*. *The Civilized Man*, drawing on Plato and Aristotle, represents form as an absolute above the naturalistic flux, expressive of the divine element in the universe. Form moulds and restrains natural expression in art just as human character moulds and restrains instinctual impulse in human life. Form is the universal which represents the ethical character of the artist over and above what he actually says. In *The Civilized Man*, McEachran writes, 'it is precisely on the strength and quality of this form that degrees of value in artistic works may be traced'.[23]

IV

Auden's conception of the 'Lords of Limit', first mentioned in 'A Happy New Year' (1932), originated with McEachran. It makes sense that the mythical patrons of schools should originate with a schoolmaster. The 'Lords of Limit' were transformed into 'The Witnesses' and reappeared in *The Chase* (1934) and *The Dog Beneath the Skin* (1935). McEachran always differentiates his understanding of civilized freedom from unrestrained, primitivist or purely romantic notions of freedom. For Auden and McEachran, the 'Lords of Limit' ensure that the basic human will to power, which is almost inseparable from the *élan vital*, is kept in check.[24] They delimit, delineate, and define nature's formlessness

---

[23] (London, 1930), 116. Cited hereafter as *CM*.
[24] I believe that McEachran and Auden discussed Nietzsche together at Gresham's. Although McEachran criticizes Nietzsche in *CM*, Nietzsche (in particular his views on

and chaos. The 'Lords of Limit' operate both cosmically and, as the transcendent Will, in man.

The gamekeeper in 'No Change of Place', written in the summer of 1930 shortly after the publication of *The Civilized Man*, is a progenitor of the 'Lords of Limit', as Edward Mendelson has pointed out.[25] When at the end of the poem the gamekeeper shouts 'Turn back',[26] he echoes McEachran on the powers that limit human endeavours, the powers that say to man:

'So far shalt thou go and no further, and here shall thy urge be restrained'. This is the power which is the will and which constitutes the really human element in man. Scientifically speaking, it cannot be said to exist at all, for, as we have seen, it has no positive content. It says 'stop' and nothing more . . . Yet in spite of its negative content it is responsible for all that is noble in man . . .[27]

In 'A Happy New Year' the 'Lords of Limit' are experienced in a more positive and religious way. They are an amalgam of McEachran's God in *The Civilized Man*, the circumscribing element of the world, 'a force and limitary means of control',[28] and D. H. Lawrence's biblical witnesses in *Apocalypse*, 'gods of limits . . . enemies . . . of licentious freedom'.[29] The teaching of *The Civilized Man* culminates in the attainment of religious peace. For McEachran, man's will circumscribes the flux of nature, but there must be an end for the will to aim at, and in the classical understanding of nature there is no aim at all. The will points to man's absolute aim, end, or limit, which is God. Here McEachran's God is similar to the Greek 'one behind the many', the ultimate universal which is revealed in the religious peace on the other side of tragedy. Tragedy reveals that the human will is really aiming at religious peace. Thus, the 'Lords of Limit' hark back to the Greek chorus. Their later title, 'The Watchers', may have been suggested by the idea of the Lords keeping watch like the Greek chorus, representatives of a divine justice in the universe.

V

Let us now turn to a related concept. Auden and Isherwood shared the conception of the Truly Strong Man as early as 1929—a time when

Goethe) may be a veiled presence behind the work, and several references in McEachran's *Spells* (Oxford, [1954]) suggest that he thought Nietzsche influenced the young Auden more than is usually realized.

[25] *Early Auden*, 126.   [26] *EA* 54.   [27] *CM* 83.
[28] *CM* 152.   [29] (London, 1932), 148–9.

McEachran's influence on Auden was still strong. I believe the conception was influenced by McEachran. Auden's idea of a self-sufficient man of integrated power who does not feel the need to act or to prove himself was almost certainly influenced by McEachran's 'civilized man' who lives in accordance with the restraint of the higher will. The Truly Strong Man recognizes the 'Lords of Limit'.

Behind the Truly Strong Man is McEachran's classical gentleman ideal, the civilized man of 'harmoniously balanced personality'.[30] In one sense both the 'Lords of Limit' and the Truly Strong Man accommodate Auden's sense of the heroic to a reality which is anti-heroic. Civilized restraint and the mastery of instinctual impulse are more truly noble than conventional heroics. The conception is similar to Auden's later 'Contemplative Hero' in 'The Greeks and Us' (1948) in that simply 'to learn how to keep the Law has become a heroic task which is beyond the power of the average man'.[31] McEachran's 'civilized man' has, like the spectator of Greek tragic drama, seen the catastrophes wrought in the lives of traditional heroes. He has seen the worst and is unafraid. His will is directed beyond the range of conventional human heroism. He is 'truly' strong, not merely physically powerful like the hero of Greek epic.

McEachran's 'civilized man' is also a Christ figure who is the apotheosis of the gentleman. The tragic hero acts and thereby falls. Christ does not act. He passively suffers the evil in nature, deferring to the higher will of God. Christ is 'the *supremely civilized* man'. He most completely 'restrains' nature and is 'on the edge of divinity'.[32] The only other type of man who can give true spiritual leadership is the great artist who ethically 'restrains' nature.

I am convinced it was McEachran at Gresham's who first introduced Auden to Dante. Between 1928 and 1933, McEachran published five articles on Dante—the first two before Eliot's famous essay.[33] Both in these articles and in his reference to Dante in *The Civilized Man*, McEachran's interest is clearly centred on the passage of Dante that is also most important to Auden, the Ulysses episode in Canto XXVI of the *Inferno*. In *The Civilized Man* McEachran says of the Ulysses episode: 'It is a symbol of the first European renaissance'. He refers to this renaissance as 'the age of Dante'. After the Dark Ages, McEachran says, the human individual is reborn and the world again grows civilized: 'No

[30] McEachran, 'The Gentleman Ideal', *The Nineteenth Century and After*, 104. 622 (Dec. 1928), 825.
[31] In *The Portable Greek Reader* (1948), repr. in *FA* 26.   [32] *CM* 175.
[33] 'Dante' (1929), repr. in *Selected Essays 1917–1923* (London, 1932), 199–237.

one who has read the account in Malbolge, of the last voyage of Ulysses, can fail to feel a feeling of human endeavour and the spirit of men who are free.'[34] For McEachran, Dante is the highest exemplar of liberal Christian humanism in the Middle Ages. He represents the first of the great 'imitations' in a Christian mould of Greek culture and civilization. McEachran never ceased hoping for a further European renaissance in this sense.

The Ulysses episode appears to have been in the front of Auden's mind whenever he thought of Dante. He refers to it in the 1932 poem beginning 'O Love, the interest itself in thoughtless heaven', in *The Ascent of F6*, and again in Part I of 'New Year Letter'. In 'O Love, the interest itself . . .', Auden uses imagery from the Ulysses episode to describe the mythical origins of England. He envisages a transformed England where love will bring about a new unity of purpose and a new stage of evolution:

> As when Merlin, tamer of horses, and his lords to whom
> Stonehenge was still a thought, the Pillars passed
>
> And into the undared ocean swung north their prow,
> Drives through the night and star-concealing dawn
> For the virgin roadsteads of our hearts an unwavering keel.[35]

The founding of England, where Auden centres his evolutionary hopes, is the only occasion in his work when the Pillars of Hercules, symbolically connected with the 'Lords of Limit', are truly passed. The positive limits of the Herderian *Gefühlmensch* (the man of fully unified being) are implied here. Herder taught that the *Gefühlmensch* has to assert himself to discover in an intuitive and religious sense what his true limits are. He thereby discovers true unity and wholeness of being.

McEachran's influence also throws fresh light on *The Ascent of F6*, which is on one level a modern psychological drama of Ulysses. Significantly, the play opens on 'The Summit of the Pillar Rock, above Wastdale'.[36] At the beginning of the play, Ransom lacks both self-knowledge and unified being; he mocks Dante's words in the Ulysses episode. Isherwood thought of Ransom as an anti-hero, but he is more a romantic hero of self-deluding hubris engaged in a self-absorbed battle. In his way he acknowledges the 'Lords of Limit'. He knows that in climbing the mountain (symbolically passing the Pillars of Hercules) he has exceeded his inward limits. Still, like Ulysses, he 'finds his death,

[34] *CM* 60.   [35] *EA* 119.   [36] *PDW* 295.

wrecked on the shores of salvation, the mount of Purgatory'.[37] A related figure, Prince Alpha in the earliest version of 'The Witnesses', lies down in the desert next to two great pillars of stone and weeps in despair. He will not acknowledge the 'Lords of Limit' and is brought to his knees.

VI

Both McEachran and Herder influenced Auden's early Utopianism. They helped to foster his belief in the essential goodness of man and also his belief in meliorative purposeful History. Edward Mendelson suggests that Auden first encountered the idea of meliorative purposeful History in 1932.[38] I think it is more likely that he first encountered it through McEachran in 1925. Like Herder, McEachran saw rapacious governments as the cause of most evil, and so he was partially blind to the fact of sin. Unnatural society had distorted the image of God in man. In McEachran's view, if History were put back on its God-given course toward realizing the *Humanitätsideal*, nothing would be able to withstand its benevolent evolutionary force.

Auden's biological studies corroborated his early belief in evolutionary natural order. Here again the influence of Herder was important. Herder's historical thought is often said to anticipate Darwin's. In Herder's view, both man and society should constantly evolve. Reacting against the mechanistic philosophy of the eighteenth century, Herder emphasized the realization of the immanent deity by man, physically and spiritually at one, in his natural historical setting. He wedded his evolutionism to religious belief, but he still maintained the value of the positive sciences and the natural law tradition that Hegel wanted to destroy. Herder is, in fact, less a typical Utopian thinker than he is an evolutionary optimist, and he is the true modern progenitor of a non-revolutionary dialectic.

Auden and McEachran may have first discussed at Gresham's the Marxist challenge to liberal values. This period was alive with the challenge. (James Klugmann, the future English Marxist leader, was both a contemporary of Auden's at the Gresham's School and an admirer there of McEachran.) Auden and McEachran agreed that there were two ways to counter the Marxist challenge. The first way was to study collectivism scientifically, because collectivism, like liberalism, is subject to impersonal natural law.

[37] McEachran, *More Spells: A New Anthology of Words and Comment* (London, 1970), 219.   [38] *Early Auden*, 308.

At this time, Auden saw History as the immanent deity or the natural law at work. This idea of History is based on the evolutionary and biological model of order. Auden was to refer to it in 'Spain' as 'the life'.[39] Marx did not give a truly 'scientific' account of History, although he claimed to. The truly scientific account began with Herder. His original model of historical order was biological change, and he often used the biological organism as an analogy for society. Biology studies individual units in the natural order; it knows of nations but it knows nothing of states, these are outside the natural order. Collectivism and states represent unnatural blind forces manipulated by power politics. But History, the overall evolutionary urge forward of 'the life', is beneficent.

'Spain' was one of McEachran's favourite poems. (He went to Spain as a civilian in 1937 to support the Republican cause.) He interpreted the poem as Auden's last great appeal to the natural order, in which the individual was still vital, of Western civilization. He said that 'The poem is not so much about Spain as about the human race'.[40] Later Auden was to change so much that he actually forgot what he originally meant in 'Spain'. In fact, 'Spain' is an attempt both to celebrate and to plead for a natural order in which the private and the public spheres are in harmony. In 'Spain' Auden attempts to validate the natural law tradition of History in which 'Time' is 'the refreshing river'. The poem suggests that mankind must return to History's natural evolutionary order so that the individual can shape his own life and make his own decisions. The chaos resulting from power politics and war has caused man to question whether History really is a purposive beneficent force. Auden feared that the choice and the 'proposal' of many at that particular crucial moment of History would be 'the suicide pact, the romantic / Death' rather than 'To build the Just City'. 'Spain' is in this sense a call both to action and to faith. 'To-day the struggle' in order that tomorrow we may readjust to the vital and natural course of historical evolution.[41] By reasserting History in this sense, Auden was resisting Hegel's denial of individual ethical will. He was disillusioned by the conduct of the Spanish Civil War, but he believed, despite Hegel's teaching, that individual choices could return History to the order of natural law. It is probably significant that in 'Spain' the actions of the volunteers are described in terms of natural metaphor.

The second means to counter the Marxist challenge to liberal values

---

[39] *EA* 211.   [40] *Spells*, 195.   [41] *EA* 211.

has already been touched on. It is to show that the true dialectical movement of History is not Hegel's and Marx's dialectic, but a dialectic of natural growth. When Edward Mendelson says that 'When [Auden] wrote about politics in Marxist terms, he tended to replace Marx's materialist base with an idealist one, as in his accounts of History moving towards the reign of Love',[42] he is pointing to McEachran's influence. What Auden was doing is most clearly shown by McEachran's article 'A Pattern for Reality'.

In this article McEachran gives his fullest account of the concept of the 'natural dialectic' whose basis he and Auden had first discussed at Gresham's. After Auden's Marxist phase this natural dialectic was to contribute to his return to Christianity. McEachran summarized its aim as attempting 'a re-statement of Christian idealism on a dialectic basis'[43] or, we might say, using Marx's methodology for idealist Christian ends.

The 'natural dialectic' is the dialectic of birth, death, and rebirth in the primordial rhythm of life. At its simplest level it is the pattern of the seed which after flowering dies and 'triumphs in defeat by reproducing more life'.[44] It is the agricultural rhythm and the rhythm of the seasons. McEachran calls it 'the oldest and strongest tradition of the human race'.[45] Present in ancient religion and ritual (whence it becomes the primary dialectic of the tragic drama), it provides the dialectical framework of the Christian religion. Philosophically its father was Heraclitus, who was the first to represent nature as the balance and integration of contending opposites. Some of the neo-Platonists and Stoics and then Herder developed the natural dialectic. Herbert Spencer was the greatest of the nineteenth-century inheritors of the tradition. McEachran maintained that the abstract Hegelian dialectic was essentially a borrowing and perversion of the dialectic of organic growth. Hegel took his dialectic from many sources 'without realizing to what extent he was borrowing from the conception of growth'.[46] It is important, then, that Auden came to Hegel and Marx via Herder.

In 'A Pattern for Reality' McEachran stressed that bourgeois liberal ideologists were not living an illusion, nor was it necessary for them to form an alliance with the proletariat at that moment of history. Communist society would not restore freedom in the sense that liberal Christian civilization had valued it. McEachran aimed to show that a realistic

---

[42] *Early Auden*, 307.
[43] 'A Pattern for Reality', *The Criterion*, 17. 67 (Jan. 1938), 218.
[44] Ibid. 220.
[45] *Freedom—The Only End*, 18.   [46] 'A Pattern for Reality', 230.

Christian world-view both includes and transcends the Marxist dialectic. The basis of all reality, he affirmed, is the vital experience of the individual. The natural dialectic expressed this. The abstract dialectic of Hegel was the illusion.

For Auden, World War II demonstrated the failure of liberal Christian humanism. By the time the war began he had ceased to believe both in the goodness of man and in purposive History. In America he was already reading another dialectic—Kierkegaard's. Auden had turned to a dialectic cut off from nature almost entirely, a dialectic of pure subjectivity. He now concentrated increasingly on the private role of the responsible Christian individualist fully conscious of the price that had to be paid for civilized freedom in a modern democratic society. The Church replaced the public school as the community where he belonged. The individual was still important, but not in the kind of vital contact with nature that McEachran desired. McEachran used to say that he felt Auden's poetry lacked real vitality from the time he moved to America. Indeed, Auden rejected natural law in favour of absolutist revelatory truth. After his conversion to orthodox Christianity his whole understanding of history and time changed. In Babbitt's terms, the religious plane of life took precedence over both the human and the naturalistic. Soon after his move to New York, Auden closely identified his Christian thinking with Reinhold Niebuhr's. This marked a decisive move away from the viewpoint that he had once shared with McEachran. But his new thinking actually followed on from that viewpoint. Indeed, Niebuhr's *The Nature and Destiny of Man*[47] was in a very real sense for Auden a new version of *The Civilized Man*.

[47] (New York, 1941–3).

'The Hero': Auden and Flaubert

JOHN FULLER

AUDEN's earliest references to Flaubert occur in two letters to his brother, John Auden, written probably in 1927. They both make very much the same point (and quote the identical dictum from Flaubert) about the artist's withdrawal from participation in the life that he must none the less write about. Auden's context is the trouble that marriage would entail in terms of financial and sexual compromise. The answer, he believes, is celibacy. A passage from one of the letters runs:

As to sex I am becoming convinced that for myself, asceticism is the only thing ... qua writer, I think celibacy's indicated. Flaubert wrote 'You shall paint wine, women and glory, on condition my good man that you are neither husband nor lover, drunkard nor cuckold.' This of course does not I expect apply to the heterosexual, yet personally if I discover a heterosexual trait in myself, I shall not marry, as it makes the demand for money so imperative, that one will write anything to get it. As you may imagine, I shall not enjoy asceticism, even if I achieve it. I have anyway for the last year.[1]

Flaubert had made the remark in a letter to his mother of 15 December 1850:

For me, marriage would be an apostasy: the very thought terrifies me ... If a man, whether of low or high degree, wishes to meddle with God's works, he must begin, if only as a healthy precaution, by putting himself in a position where he cannot be made a fool of. You can depict wine, love, women and glory on the condition that you're not a drunkard, a lover, a husband, or a private in the ranks. If you participate actively in life, you don't see it clearly; you suffer from it too much or enjoy it too much.[2]

---

[1] In the possession of John B. Auden.

[2] *The Letters of Gustave Flaubert 1830–1857*, ed. and trans. Francis Steegmuller (Cambridge, Mass., and London, 1980), 132. For some reason Steegmuller does not translate the French text's 'bonhomme', which Auden gives as 'my good man'. The word that Auden, probably reading the French, mistranslates as 'cuckold' and that Steegmuller gives as 'private in the ranks' is 'tourlourou', a soldier on leave, a soldier-boy, *Œuvres complètes de Gustave Flaubert* (Paris, 1926), *Correspondance*, 2. 268–9.

The iteration of these words of Flaubert suggests that the novelist might have been in Auden's mind as a role model. However, the whole notion of asceticism was before long abandoned.

Flaubert first surfaces in Auden's poetry in a poem written on Easter Day 1930 and, as far as I can discover, does not appear again until the 'New Year Letter' of 1940. The occasions of both these poems naturally help them to be poems of resolve. In the first, 'Get there if you can and see the land you once were proud to own', the nature of the resolve is similar to that in Auden's Easter Day poem of the previous year ('It was Easter as I walked in the public gardens', 1929) and involves a challenge to try to start living. The forms of 'death' that provide a comfortable alternative to this challenge are various in the poem (and were to be Auden's major subject for the following few years) but perhaps the most striking is the list of private and public enemies of the achieved life:

> These were boon companions who devised the legends for our tombs,
> These who have betrayed us nicely while we took them to our rooms.
>
> Newman, Ciddy, Plato, Fronny, Pascal, Bowdler, Baudelaire,
> Doctor Frommer, Mrs. Allom, Freud, the Baron, and Flaubert.
>
> Lured with their compelling logic, charmed with beauty of their verse,
> With their loaded sideboards whispered 'Better join us, life is worse.'[3]

The list collocates the multiple spheres of operation of these false mentors (private and public, sexual and educational, philosophical and literary). Brothel-crawling in Berlin, Auden brandished a cigar and pictured himself as the Baron Charlus ('Actually I was a middle-class rabbit'). Reading Proust and Gide brought Auden face to face with the modern novelist's problem of transmitting the truth about life ('If Proust meant the first part of Sodom and Gomorrah to be a full analysis of the bugger and not only a beautiful piece of writing, it is very inadequate') and clearly an essential aspect of this truth (indeed, the crucial aspect of the new life that must be lived) was the sexual. For Auden at this time the sex-act was a piece of sympathetic magic like taking Bovril: 'a beautiful piece of writing' was inevitably suspect.[4]

We cannot tell what precise aspect of Flaubert's work turned that father of the modern novel into a betrayer at this date, but Auden may have felt that his perfectionism of documentary preparation and verbal texture were tell-tale signs of an aesthetic withdrawal. It is also quite

---

[3] *EA* 48.
[4] This and other quotations and allusions in the paragraph are from Auden's 1929 Berlin journal (Berg).

clear that Auden's reaction from asceticism in Berlin, bringing in its wake as it did a critical analysis of homosexual novelists like Gide and Proust, would induce no less of a reaction to a writer he had once enlisted as a spokesman for such asceticism, a writer, moreover, who himself was not only not an ascetic but was not even a homosexual. Auden's letter to his brother appears to claim him as one, and he continued to muse on the possibility. In a review as late as 1973 of Francis Steegmuller's *Flaubert in Egypt*, Auden went out of his way to speculate on Flaubert's unhealthily close relationship with his mother, and on his fascination with brothels

where sex could be divorced from emotion. Indeed, one would not have been surprised if it had made him a homosexual, though it did not. In a letter to Louis Bouilhet, he tells of going to bed with a *bardash*, or a boy prostitute. Sartre, Mr. Steegmuller informs us, wrote an article in which he argues that this was impossible, but, from what one knows about Flaubert's character, I would say that he was a man who would try anything once.[5]

As for the purely aesthetic withdrawal, the Auden who was to stress a crucial distinction between escape art and parable art did at times prefer the directly parabolic. 'Le mot juste', for example, was a particular temptation for him as he recognized himself, at least in his version of it as 'the picked word' about which there was 'something exhibitionistic, and Society for Pure English'.[6] Eventually, however, it was this very withdrawal that was to turn Flaubert back into a type of the artist-hero for Auden, and, incidentally, to license once again this particular lexical temptation.

The change in Auden's thinking can be demonstrated in a series of poems that take his friend Isherwood as a model for the novelist, a class of writer that for Auden invariably demonstrated superior powers (e.g. in *Letter to Lord Byron*: 'novel writing is / A higher art than poetry altogether / In my opinion, and success implies / Both finer character and faculties').[7] In 'August for the people and their favourite islands' of August 1935, Isherwood's 'strict and adult pen' is invoked as best able to 'make action urgent and its nature clear'.[8] The implication is that the sort of 'full analysis' that is not merely 'a beautiful piece of writing' will allow the reader to come to a better understanding of life and to make choices. On 3 September 1937 Auden gave Isherwood a copy of D. H. Lawrence's *Birds, Beasts and Flowers* in the preliminary pages of

[5] 'Responses to the Near East' in *The New Yorker*, 49. 19 (2 July 1973), 73.
[6] 1929 Berlin journal. This passage is printed in *EA* 300.
[7] *EA* 171.   [8] *EA* 157.

which he had written a poem for him. This charming Lawrentian pastiche takes a rather different position. Instead of pointing to the obligation of warning and insight, Auden now stresses the novelist's need to appear commonplace, 'pretending to be nobody, to be quite humdrum and harmless', in order to act as 'our great ambassador to the mad'. There is an interesting phrase in the poem that encapsulates this idea ('Anonymous, just like us')[9] and appears to be the seed of the famous phrase in the Yeats elegy, 'silly, like us':[10] the writer in his person alone has no moral distinctiveness. This function of social camouflage is taken even further in the sonnet 'The Novelist' of the following year, where Auden claims that the novelist must actually and perhaps mysteriously *become* the experience that is the material of his art. This, perhaps, is a greater effort of imagination on the writer's part than Isherwood's 'anonymity', which in the Lawrence poem seems simply to be an aspect of his general pose of disguise and temperamental detachment.

In the following year Francis Steegmuller published *Flaubert and Madame Bovary*.[11] Auden, reading this book and making use of it in *New Year Letter*, must have been struck by the way in which Flaubert exemplified the vocation of the novelist as it had been delineated in that sonnet:

> For, to achieve his lightest wish, he must
> Become the whole of boredom, subject to
> Vulgar complaints like love, among the Just
>
> Be just, among the Filthy filthy too . . .[12]

This is the provincial life that Flaubert, in creating Emma Bovary, could so instinctively inhabit that he claimed to understand the tiniest nuance of her experience of it, whether within the text of the novel or not ('Madame Bovary, c'est moi'[13]). It was not only the creative endeavour behind this novel that was to seem heroic, but also the self-abnegation. It fitted perfectly with Auden's long-held psychological view that heroic resistance was ultimately a weaker position than enlightened acceptance. A series of major works from *Paid on Both Sides* (1929) to *The Ascent of F6* (1936) had explored this predicament in tragic terms: the writer struggles with his conditioning and motivation and fails. In particular, the last of

---

[9] The poem is printed in Finney, 287.   [10] *EA* 242.
[11] (New York, 1939).   [12] *EA* 238.
[13] In full: 'Madame Bovary, c'est moi.—D'après moi', reportedly said to the Rouen writer Amélie Bosquet; see René Descharmes, *Flaubert, sa vie, son caractère et ses idées avant 1857* (Paris, 1909), 103 n. 3.

this series had probed in allegorical form another of Auden's particular temptations: being seduced into the political attitudinizing that his audience required of him, and doing it, moreover, simply to please his mother. Auden still wishes to write poems of resolve, but he knows very well that the Truly Strong Man refuses to attitudinize.

Auden's biographical poems of the immediately pre-war years show him testing out this conclusion on writers who in one way or another exemplified the duties towards the artist's 'gift'. Rimbaud and Arnold, for example, deny it in their different ways, in efforts to be model sons. Melville survives the paternal storm in order to 'sail into an extraordinary mildness'.[14] Yeats's gift survived all that otherwise characterized him as ordinarily human. In Housman suppression is itself a stimulus to a creativity that compensates, along Freudian lines, for sexual failure (Auden told Dodds that he thought that if Housman had had self-knowledge we shouldn't have had the poems).[15] In a review written at about this time, Auden sets Housman up as a classic case-history of dualism:

Does Life only offer two alternatives: 'You shall be happy, healthy, attractive, a good mixer, a good lover and parent, but on condition that you are not overcurious about life. On the other hand you shall be attentive and sensitive, conscious of what is happening round you, but in that case you must not expect to be happy, or successful in love, or at home in any company. There are two worlds and you cannot belong to them both'[?][16]

It is no accident, I think, that the tone and substance of Life's conditional advice here are remarkably like the tone and substance of Flaubert's advice quoted by Auden in the 1927 letter to his brother.

These, and other examples written between December 1938 and May 1939, begin to establish what for Auden became the ambiguously privileged position of the artist. With insight into his gift the artist may momentarily resolve the duality implicit in his condition as a human being, and seek a purely aesthetic perfection. But is this enough? The good writer is not necessarily a good man, and Auden's thinking, as we know, was moving towards the necessity of Christian revelation. In August 1939 Auden found a crucial example of a writer who was also a scientist and a mystic, and whose employment of his 'gift' could more particularly be seen as a preparation for belief.

[14] *CP76* 200.
[15] Letter to E. R. Dodds, 8 Dec. 1936 (Bodleian, MS Eng. Lett. c. 464).
[16] 'Jehovah Housman and Satan Housman' (1938); repr. in *EA* 361.

This was Pascal (along with Flaubert, one of the boon betrayers of the 1930 Easter poem). Auden was obsessed with Pascal during the summer of 1939, writing not only the 96-line poem about him, but a whole book modelled on the *Pensées* (the posthumously published *The Prolific and the Devourer*).[17] It is not Pascal's role as a literary model that is important here. It is his role as a personal model, the type of the 'genius attempting sainthood' (the view put forward in Morris Bishop's study of 1937, which Auden had surely been reading).[18] The essence of Pascal's story is that the mathematical prodigy had a two-hour vision on the night of 23 November 1654, at the age of thirty-one, which prompted him to abandon science for the writing of Christian apologetics. The appeal of this to Auden at this date is obvious. Of all his biographical poems of these years, with their examination of how a creative genius can be true to his gift, only this poem finds the redeployment of the gift wholly satisfactory:

> Yet like a lucky orphan he had been discovered
> And instantly adopted by a Gift;
> And she became the sensible protector
> Who found a passage through the caves of accusation,
> And even in the canyon of distress was able
> To use the echo of his weakness as a proof
> That joy was probable . . .[19]

Auden is referring here, appropriately in the language of mathematical or logical proof, to those arguments for Christianity in the *Pensées* which were drawn from gaming and chance. The Gift is inalienably a gift of the Enlightenment, I think, letting Pascal believe that it was his own 'finesse', i.e. intuition, which prepared for his restoration of faith (the reference in the following stanza is to the distinction in Pensée 21 between *esprit de géometrie* and *esprit de finesse*).[20]

There is another difference between 'Pascal' and the earlier biographical poems, evidenced by the quest imagery in the same passage: Auden is abstracting from the facts of Pascal's career in order to discover the essential lineaments of a life involved in religious discovery. He is indeed rather particularly in this case (and unlike the vividly presented cases of Rimbaud, Housman, Lear, and others) not much interested in the facts at all. For example, referring to Pascal's transcription of his

[17] *EA* 451–3 and *PD*.
[18] Morris Bishop, *Pascal* (London, 1937), 353.   [19] *EA* 452.
[20] Blaise Pascal, *Œuvres complètes*, ed. Jacques Chevalier (Paris, 1954), 1091.

vision which he wore sewn into his doublet for the last eight years of his life, Auden writes:

> . . . round his neck
> Now hung a louder cry than the familiar tune
> Libido Excellendi whistled as he wrote
> The lucid and unfair.[21]

'Libido Excellendi' (intellectual pride) is a version of 'Libido dominandi' which Bishop chooses to use in his discussion of Pensée 696.[22] Pensée 696 refers to the *libido sentiendi, libido sciendi,* and *libido dominandi* ('the lust of the flesh, and the lust of the eyes, and the vainglory of life') of 1 John 2: 16.[23] Auden implies, therefore, that Pascal's scientific achievements (such as his invention of the calculator, proof of the vacuum, or early work on conic sections) were entirely a product of his worldly egotism. But Auden actually refers to none of these. His total silence on the colourful details of Pascal's secular career is replaced by an odd concentration (throughout the first four stanzas) on Pascal's mother, about whom almost nothing is known except that she was very pious, and that she visited and loved the poor. She died when Pascal was three. The point of this, and of the marvellous description of pregnancy with which the poem opens, is, I think, to establish her as a typological representative of the Virgin ('Love' lifting up 'Knowledge') and the infant Pascal as Christ announced to a superstitious and barbaric age, a Christ leaving her maternal comfort to 'build a life upon original disorder' (there is a hint for this in Bishop: 'After all, he was a little like Jesus').[24] There is an evident foretaste here of the method of the sonnet sequence 'The Quest' in *New Year Letter*.[25] Auden's process of abstraction allows the struggles of the heroes and false heroes of the religious life to be presented as generalized symbols applicable to us all, though in the first place, perhaps, they are to be applied to the poet himself. This is no doubt what Auden meant when he said of the sonnets that the 'He' and 'They' referred to should be regarded as both objective and subjective.[26] In 'Pascal', the role of the mother, of the Gift, and of the *libido dominandi* suggest that elements personal to Auden's own life could be used to dramatize the religious predicament of the dualist.

[21] *EA* 453.
[22] Bishop, 197 (see also 307, 338, 353).
[23] *Œuvres complètes*, 1302.   [24] Bishop, 339.
[25] I shall refer throughout my discussion to *NYL*, the English edn. of the book published in the US as *DM*.
[26] Prefatory note to 'The Quest', *The New Republic*, 103, 1356 (25 Nov. 1940), 716.

But when he came to assemble 'The Quest' Auden found that he was still writing about religious discovery in literary terms, not only in the imagery of 'fairy tales, legends like the Golden Fleece and The Holy Grail, boys' adventure stories, and detective novels' mentioned in the same prefatory note, but in terms of the experience of writers like himself. It is clear, for example, from his treatment of the three temptations (sonnets VI, VII, and VIII) that the source in Matthew 4 has been liberally reinterpreted. In *The Prolific and the Devourer*, Part 2, Auden discusses them as the temptations of childhood, adolescence, and maturity, and they are treated in artistic and intellectual terms. Commenting in *The Prolific and the Devourer*, Auden said: 'There is only one way in which stones can be turned into bread, and that is by phantasy, stimulated by hunger'[27] and in sonnet VI he dramatized his own temptation to poetic attitudinizing ('rowdy stories') and consequent fear of the Truth. The second temptation of sonnet VII is close to the *libido dominandi* examined in the Pascal poem. The third temptation, with imagery from Henry James, examines the fatal detachment of the artist.

Detachment became a subject of key interest, not least because the outbreak of war forced Auden to re-examine his own revulsion from political attitudinizing. He may also have been encouraged to reappraise his views on James, Proust, and Flaubert through Chester Kallman's admiration of them.[28] Auden's long poem to James ('At the Grave of Henry James', ?spring 1941) has gone so far beyond the biographical that it is unashamedly in the form of a prayer. There are few allusions to James's novels, but a good deal of praise for the Master's lofty sense of discrimination. The true artist hero is still the novelist, who must be anonymous and 'become' his material, but he has turned into a quasi-religious figure as well, immensely purified, innocent, an agent of intercession:

> Who opened such passionate arms to your *Bon* when It ran
> Towards you with Its overwhelming reasons pleading
>   All beautifully in Its breast?
>
> .   .   .   .
>
> . . . your heart, fastidious as
> A delicate nun, remained true to the rare noblesse
> Of your lucid gift and, for its own sake, ignored the
>   Resentful muttering Mass,
>
> .   .   .   .

----

[27] *PD* 35.   [28] Carpenter, 259.

All will be judged. Master of nuance and scruple,
Pray for me and for all writers living or dead.[29]

James's priestly role might, then, have suitably presided over 'The Quest'.
Given the literary context of its exploration of religious enlightenment,
the sequence needed at a certain point an example of a successful 'hero'
who, in his withdrawal and modesty, could provide an amalgam of the
psychologically Truly Strong Man, the great artist true to his gift, and
the saintly imitator of Christ. As it turns out, Auden reserved James for a
memorial poem of his own, and, when he came to write sonnet XVI of
'The Quest' (entitled 'The Hero' in the US edition), clothed his
message in formulae which are notoriously obscure even for a sequence
which has already decided to make a virtue of obscurity. The quite
different subject of this poem has not hitherto been identified:

> He parried every question that they hurled:
> 'What did the Emperor tell you?' 'Not to push.'
> 'What is the greatest wonder of the world?'
> 'The bare man Nothing in the Beggar's Bush.'
>
> Some muttered: 'He is cagey for effect.
> A hero owes a duty to his fame.
> He looks too like a grocer for respect.'
> Soon they slipped back into his Christian name.
>
> The only difference that could be seen
> From those who'd never risked their lives at all
> Was his delight in details and routine:
>
> For he was always glad to mow the grass,
> Pour liquids from large bottles into small,
> Or look at clouds through bits of coloured glass.[30]

Clearly this hero has a Kierkegaardian patience and humility. Auden
was later to describe Kierkegaard's ideal Christian as 'happily married,
looks like a cheerful grocer, and is respected by his neighbours'.[31] However, these 'neighbours' feel that the hero 'owes a duty to his fame'. They
are like the 'astonished critics' of the popular hero described in the sonnet
'Who's Who', who cannot believe that having been the greatest figure of
his day he can long for someone who does little more than potter around
the garden.[32] This earlier sonnet (1934) appears to be contemporaneous

---

[29] *SP* 121–3.
[30] *NYL* 178 (punctuation emended following *CP76* 229).
[31] 'A Knight of Doleful Countenance' (1968), repr. in *FA* 192.
[32] *EA* 150.

with Auden's review of a biography of T. E. Lawrence: the contrast between the athletic and the suburban conforms absolutely to Auden's theory about the Truly Weak and the Truly Strong Man'.[33] By the time he comes to write 'New Year Letter', as we have seen, the theory has received a theological underwriting: 'only God can tell the saintly from the suburban'.[34] The world of neighbours and critics has no conception of the difference.

This ambience of critical fools becomes the undiscriminated 'They' of the sonnet sequence (not unlike the 'They' of Lear's limericks, described by Auden in his Lear sonnet as 'legions of cruel inquisitive They')[35] and stands for the moral and cultural philistinism of the nineteenth-century bourgeoisie. Auden's historical account of their social antagonism to post-Romantic art is amusingly sketched in 'New Year Letter':

> . . . *Baudelaire* went mad protesting
> That Progress is not interesting
> And thought he was an albatross,
> The great Erotic on the cross
> Of Science, crucified by fools
> Who sit all day on office stools.[36]

His note to this passage, however, interestingly refers not to Baudelaire but to Flaubert, and consists of a quotation from Steegmuller's book about Flaubert and *Madame Bovary*:

'Gustave Flaubert? Nothing but an eccentric,' a respectable Rouen business man once replied when asked his opinion. 'One day he's living quietly at Croisset, and the next day he packs his trunk and is off to Carthage. We don't like that sort of thing much, in Rouen.'[37]

Auden's notion that 'They' will confuse the great artist with a grocer may also refer to Flaubert, for Flaubert was much aggrieved at a misprint of his name at the time of the publication of *Madame Bovary*: 'Gustave Faubert' was the name of a grocer in the Rue de Richelieu, as Steegmuller points out.[38]

Other details of 'The Hero' would appear to have been suggested by Steegmuller's book[39] and by other Flaubertian sources. Flaubert's letters to Louise Colet reveal an ambivalent attitude to the Emperor Napoleon III's coup and its resulting literary censorship. The lesson

---

[33] 1934 review of B. H. Liddell Hart's *T. E. Lawrence*, repr. in *EA* 320–1.
[34] *NYL* 137.   [35] *EA* 239.   [36] *NYL* 60.   [37] *NYL* 136.
[38] Steegmuller, 368.   [39] Ibid. 309, 324–9, 368.

that Flaubert learns from the Emperor ('Not to push') is, therefore, a carefully cultivated independence from commitment. As he wrote to Louise Colet in 1853 in terms close to those quoted by Auden in the 1927 letters to his brother: 'I believe that at the present time a thinker (and what is the artist if not a thinker in every possible sense of the word?) should have neither religion nor fatherland nor even any social conviction.'[40] I take it that Auden is allowing his religious quest hero (who is, as explained above, both objective and subjective) to 'become' Flaubert for this sonnet, but to become Flaubert in the sense of being a viable model for Auden in New York. Auden is 'parrying' the expectations of his thirties audience, the audience of critical fools who expect him to remain the court poet of the Left. In effect, that experience has taught him 'not to push' (i.e. to conclusions). This is obviously a version of Flaubert's 'ne pas conclure', that ability to express a variety of points of view, like Negative Capability, which he considered the only motto for a sensible man.[41] Auden in New York was very much a writer who was deliberately, and in a sense heroically, cutting himself off from his fatherland. The hero's answer to 'Their' second question does in a sense absolve him from the charge (to which a work like *New Year Letter* would be particularly sensitive) of having cut himself off from religion, but it does so in a markedly oracular way. Someone who consorts with emperors might be supposed to have a view about the greatest wonder of the world, but the answer is no secular monument. Its immediate meaning is something like: 'Mind your own business.'[42] However, in a commoner proverbial sense it is an answer more appropriate to King Lear's Fool, suggesting (I think) the utter poverty, and perhaps the crucifixion, of Christ (to go home by Beggar's Bush means to be ruined). This would conform perfectly well to the other guarded and emblematic references to Christ in *New Year Letter* (as unicorn, dove, fish, and so on).

The Flaubertian persona is confirmed by the allusions in the last two lines of the sonnet (giving details of the 'suburban' recreations of the enlightened hero) to Flaubert's researches for *Madame Bovary*. As Steegmuller writes, 'another afternoon he spent staring at the Norman countryside through pieces of coloured glass, to be able to describe the effect'.[43] This was for an omitted episode where on the day after the ball

---

[40] Quoted ibid. 324.   [41] Quoted ibid. 329.
[42] In a letter of Sept. 1965 to his Italian translator, Aurora Ciliberti, Auden described the line as: 'An English proverbial way of refusing to answer an impertinent personal question. I think you could translate it more or less literally.'   [43] Steegmuller, 309.

Emma walks in the grounds of La Vaubyessard and looks at the country-side first through the stained-glass window of a small pavilion, and then through its window of clear glass in order to see things as they really are, and it was intended to symbolize the point-of-view technique.[44] The immediate source of the mundane decanting of the penultimate line was probably a letter of Chekhov ('I have just poured castor oil from little bottles into a large one. A pleasant occupation.'[45]), but a Flaubertian context is very suggestive: Flaubert could just as easily have tried such pouring of liquids in an attempt to 'become' the pharmacist Homais as he clearly felt he could 'become' Emma. Homais is, perhaps, the fullest representative of the bourgeois in *Madame Bovary*. He wishes to label all experience and contain it in his bottles ('Often he spent long hours there alone in labelling, decanting, tying up again with string').[46] Homais' objective decanting is, in a sense, the opposite of Emma's subjective vision through the glass, but Auden shows that the novelist must transcend both attitudes by absorbing them, just as he must maintain an aesthetic detachment from religious or political positions. Auden is doing this, of course, in a verse form which traditionally requires argument, condensation, parallelism, and effective conclusion. In these last two lines the whole of the bourgeois tragedy of the novel is implicated (it is with Homais' arsenic that Emma kills herself) so that Auden's Flaubertian 'hero' is enabled to reach his strange Christian conclusion beyond the self-destructive scenario of dualism. He wants to be not the Double Man, but the bare man Nothing. He will be able to transcend the paradox of romanticism and materialism represented by Emma/Homais, through art such as that which Flaubert created from the materials he researched with such diligence and detachment. Auden was to tackle in *The Sea and the Mirror* (written 1942–4) the difficult question of the role of art in Christian belief, and even there he could not treat Prospero's abdication without qualification. For a time, however, he still needed a type of the artist hero to represent him, and the Flaubertian distance once more suited him as a model in these dark years.

---

[44] *Madame Bovary: nouvelle version précédée des scénarios inédits*, ed. J. Pommier and G. Leleu (Paris, 1949), 215–17.

[45] Letter to A. S. Souvorin, 1 Dec. 1895, in *The Life and Letters of Anton Tchekhov*, trans. and ed. S. S. Koteliansky and Philip Tomlinson (London, 1925), 232. Auden more than once quotes from Chekhov's letters in the Notes in *NYL*.

[46] *Madame Bovary: mœurs de province*, part 3, ch. 2, *Œuvres complètes de Gustave Flaubert* (Paris, 1930), 341. My trans.

Louis MacNeice's Early Poetry
(1924–1930)

PETER MCDONALD

I F some poets prefer their earliest work to be given a quiet burial, there are others who find youthful productions, and mistakes, serviceable in their mature careers. Louis MacNeice belongs to this second category. The poetry of his early years, though for the most part dropped from the collected editions of his work, has distinct relevance for his writings from the 1930s until his death in 1963. Indeed, MacNeice gave public burials to his early work with some regularity in his critical essays. The reasons for this have largely failed to interest his critics, but the juvenilia have enough inherent value to be of interest outside the small circle of MacNeice scholars. This largely forgotten body of work casts a revealing light on the poetic experience of the 'thirties generation', the first poets in England whose encounter with Modernism was, in the phrase T. S. Eliot used for his generation's reading of Shelley, 'an affair of adolescence'.[1] This article will survey MacNeice's creative writing from 1924, when he was a pupil at Marlborough School, until 1930, when he left Oxford with a First Class Honours degree in 'Greats' (specializing in philosophy and classical literature) to take up an appointment as a lecturer in Greek at Birmingham University.

The seventeen poems making up the 'Juvenilia' section of MacNeice's *Collected Poems*, as edited by E. R. Dodds in 1966 and still in print, do not tell the whole story of the poet's development. Besides the considerable number of poems printed in *The Marlburian* from 1924 to 1926, MacNeice's work appeared in many Oxford publications between 1926 and 1930, and a substantial volume of his poetry, entitled *Blind Fireworks*, was published by Gollancz in 1929.[2] In addition to the published work,

Textual Note: In transcribing manuscript material, I have retained MacNeice's spelling, punctuation, and abbreviations. Obvious misprints in published material have been silently corrected.

[1] *The Use of Poetry and the Use of Criticism* (London, 1933), 89.
[2] C. M. Armitage and Neil Clark, in *A Bibliography of the Works of Louis MacNeice* (London, 1973; 2nd edn. 1974), give an incomplete list of uncollected juvenilia; a selection of school poems appeared in the Michaelmas Term 1975 issue of *The Marlburian*, edited with notes by MacNeice's friend, John Hilton.

some manuscript material survives which gives a fuller picture of MacNeice's development, particularly in his last year at school, when, along with friends such as Anthony Blunt, he was patching together an eclectic and eccentric approach to life and art. Dodds is not responsible for the slimness of the 'Juvenilia' section of MacNeice's *Collected Poems*. MacNeice himself made a selection from his early poetry for the *Collected Poems 1925–1948* (1949), and this was repeated by his posthumous editor. There is, however, a significant difference between the 1949 and the 1966 *Collected Poems*: in the earlier book, MacNeice positioned the 'Juvenilia' after an opening group of longer poems from the thirties and before a group of shorter lyrics from his *Poems* of 1935; Dodds restored the early work to its chronological position at the beginning of the volume. In 1949, MacNeice had implied by his positioning of the early poems that they might be read more profitably in the context of his thirties work, and might in their turn offer sidelights on his poetry of that period. For this reason, his selection is more than usually careful. However, it is worth looking beyond the perspectives offered by MacNeice himself, and to do so more material must be considered than simply the work which he himself chose to preserve.

MacNeice spends more time than many of his critics talking about his early writings. Both *Modern Poetry* (1938) and *The Strings Are False* (written 1940–1) devote considerable space to early poems and intellectual development, while later articles such as 'Experiences with Images' (1949) or 'When I Was Twenty-One' (1961) treat the early writing in some detail. But, not surprisingly, his perspective on his past work is coloured by his literary concerns at the time of his recollection. MacNeice's declaration in *Modern Poetry* that in the twenties 'I attempted to dope my mind and see what would come out of it'[3] is related to the determination of 'Ode'[4] to 'put away this drug', and brings his early writing into line with a conception of literature as primarily 'communication', a key MacNeice term of the thirties. In recalling his early work, MacNeice tended to shift the emphasis from the poetry itself to the psychological state which produced it; in this respect, he was engaged in something of a misreading, or at least a distortion, of his juvenilia. Thus, in attributing to a reaction against his childhood in the Rectory at Carrickfergus 'what I now think an excessive preoccupation in my earlier verse with things dazzling, high coloured, quick-moving,

---

[3] *Modern Poetry: A Personal Essay* (London, 1938), 61.
[4] *Poems* (London, 1935), repr. in *Collected Poems*, ed. E. R. Dodds (London, 1966), 54–8.

hedonistic or up-to-date',[5] MacNeice obscured other important elements. The line between personal, obsessive brooding and bravura intellectual display, which the later MacNeice invites readers, to see in his early writing, is in fact much more difficult to discern there than his retrospective accounts suggest.

As in a great deal of MacNeice's writing, personally rooted tensions and obsessions are important elements of the early poems. One untitled piece, published in *The Marlburian* in 1924, presents its nightmare imagery with a particular directness:

> The ways are green and gorgons creep
> In and out among the hay—
> Rotten hay, sunken hay;
> And the creatures of the bay
> Mourn a dismal roundelay
> To their accompanist the deep.
> In my dreams that flit and flow,
> Flit and flow, flow and flit,
> I cannot help but think of it,
> When I am dead that I shall sit
> Crumbling, crumbling, bit by bit,
> Where the yellow gorgons go.[6]

The 'yellow gorgons' inhabiting a pastoral landscape here are part of MacNeice's own remembered imaginative landscape. Throughout his work, the childhood scene of Carrickfergus is associated with images of petrifaction; the gorgons in this very early poem are in MacNeice's work to stay. Recalling in 'Experiences with Images' the surroundings of his childhood and their influence upon his writing, MacNeice remembered the sea as 'something alien, foreboding, dangerous, and only very rarely blue'; here, the 'early stratum of experiences which persists in one's work just as it persists in one's dreams' also includes 'the very small, very green hedged fields of Northern Ireland' and 'my father's medium-sized lush garden with a cemetery beyond the hawthorn hedge'.[7] Far from being a green world of remembered innocence, this scene often represents a place of danger and fear in MacNeice's poetry.

If one aspect of the young MacNeice's poetry is rooted in the nightmare imagery of his early childhood, another is altogether more artificial and self-consciously sophisticated. MacNeice himself later

[5] 'Experiences with Images', *Orpheus* 2, ed. John Lehmann (London, 1949), repr. in *Selected Literary Criticism of Louis MacNeice*, ed. Alan Heuser (Oxford, 1987), 160.
[6] *The Marlburian*, 59. 855 (20 Nov. 1924), 160.   [7] 158–9.

deprecated the premature and dandified intellectualism which still mars the poetry, all too often ruining its more acute and individual features. Towards the end of his time at Marlborough, MacNeice was both a brooding, nightmare-haunted adolescent and a self-possessed aesthete and wit. Above all, there, as at Oxford, he was determinedly 'modern', gathering and displaying what seemed to him the most attractive elements of a distinctively up-to-date intellectual stance. The structure of the school year made the difference between the aesthetic ambience of his Marlborough set and the sterner, more troubling surroundings of his home life in Ulster especially pronounced. Modernity was, in an important sense, a way of escape from the nightmarish 'yellow gorgons' with their disabling gaze. The artist's pose, the inclination towards the world of what MacNeice called 'Romance' throughout his early writings, was also a gesture of defiance. It is not enough to describe many of the early poses adopted by the poet as aspects of a pervasive affectation: they are parts of a deliberate, almost aggressive decision to be 'difficult', a refusal of, and sometimes a confrontation with, an unhappy past.

MacNeice certainly took his 'difficulty' seriously; indeed, for him, as for Auden, also born in 1907, modernity in thought implied intellectual difficulty. However, the kind of difficulty encountered in Auden's post-1927 poetry, which has been seen by Edward Mendelson as 'an extreme extension of modernist ideas',[8] cannot be dissociated from the kaleidoscopic jumble of mythological and personal imagery which MacNeice was to employ in *Blind Fireworks*. If MacNeice was slower than Auden in arriving at the style which was to serve as a basis for his thirties writing, he was remarkably quick in finding the themes, images, and even forms which were to be at the core of his later work. MacNeice's recollection that he had, before leaving Marlborough, 'become interested in being fashionably modern'[9] means to imply the superficiality of his tastes then. This modernity entailed a belief in what MacNeice referred to at the time as Significant Form, an idea derived by way of Anthony Blunt from the writings of Clive Bell. The notion is made to seem simply whimsical and adolescent by MacNeice in his later accounts, but its implications were not quite so limited as 'that People were of minor importance compared with Things'.[10] In however crude a form, the idea was part of a more general Modernist understanding of art as partly self-referential, in

---

[8] *Early Auden*, 11.
[9] *Modern Poetry*, 51.
[10] 'When I Was Twenty-One', *The Saturday Book 21*, ed. J. Hadfield (London, 1961), 236.

some ways hermetic and autotelic. In an early Marlbor(
of his ideas, Blunt had written:

The difficulty is to decide what is the most essential and ir
natural object. To do this it is necessary to imagine it isolate
and human connections, and to determine what is left. Tak
boat: imagine it completely isolated from all human connections. What remains?
What but significant form?[11]

The artistic puritanism of this goes several steps further than Pound's
description of the vortex which 'purges [the external scene] of all save
the essential or dominant or dramatic qualities,' so that 'it emerges like
the external original'.[12] By 1926, Blunt was announcing that 'the
imitative part of a painting has no aesthetic value' and that the artist 'is at
liberty to use nature exactly as much or as little as he pleases'.[13] The
young MacNeice spoke along very similar lines, claiming in 1925 that
'Facts are the foundation of everything but for most people they have to
be touched up to mean anything'.[14] In the same year, speaking in a
debate in favour of Sir Jacob Epstein's then controversial panel *Rima*
(1925), he 'pointed out that art is not merely imitative, as is generally
believed . . . The panel expresses the noble rather than the petty side of
nature, a result achieved largely by the recovery of the qualities of
primitive art.'[15] Less thoroughgoing than Blunt, MacNeice shared his
assumption in believing that 'Primitive art is superior to developed, in
that it has the essential qualities more clearly shewn'. 'Distortion' was
justified, since 'if it is not allowed most good art goes'.[16] Blunt, too, had
asserted that 'All artists have distorted and the only distinction that can
be made is one of degree.'[17] There is an obvious conflict here between
sophistication and primitivism, which Blunt was able in some degree to
resolve through his interpretation of Cubism, but which MacNeice
found more difficult to handle in literary terms. For him, of course, the
'primitive' levels of experience were no mere abstractions, since they led
back to early memories of the Carrickfergus Rectory, a brother suffering
from the condition recognized now as Downs Syndrome, and a mother
who left mysteriously for hospital and died when MacNeice was aged

[11] 'Some Aspects Of Modern Art', *The Heretick*, Marlborough, 1 (Mar. 1924), 11.
[12] 'Affirmations' (1915), repr. in *Selected Prose 1909–1965*, ed. W. Cookson (London,
1973), 345.
[13] 'De Cubismo', *The Marlburian*, 61. 870 (23 June 1926), 88.
[14] 1925 paper, quoted in *Modern Poetry*, 53.
[15] Report of debate, *The Marlburian*, 60. 864 (19 Nov. 1925), 136.
[16] Ibid. 137.   [17] 'De Cubismo', 88.

en. MacNeice's rather reductivist Modernism was intended as the means to a desirable sophistication, and he seized upon the primitivism it sanctioned as an excuse for what he called 'Romance': 'the stuff of personal dreams made sufficiently impersonal to be palatable to others than oneself'.[18]

This division of allegiance, between what was 'either stark and realistic or precious and remote',[19] shows in MacNeice's schoolboy writing, where a prematurely jaded modernity combines with a flamboyant mixture of mythological references. In the poetry, two distinct elements may be seen: an habitual association of myth with images drawn from the experience of early childhood, and a reluctant acceptance of both modernity and art itself as inevitably impoverishing the imaginative scope of mythic antiquity and infancy alike. MacNeice devoured Robert Graves's *Poetic Unreason*, and followed its contention that 'Since the nursery is the one place where there is an audience not too sophisticated to appreciate ancient myths and so-called nonsense rhymes of greater or lesser antiquity, it happens that when we remember a dream, or write a poem in which we afterwards discover this emotional mode we say we are making a regression to childhood.'[20] However, the personae often adopted by MacNeice in his early poems tend to be preoccupied with their own obsolescence rather than with the privileges inherent in their nursery-mythic perspectives. In one poem of 1925, the speaker complains that 'I am left to tell my beads / In this gaud-faded old band-stand / Where I alone have no sweet sleep'.[21] The conflict between the rationalism of the modern world and the ingredients of Romance could be dramatised easily into one between philistinism and art. In a sonnet of 1925/6, 'The dark empoppied gypsy's daisy chain / Stretches across the barge-begrimed canal', leading back from the present with its 'plump workhouse' to a mythic heart, 'To find a Queen upon the Sphinx's knee / Weaving a lotus wreath of Why's and How's'.[22] This should be compared with a short prose piece of 1924 where the world is 'so glutted with knowledge of the "hows" and "whys" of things, so determined to put everything in its right place as in a well-oiled engine, that it is becoming itself an engine—and a poor one at that'.[23]

[18] 1925 paper, *Modern Poetry*, 98.
[19] MacNeice, *The Strings Are False: An Unfinished Autobiography* (London, 1965), 98.
[20] *Poetic Unreason and Other Studies* (London, 1925), 126.
[21] 'Cradle Song', *The Marlburian*, 60. 864 (19 Nov. 1925), 150.
[22] 'And the Spirit Returns . . .', *The Marlburian*, 60. 866 (17 Feb. 1926), 17.
[23] 'The Story of the "Great Triobol Clan" as Created by Mr. Schinabel', *The Marlburian*, 59. 854 (23 Oct. 1924), 135.

This relocation of the origins of rationality within the realm of myth is a characteristically crude retort to empiricism, but MacNeice was capable of still more direct confrontations. In another sonnet of 1925/6, he dropped the mythological element in favour of direct satire of 'Common Sense':

> Yes! Insulate your souls in cotton wool
> Like real good fellows; prime yourselves with beef
> And sentimental novels and a sheaf
> Of popular songs. Go on, enact John Bull,
> Bear round the bowler hat and gaily pull
> The purse strings of men's brains, beyond belief
> Forced blind, forced dumb, forced brutish & forced deaf.—[24]

MacNeice's desire 'to outrage the Boy in the Street'[25] leads him in the poem's final line to identify the hostile audience with the murderers of Socrates, but the sonnet is revealing for the lack of substance in the young man's ideas, laid bare by the removal of the customary mythological paraphernalia. Like Thersites, a prominent member of the MacNeice pantheon at this time, the writer entertains scorn for its own sake. MacNeice was evidently aware of the limitations of such an attitude, and was thus all the more keen on finding a way, through 'Romance', to an art unpolluted, as he saw it, by 'external' connections, close to Blunt's 'significant form'. He tried to make his early attempts at writing vehicles for, or assemblages of, what might be styled 'significant myth'; however, the problem that ' "significant", on any analysis, ought to mean significant of something outside itself '[26] became more troublesome as his writing gained in assurance and he began to recognize an impasse in the second-hand Modernism by which it had been influenced.

Despite MacNeice's implication, in *Modern Poetry*, that 'Literature had become miles removed from life' because his personal life was 'so inadequate to my emotional demands that I fled towards euphuism on the one hand and a dream world on the other',[27] the actual representation of 'Romance' in his juvenilia always leads back to the world from which it attempts to escape. It is always defeated as an impulse. In a short play, 'Third Time', written probably in 1925, a figure called Romantic Temperament elaborates upon his identity and foresees his own end:

[24] Contained in MS notebook of 1925–6, given by John Hilton to E. R. Dodds, MacNeice's literary executor, in 1964, and at present deposited in the Bodleian (cited hereafter as 1925/6 notebook). The poem is found on fo. [26]ᵛ.
[25] *The Strings Are False*, 97.
[26] *Modern Poetry*, 60.   [27] Ibid. 52–3.

I am Merlin. I am Apuleius. I am the Wizard in the Bystreets and the Enchanter in the Side-Alleys. I was born in a cave of the Atlantic, I was reared on the crests of the rocks; I was fed on the sound of piping, Pan and the pennywhistle; I whirl round the bowl of the world on my hairy mat of imagination . . . I shall die, I the wind, the fire, the foam, on a palliasse in a cottage with cigarette ends on the floor and the window pane stuck up with candle-grease.[28]

As often with MacNeice, Romantic Temperament's lineage here suggests a Celtic Twilight gone to seed; the dandified 'Pan and the pennywhistle' ends up in the unromantic poverty it has never really transcended. In the play, these claims go unregarded by the central character whom Romantic Temperament tries to influence. In claiming access to a romantic heritage (for which a degree of Irishness came in handy), MacNeice always emphasized his own belatedness; in one poem, a Norseman and a Gael, who have lost 'power', 'gods', and 'home', pass their knowledge on to the poet:

> Then they raised a lament by the Western Sea
> And set the seagulls keening;
> The song they sang is sense to me
> Though for you it may have no meaning.[29]

MacNeice's schoolboy writing is remarkably reluctant to expand upon what this 'sense' may be, other than a rejection of rationalism and a recourse to myth.

A distancing of the persona from the Romantic pursuit can be felt in one important piece of 1926, entitled 'Sentimentality'. Here, the lover of Romance is presented in the third person as an 'old grey dotard straddling times abyss' who searches through a cupboard full of mythic props. The poem, extant in manuscript, is reproduced here in its entirety:

Sentimentality

> Mona Lisa among yellow roses
> Ever blows her faint peach blossom kiss:
> The old grey dotard straddling times abyss
> Feeds his quick soul on those pressed kisses: posies
> And sentimental spiders ~~drape him round~~
> With love-letters inscribed in their drab thread
> Sing, Old Cat by the Fire, thy hardihead
> Grasp sugar pennies & scrap paper pound.

---

[28] 1925/6 notebook, fos. [15]ᵛ–[16]ʳ.
[29] 'The Hope Of The Present', *The Marlburian*, 60. 861 (24 June 1925), 71.

Have you not a cupboard full of mysteries,
Diadems wrought of long-surrendered hearts
And all the riotous jams of animal marts
And all the preserved fruits of histories?
Do not the ~~bottles~~ [   ] stand like marble towers
Of cold, imperial, variegated shine?
Are these not dusty bottles of good wine
Mellowed by many melodramatic hours?
He goes to the cupboard, that old man:
The cupboard behind her tapestry fan
I search, for who knows what lies hid
In Pharaoh's dusky pyramid.
Souls will rise like a pack of cards,
Scented with nard and spikenard,
Bright as leopard and camelopard
And all the constellate of pards.
Hearts will flaunt like lampshades bright
(And the wizards will light the lamps again.)
We will see the guitars of Aramaine
And the old toys of the infant night
The phoenix feathers, the mitred Popes
In open coffins on mothfull shelves;
The stamp albums stuck full of elves
The postcard albums of cracked hopes.
And the autograph album vellum-gilt
And the names of [mockery] chessboard kings
And Guinevere imaginings:
And ladies who flutter & knights who tilt;
That heap of gramophone records too,
Black crinkled halos of old tales,
More mournful than the north wind wails
When he comes the South to woo.
With a grating sound the key unlocks
The cupboard grained like chickenpox
Out flops the wan old pendulous air.
What has the old man found in there?
Found after many centuries
Found of his silken mysteries?
He has found nothing. The cupboard is bare.[30]

---

[30] 1925/6 notebook, fos. [16]ʳ–[17]ʳ. This is a pencil draft, often smudged, which
MacNeice partially revised. I incorporate his revisions here, except in l. 13, where 'bottles'
has been replaced by an indecipherable word. The reading 'mockery' in l. 34 is uncertain.

'Sentimentality' is a compendium of images MacNeice used habitually throughout his juvenilia, but shown in a less gaily coloured light. Besides the devaluing of childhood memories into 'old toys of the infant night', the elements of Romance are presented as 'preserved fruits of histories' and wine in 'dusty bottles', while the poem's bathetic ending intensifies its atmosphere of sterility and decay. It is a reductive poem, an enumeration of features of Romance myth, from 'Pharaoh's dusky pyramid' to 'Guinevere imaginings', which finally signify nothing but their own dead antiquity. The poet's position, despite the third-person distancing, is uncertain, and even, at the end of the poem, redundant. The poem's only escape from the sentimentality of its title is the rough bathos of the ending, which is unsatisfactory as a basis for development in other directions.

The solution to this problem was already implied in some of the early poems, and perhaps even in the sinister atmosphere of 'Sentimentality' itself. In MacNeice's schoolboy verse, as well as in the poetry of *Blind Fireworks* and after, mythological allusion functions as a kind of deferral of direct imaginative access: that is, access is generally implied to be possible rather than actually achieved. This deferral is recognized as such by the poet, who controls, to use the most economic terms, different configurations of signifiers without a definite signified. The poet does not regard the signified as non-existent, or even as irrelevant, but rather as lost. This attitude leads to the impasse encountered in poems such as 'Sentimentality', and it prompts MacNeice to make use of an alternative mythic frame of reference. MacNeice's 1925 claim, reproduced in *Modern Poetry*, that 'My earliest memory is one of memories and they were melancholy',[31] is one of his many mythopoeic darkenings of personal history, and suggests the direction in which he attempted to develop Graves's sanctioning of 'nonsense' and the nursery. In 'Spring' (1926), the figures of Pythagoras and Adonis are set alongside images of modernity—a mowing-machine and a petrol-pump. The effect is disconcertingly incongruous:

> But the mowing-machine upon the lawn is calling
> With whirring chirp her welcome to Adonis—
> (Yet they cannot stop the clock to keep Adonis;
> From the felt roof the drops of time are falling).[32]

---

[31] 1925 paper, *Modern Poetry*, 54.
[32] *The Marlburian*, 61. 868 (29 Mar. 1926), 53.

Adonis, in falling victim to the time dispensed by Pythagoras, enters the worlds both of 'modern' imagery and of the poet's own history. In his 1925 paper attacking 'Common Sense', MacNeice had made the mowing-machine one of the elements in a personal memory-store of interacting symbols:

When I was little I lived in a perpetual chiaroscuro; noises ticked themselves into other noises, the cracks in the ceiling slid into faces and the marble markings on the mantelpiece became an epic with a hundred plots. Mowing-machines reappeared in dreams to chase me; they lived in the hen-house; without drums were beating and soldiers marched about, very stiff and wooden and red.[33]

'Spring' brings together the mowing-machines and Adonis to explore the point at which 'Memory cannot go back' and 'fades into myth'.[34] By locating the significance of the mowing-machine firmly in memory, as an image of inescapable pursuit, MacNeice is able to fuse covertly the victim-figure of Adonis with his own remembered nightmares, associating both with the inevitable victory of time. The poet's adaptation of his own memories into a shifting and rich pattern of myths enables him to sidestep the problem of a mythic vocabulary in which multiple deferrals of the signified effectively close off the field of reference. If the 'lost' signified is to be found anywhere, it is in the imagination's transformation of personal experience. This habit was to persist long after Marlborough and Oxford, in the mythic co-ordinates of *Autumn Sequel* (1954), for instance, or in MacNeice's application of his ideas of parable to the late poetry. The (mistaken) conception of MacNeice as a slice-of-life thirties realist dogged him throughout his career; in fact his insistence on poetry's relation to myth goes back much further than the procedures of *Autumn Sequel*, to the early poetry.

Once at Oxford, MacNeice's pronounced self-consciousness in writing started to give way to self-confidence: the external trappings of modernity seemed to him to be satisfactory camouflage for the raw and painful areas of his experience. A belief that form guarantees impersonality, which was always to some degree to remain with MacNeice, had begun at Marlborough in the development away from 'significant' myth and Romance. Any belief in 'blind inspiration' was qualified by a need for form. In a poem of 1926, MacNeice wrote of how 'Aganippe's stream / Is somewhat strong for most unless diluted', and continued:

[33] Quoted in *Modern Poetry*, 55.
[34] *The Strings Are False*, 36.

> One needs the power to realise one's dream
> To reign the divine madness Plato bruited;
> The inspiration-mongers are confuted
> If they deny the miller to the stream.[35]

'Realise' here, which has been substituted in the manuscript for 'express', perhaps indicates the literariness at this time of MacNeice's notions of reality. Yet the insistance upon formal qualities brought the poet back to the problem of 'significant form' and self-defining systems. Writing to Blunt just before going up to Oxford, MacNeice could declare that 'I don't believe in pure form, I don't believe in pure anything. Anything pure is an abstraction.'[36] At Oxford, composing the poems which were included in *Blind Fireworks*, MacNeice worked elements of private symbolism into a mythology which was kept both fluid and personally anchored. In one sense, this left what the poet called the 'earlier stratum' of his instinctive images 'the most uncovered', but the poems were also 'in spite of that the most artificial or literary'.[37] However, for MacNeice that very artificiality tended to imply the genuineness of the material it contained — 'You are, to start with, irretrievably artificial when you set pen to paper, when you select, when you limit a book by beginning or end'.[38] He resisted the inclination to see the very act of writing as distinct from some pre-existent essence or idea, but he remained aware of form as a defence against what might otherwise defy control, and this may be felt in the problems and tensions of formal closure in some of MacNeice's later writing. In *Blind Fireworks*, the artificiality is highly pronounced because it is, in some ways, desperate.

A reviewer of *Oxford Poetry 1929* saw in MacNeice 'a double self . . . trying to play the censor on the threshold of the unconscious';[39] this is perhaps the impression which the poetry of MacNeice's Oxford years is intended to create. Certainly, the 'Foreword' to *Blind Fireworks* emphasizes the individuality of the 'esoteric mythology'[40] upon which the poems are founded, and the recurrence of the same symbols in a number of different poems tends to suggest the presence of personal obsessions without

[35] Sonnet entitled 'Moral', possibly intended as a coda to MacNeice's 1926 entry for a school poetry prize on the theme of 'Inspiration', among John Hilton papers, Bodleian, (MS Don. c. 153), fo. 88ʳ.

[36] Letter to Blunt, 25 Sept. 1926, quoted in William T. McKinnon, *Apollo's Blended Dream: A Study of the Poetry of Louis MacNeice* (London, 1971), 95–6.

[37] 'Experiences with Images', 161.

[38] 'We Are the Old', 1930 paper, quoted in *Modern Poetry*, 71.

[39] M. C. D'Arcy, *The Oxford Outlook*, 10. 50 (Nov. 1929), 380.

[40] 'Foreword', *Blind Fireworks* (London, 1929), 5.

making them explicit. 'Child's Terror' (which MacNeice dismissed in
Modern Poetry on account of its Sitwellian opening) is cast in the mode of
first person recollection, and it is in fact one of the most direct of these
poems, though suffering from occasional rococo decoration. The memory
of a broken swing in a park beside a cemetery (a version of 'my father's
medium-sized lush garden with a cemetery beyond the hawthorn
hedge') opens up into nightmare:

> I fell into a nightmare down suddenly
> Into a hole without a bottom. Music
> Died above my head, died in silence.

MacNeice retreats at once from this directness into more artful
composition:

> Mute is the lute and the flute and the drum
> And the trumpet dumb; and I have lost my swing
> That I thought would climb the sky. But now falling,
> Dropping plumb, listening to silence . . .

This a typical instance of artificiality attempting to function as impersonality, though in fact the clumsy internal rhymes and repeated assonances
achieve only inept evasion. The poem is stronger, however, in its use of
images as intensifying elements; snow turns into the marble of tombs,
and clocks tick menacingly, leading to the final lines:

> Nurse, nurse, drive away the nightmare,
> Turn a light on my snowy counterpane,
> Tell me it is linen, it is not rock,
> Only tell me I am alive again,
> And the pampas grass will raise plume aloft again—
> And stop the clock, nurse, stop the clock.[41]

The images of time, sleep, and petrifaction are here already fully formed
into what were to be their characteristic expressions in MacNeice's work,
foreshadowing poems of the thirties, such as 'Perseus' (1934) or
'August' (1935), in which the fear of stasis refers to more than private
obsession. The poem is explicit in its use of personal symbolism without
thereby becoming obscure, though the same could not be said for some of
the other pieces in the volume. MacNeice uses the amalgamated casts of
classical and Norse mythologies in a manner that is not merely post-
Frazer, but consciously post-Eliot in its assimilation of legend. He has
learned from his schoolboy experiments to deal with the interrelated

---

[41] *Blind Fireworks*, 9–11.

sign-systems of mythological reference as modes of deferral rather than simply ornament. In order to approach the imaginative core of the writing, whether 'personal' or not, MacNeice regarded the artificial, deferring mode as the only one still possible:

we who are sailing between Scepticism & Stupidity as in a nightmare never make headway, but are caught in this narrow strait for ever, with the alternative prospects of eternal deafness with stoppers of cotton wool or else a little music & foamsplashed nudity & foamsplashed bones thereafter. As for Odysseus he had a head for business . . .[42]

Self-consciousness, a recognition of artifice as strategy, lies behind MacNeice's undergraduate writing. Critics have been too quick to dismiss his 'head for business' in this respect. It was never really to desert him, however greatly his aims were to change.

'Summer Remembered', a short prose poem of 1927, reveals some of the difficulties for MacNeice in representing the personal by the artificial. This short meditation sets the first-person voice in a passive relation to its surroundings, the imagery strikingly anticipating later poems such as 'Ode' or 'Hidden Ice':

Summer Remembered

The dimly gaudy drums of summer thumping in the distance and noises rising hazily like sea-drowned bells. The scent of mown grass lulled and lullabied and lapped me in a cradle, eiderdown'd with mottled blue. I could see nothing but the clouds lifting, sinking, drifting over the sky. A tap dripped music on the thirsty silence. The flies answered with their distant music, virelays and yawns and roundelays. The sun had shot me through and through with arrows, Sebastian fallen on his back. When I shut my eyes I retired behind heavy curtains into a chapel; incense hung about and there was a laver of water flecked with rays from a stained glass window. The cool, marble saints were nodding, drowsing, were dozing; the candle flames were sloping, drooping, were sleeping. Then again the drums of summer like red-hot-poker flowers beating on parchment. The sun was stretching down dog-like to lick Sebastian's wounds with a hot and hairy tongue. A lawn-mower droning, a butterfly flapping, a wheelbarrow trundling. The tap was dripping again like peaches or strawberries. If I were lying beneath a fruit tree the juices would be dripping on my lips. Coolness would pervade me like the vans of shadow, dissolve me like a pearl in wine. When I pressed my eyelids peacocks came with constellated tails. It was too hot to move; they had hardened in their moulds. So I lay all afternoon, and the sun yawned on his cushioned chariot behind the foaming horses, whose feet were

---

[42] From fragmentary minutes of a paper, 'The Policeman', read by MacNeice in Corpus Christi College, Jan. 1929, Hilton papers, fol. 81ʳ.

shod with sparks. So all afternoon I lay encrusted in sunlight, taut on my blazing wheel that cycled through the blue. The jagged blue of the sky bit me like a toothed collar. The fruit had shrivelled on the trees, the watertap was silent, only the drums of summer kept up their stupid beating while the butterflies were fainting. I lay all afternoon.[43]

The sun is for MacNeice one of the 'great symbols of routine'[44] and here Sebastian is its victim. The retreat into the self prompts images that are equally sinister; the self's complete passivity brings MacNeice back to the images of obsolescence that had haunted some of his schoolboy verse. The aspects of the natural world in the garden have 'hardened in their moulds' and the self is 'encrusted in sunlight' while 'The jagged blue of the sky' bites 'like a toothed collar'. The attempt to 'remember' summer entails the internalization of descriptive metaphors so that they become parts of a disabling stasis, leaving no room for the self to move freely.

The alternative to this process would be to pin down metaphorical usage to direct correspondence (the correspondences in 'Summer Remembered' run out of control). One of MacNeice's relatively few attempts at this is a poem of 1928, 'En Avant: A Poem suggested by Marco Polo', in which he drily follows Eliot's 'objective correlative' formula with imagery taken second-hand from Eliot himself. An Emperor's funeral procession, and its horsemen 'Dead upon dead horses / With lances at rest and cakes in wallets' is juxtaposed to a contemporary street scene where 'buses / Pass full of passengers' who are 'Wooden upon seats of wood, / With pipe in mouth and coppers in pockets'. A third stanza ends the poem by bringing the two scenes together:

> Foot in stirrups, clutch releasing,
> Horse procession, bus procession,
> Mummy-head, wooden head,
> Never ceasing, never ceasing,
> All dead, dead.[45]

As the two images move syntactically towards identification, the poem gutters into negation. Neither scene adds anything to the other. The poem is worth noting, all the same, as a very early version of the death-bound journey by bus or by train which was to feature so successfully in late poems like 'Figure of Eight' (1956) or 'Charon' (1963). Indeed, one of MacNeice's most common images was to be that of the passenger

[43] The Oxford University Review, 3. 5 (24 Feb. 1927), 144.
[44] Modern Poetry, 176.   [45] The University News, 1. 4 (10 Nov. 1928), 124.

waiting for the future (in 'Corner Seat' (1948) or the last Canto of *Autumn Sequel*, for example). The failure of 'En Avant' suggests that MacNeice's deliberate mythological indiscipline in many of the *Blind Fireworks* poems was part of a strategy that left little room for direct metaphorical or symbolic correspondences. 'En Avant' and 'Summer Remembered' illustrate two poles of MacNeice's early writing, the first allowing metaphor to correspond with 'subject' so closely as effectively to obliterate it, and the second internalizing metaphor to the point of obliterating any 'subject' outside a self-crippling imagination. Between an artistic Scylla and Charybdis of this kind, the 'head for business' of an Odysseus was clearly necessary.

The strategy of *Blind Fireworks* might be characterized as an attempt to construct a Modernist 'myth-kitty' and then watch it explode, or, in the poet's own terms, to stage a series of explosive displays which 'go quickly through their antics against an important background, and fall and go out quickly'.[46] MacNeice's later attitude towards the book, as an adolescent work 'full of mythological tags, half digested new ideas and conceits put in for the hell of it',[47] concentrates on the firework display rather than its surrounding element, and leaves unclear what he might have meant (however mistakenly) by this 'important background'. MacNeice intended his poetry to convey a sense of the personal tensions behind it, and to draw attention to the forces by which it is undermined, or against which it struggles. Time, which appears in various guises, is more than just a fruitful source of 'poetic' melancholy or a good subject for stylized personification. The 'dotard Time' who 'Hobbles on a crooked stick' or Pythagoras, whose stone beard wags 'Like a clock's pendulum', are artificial representations of the same force that ends the nightmarish poem, 'A Cataract Conceived As The March Of Corpses':

> And the beat of the bells on the horses' heads and the undertaker's
> laughter,
> And the murmur that will lose its strength and blur at last to
> quietness,
> And afterwards the minute heard descending, never ending heard,
> And then the minute after and the minute after the minute after.[48]

Images of death and decay are associated throughout the book with the progression of time. MacNeice's way of countering the stasis of poems like 'En Avant' was to distinguish patterns in flux—'pattern is value and

---

[46] 'Foreword', *Blind Fireworks*, 6.   [47] 'Experiences with Images', 160.
[48] *Blind Fireworks*, repr. as 'River In Spate', *Collected Poems*, 6.

a *static* pattern dies on you'.[49] Yet the attempt to 'impose exactitude on the flux of the moment'[50] implied its own impossibility in the face of time with its endless successions of minutes after always outrunning the artificial limits of poetry. The time metaphors of *Blind Fireworks* deliberately defer direct reference to the element in which the poems exist but which they cannot pin down exactly. The awareness, or rather fear, of this is perhaps the 'important background' which survives the displays staged by the poems themselves.

The most ambitious poems in *Blind Fireworks* (the ones which also, in some senses, most seriously misfire) are the volume's final two pieces, 'Adam's Legacy' and 'Twilight Of The Gods'. In them, MacNeice forces together a great many disparate mythological motifs. The poems attempt to delineate mythic beginnings and endings of time. In the first, Adam inaugurates human history with the Fall; his legacy is seen as a rolling wheel that 'open gates that clang again too soon'. The wheel becomes a 'pain-spoked legacy' and the individual, in a sideways shift of myth, becomes Ixion:

> I straddle my wheel, and we move steadily onward,
> And as I grow the fettering pain grows more
> And the reeling wheel spins out a wake of history.

The poem reduces this 'wake of history' to images half-witnessed by the slumbering Adam in a cave (recalling Plato's) where 'shadows creep and crawl over all the cavern wall, / And one can hear the pendulum go to and fro till cockcrow'. The poem ends with Adam and all of the dead waiting for history's end, though 'The trump of doom is still deferred'. Instead of the cock that 'crew harshly out of the sepulchre', it offers only the question 'have you heard the mocking bird?'[51] Reality is kept at several removes in this poem—literally Pindar's 'dream of a shadow'—with history's momentum breaking the stasis only as a wheel, confined to repetition by its own circularity. The often irritating jingle of internal rhymes seems to complement this.

'Twilight Of The Gods' provides an ending for such cycles, but again purely in an amalgam of myth which has few points of contact outside the motifs themselves. The theme of obsolescence, to which MacNeice had been drawn in his schoolboy images of tarnished Romance, provided an attractive way of ending *Blind Fireworks* when combined with mytho-

---

[49] *The Strings Are False*, 127.
[50] Review of E. E. Cummings, *The Enormous Room*, *The Oxford Outlook*, 10. 47 (Nov. 1928), 173.   [51] 'Adam's Legacy', *Blind Fireworks*, 74–6.

logical versions of apocalypse such as those in the Norse stories. Time, as Pythagoras, is killed by a 'stone child' rising from apparent death under water:

> Stone he seems to-night turned beneath blue water:
> No hair will stir, no feature alter,
> Except when the wind sends a fond ripple over,
> Shrouding the dead whom the marble waters cover.[52]

Again, the image was to stay with MacNeice, reappearing in his 1946 radio play *The Dark Tower*, where Roland's mother bears a 'child of stone' upon her deathbed.[53] The gorgon's stare is never far away in *Blind Fireworks*. In 'Twilight Of The Gods' the end of time comes from the sea— water is identified ambiguously with both life and death throughout the book and is also, following Heraclitus, itself a symbol of flux—at the hands of that which had apparently been petrified, rendered static, by time. The poem uses its overlapping myths, which MacNeice later criticized as the product of 'junkshop minds',[54] to suggest the point at which myth gives way to its own obsolescence, to what it cannot adequately encompass or express. If the use of mythological allusion is a mode of deferral, here the acknowledgement of its artificiality is important, and the 'important background' starts to come forward. 'Twilight Of The Gods' ends in a white-out of snow, which imposes a dead uniformity, 'Covering this and that and the other thing, / Anything, everything, all things covering'. With the projected ending of time, differentiation and perception end also; again, the poem does not really conclude, but ends in an impasse, without suggesting adequately any relation between its symbols and their referents. *Blind Fireworks* itself, then, finishes with the conclusion of its conglomeration of myths, but once this goes nothing remains other than an awareness that time undermines the constructed patterns and finalities of myth and poetry alike.

Blind Fireworks, as a Modernist text of sorts, elevates the ephemeral and exemplifies it all too accurately. Its self-conscious use of mythological metaphor to defer reality entails a general retreat, which its rather precious ironies are insufficient to reverse, from reality into system. MacNeice avoids direct reference or metaphorical correspondence in order to protect the integrity of the 'self' which is hidden beneath the poetry and which is, to all intents and purposes, hermetically sealed off

---

[52] 'Twilight Of The Gods', ibid. 77–80.
[53] *The Dark Tower and Other Radio Scripts* (London, 1947), 60.
[54] 'Experiences with Images', 161.

from the forces beyond its control. In the thirties, MacNeice was to revise this strategy in favour of preserving the self through its very capacity to refer, to communicate with others and so keep safe the 'consciousness of himself as a man, not consciousness of himself as a poet'.[55] Yet the self 'as a man' cannot strictly speaking exist in the medium of writing, as MacNeice was to imply in his 1940 qualification of 'the half-truth that poetry is *about* something, is communication'.[56] Like Significant Form, significant myth was futile without something to signify; even so, MacNeice's later work shows that he never quite abandoned belief in at least the possibility of such signification.

In 1929, the year that *Blind Fireworks* was published, MacNeice's poetry was moving in more than one direction. As often, personal obsessions made for stronger work than did intellectual preoccupations. By now, the poet was able to make particularly powerful use of nightmare imagery, as for example in a piece contributed to *Oxford Poetry 1929*:

Laburnum (May 1929)

Laburnum gaily weeping
Well expresses us
Whose laughter tinkles downward.
Yellow crowns and dresses and bland insignia
Will not stem our waterfall, will not keep
Old Tom Time from peeping through our branches.

A hundred and one times the bell tolls,
Our souls are gay in yellow and green
With little mockery bells at ankles
Jingling under the motley sun,
Unseen the cold bell murders them,
A hundred and one times he damns our souls
Concludes our carnival
With a smack of the metal lip at a hundred-and-one.

Here it is we who are blinded and not him,
Peeping Tom has the best of it these days
And when the clown has laughed himself to nothing
And the shadowy ground has drunk his yellow tears,
The next act appears, to merit the praise
Of damned disillusioned impeccable connoisseurs
Whose monocle supplies a cleverly just horizon—
The skeleton of the beautiful clacks in the wind
His leprosy-blighted pods, fingers of poisoned death.[57]

[55] *Modern Poetry*, 1.
[56] *The Poetry of W. B. Yeats* (London, 1941; repr. 1967), 15.   [57] 29.

The gaily coloured images here cover other habitual nightmare symbols, notably 'the cold bell', which recurs often in MacNeice (compare 'Homage to Clichés' (1935), for example). 'Laburnum' shows how acute was the young poet's sense of the clash between surface and core, 'beauty' and death. The 'damned disillusioned impeccable connoisseurs' are forerunners of the doomed class in 'An Eclogue for Christmas' (1933), though their moral redundancy has not yet acquired its political overtones.

One of MacNeice's last poems written recognizably in the *Blind Fireworks* mould is 'Neurospastoumenos', also from 1929. The poem's epigraph and title are taken from the Greek of Marcus Aurelius: 'An empty pageant; a stage play; flocks of sheep, herds of cattle; a tussle of spearmen; a bone flung among a pack of curs; a crust tossed into a pond of fish; ants, loaded and labouring; mice, scared and scampering; puppets, jerking on their strings—that is life.'[58] The Greek word νευροσπαστουμενα is used by Marcus Aurelius to mean being jerked on a string, and refers to all the creatures of the passage. MacNeice changes the form to the singular, perhaps to suggest that the poem or the poet is being manipulated. 'Neurospastoumenos' revises and expands pieces like 'Adam's Legacy' or 'Twilight Of The Gods', giving a 'rough draft of history' from creation to dissolution with various mythological 'puppets' as its characters. It is more successful than the earlier poems, however, in its measure of ironic detachment from this puppet-world and its recognition that 'The philosopher in the stalls is also pulled by strings'. The emphasis shifts away from rococo decoration to philosophical scepticism, and symbols used in earlier poems return more clearly realized. Where 'Time on his camel passes down the steppes of sand' in 'Twilight Of The Gods', here the desert sand is used more simply as an image of oblivion, a function which it was to perform again in MacNeice's wartime poetry, notably 'Jehu' (1940). Also, the sea is stripped of extraneous symbolic significance, becoming an element which resists the patternings of imagination, a manifestation of the principle of flux: 'We regard / The sea intently but the sea intently / Regards not us'. Here the poem's language becomes explicitly metaphysical:

> Regards not us the One but plays at being Many,
> Regards not us the Point but dreams of three dimensions,
> Regards not us the Absolute.

[58] *Meditations*, trans. M. Staniforth (Harmondsworth, 1964), 105. (MacNeice quotes in the Greek.)

Anticipating 'Ode' (1935), where the sea was to play an equally complex role, this passage begins to destabilize the observing subject, so reducing the autonomy of the self behind the poem. Similarly, when Adam, who has found his toy puppets of human history in Pandora's box, is 'Banned from his theatre',

> Stood he a stylite spitting into the stars
> And set out then to face at last reality
> Without paint, gilt gingerbread, foreign gewgaws.

The stylite alone facing a blank reality (again, an image that was to remain with MacNeice, recurring in poems such as 'Stylite' (1940) or 'Spring Cleaning' (1961)), is, like the annihilating sand and the sea, resistant to metaphor, an emblem of the dissolution of the mythological world. Unlike the rather precious 'snowflakes of Nirvana' in 'Twilight Of The Gods', the ending of 'Neurospastoumenos' forms a conclusion that directs attention to verbal rather than pictorial elements: 'The world is round / The day is over / And the daily round. / . . . All / The round world is over.'[59] This is a word-game, mirroring the games played in the poem with Adam that also have to be brought to an end.

Another poem from 1929 shows a lighter touch than the *Blind Fireworks* material, though there is a serious level beneath its ironic surface:

Epitaph For Louis

> The fire's profanity
> Tickled him,
> The candle's whimsicality
> Amused him
> Till, life having abused him,
> Death came and pickled him.
>
> Born of a Bryant and May's pentecost
> Having put on the cone-cap of a dunce
> (Which, strange to say, never seemed absurd to him)
> He began to glut his burning soul on beeswax
> (Louis was a candle once.)
> That he was eating his own flesh
> Never once occurred to him.
> Louis was a candle once.

[59] *The Oxford Outlook*, 10. 51 (Feb. 1930), 421–9.

Peddling his vocabulary
Muttering, vexed
With this world, guttering
Into the next
In a white flux he dipped
His dunce-cap under
And slipped in a fit
To the crypt of it,
It was no wonder
Obiit.[60]

Two common elements of MacNeice's imagery are put to work here: the candle, which in 'Candles' is seen as a figure in a shroud, standing at the foot of the 'grave-bed',[61] and the 'grave-bed' itself, the recurring image of the 'crypt' waiting to receive the poet. The whimsicality of 'Epitaph For Louis' is tinged with nightmare. Like a great deal of the early poetry, its ironies are learned from others (here in particular from Eliot), but its tensions are distinctively MacNeice's own.

By the end of his university career, if not before, MacNeice had grown hostile to all forms of aesthetic abstraction, and had begun to regard art as that which theory could not encompass. In his article 'Our God Bogus' of 1929, he returned to the idea of Significant Form in order to dismiss it on just such grounds:

Theory begins by pointing out something which is inessential to art. We bow the head and eliminate that element (e.g., narrative content of a picture or metrical form of a poem); our art is now possibly one-sided, but still runs the risk of being art. But theory if it goes forward bravely will ban the other side also, and if the artist is still obedient he will eliminate this residue of the unessential and his art is now nothing.[62]

This anticipates the 'impure poetry' of the thirties, but reaches that position by way of reaction to the theory and artistic consequences of a kind of Modernism. MacNeice habitually associated a reaction against Modernism with the impurity of unliterary 'reality' and 'healthy vulgarity'.[63] He found this impurity lacking in, for example, Laura Riding, remarking 'How refreshing to turn from her sophistication to e.g. Mr. Auden (however bragging or bogus his nigger-cum-Lenin-cum-gearbox virility)'.[64] Yet he himself did not abandon 'sophistication' in favour of 'vulgarity'

[60] *Sir Galahad*, 1.1 (21 Feb. 1929), 9.
[61] (1927), printed in *Blind Fireworks* and retained thereafter, repr. *Collected Poems*, 6–7.
[62] *Sir Galahad*, 1. 2 (14 May 1929), 3.   [63] 'Preface', *Modern Poetry*, 1.
[64] Review of Laura Riding, *Life of the Dead*, *New Verse*, 6 (Dec. 1933), 19.

quite so neatly as his account in *Modern Poetry* might suggest. *Poems* (1935), for example, relies in some respects upon the heightened awareness of flux, artificiality, and closure which MacNeice developed in his earlier work, and his later writing returns to the experiments in the relation between self and myth by which *Blind Fireworks* had been dominated. The uneasiness of MacNeice's common sense increases after the 1930s (though it was hardly negligible then), and in this respect especially the early work's 'sophistication' is relevant; as he wrote of Yeats in 1927:

While scientists picked the carcass of matter and found no soul beneath the ribs, Mr. Yeats with a borrowed, antiquated marsh-light of magic followed the *Anima Mundi*. We, of course, do not believe in magic, see only a blind staircase that gapes on the night.[65]

Like the stairs in his schoolboy play 'Third Time' that 'end in a cul-de-sac' and have 'no door at the top—only a window', a 'blind end' in MacNeice's imagery is not always what it seems. There is always the chance of 'light / Before him as through a window / That opens on to a garden'.[66]

The two elements that contributed most to the failure of much of MacNeice's early writing were to prove abiding stimuli as well as problems. Firstly, in handling myth, the self as the centre of coherence had its difficulty 'controlling', 'ordering', and 'giving a shape and significance', in Eliot's terms,[67] to an almost arbitrary system. Secondly, the awareness of time as a subversive element in writing and theory alike, along with the personal fears and obsessions linked to this, subverted the stability of any self in MacNeice's poetry. In the 1930s, questions of individuality and time were translated by the Left into ideological issues. MacNeice had been preoccupied with such problems from an early stage, and he was not to leave them behind him when their political implications became *vieux jeu*.

One poem from 1930 shows MacNeice's early style at its most effective, bringing to a kind of maturity the ironic, half-wistful mode which had attracted him since his schooldays. In 'Threnody', the procedures of a poem like 'En Avant' are used more subtly, bringing together the major images of the lover, the miser, and the dandelion to a single point, the relentless progress of time:

[65] Review of W. B. Yeats, *Autobiographies*, *The Cherwell* (29 Jan. 1927), 28.

[66] 'The Wall', *Solstices* (1961), repr. in *Collected Poems*, 506.

[67] 'Ulysses, Order, and Myth' (1923), repr. in *Selected Prose of T. S. Eliot*, ed. Frank Kermode (London, 1975), 77.

Threnody

Any amount of fine writing
Will never bring me back the ghost I loved
For she has moved beyond words or wishes.

My wordy soul like a fat puff-ball wags
Where once were yellow tongues. Lips not hers
Will tell the time by me and leave me dead.

His head empty of clapper, the miser's bags
Are full of murdered tongues. The stalk
Holds neither brass crown nor snow globe.

Dandelion tea is death of dandelion.
Miser is murdered lover. Lover is
Murdered child. Minutes, blow away.[68]

'Threnody' is a reminder that time is the mainspring of MacNeice's juvenilia, and that the nightmares never far beneath the surface have time as their focus. The childish terrors remembered in *The String Are False*, or in late poems such as 'The Blasphemies',[69] of sleeping and waking in the 'grave-bed', are those of the 'murdered child'. In the juvenilia, the young poet's 'wordy soul' is revealed to be a defence, and its affectations are shown to be gestures of defiance against the nightmare values of time and stasis. That stylistic *hauteur* did not in fact suffice to contain the nightmares is equally clear. There is much more, however, to this early work than the immature posing of the precocious aesthete whom MacNeice was to describe in his retrospective accounts.

One approach abandoned after these early years was MacNeice's Modernism. This is not necessarily the same as scholarly interpretations of Modernism today. For MacNeice, 'the modern' was Significant Form, the poetry of T. S. Eliot, Edith Sitwell, and Laura Riding, the enormous canvas of *Ulysses*, the cultural shock in the aftermath of the First World War.[70] In 1961, recalling his early years, MacNeice wrote that 'However deep one's ignorance, historically, of the Decline of the West, it has been since World War I something that must hit one in the marrow at adolescence'.[71] In outgrowing the perceptions of adolescence, MacNeice saw himself as developing away from grand themes and

[68] *Oxford Poetry 1930* (Oxford, 1930), 23.
[69] *Solstices*, repr. in *Collected Poems*, 507–9.
[70] For an interesting discussion of the young MacNeice's understanding of literary Modernism, see A. Haberer, *Louis MacNeice (1907–1963): l'homme et la poésie* (Bordeaux, 1986), part 3, ch. 4, 'Les Années Vingt et *Blind Fireworks*, Romantisme et Modernisme'.
[71] 'When I Was Twenty-One', 236.

ambitions which left limited room for the individual. For this reason, perhaps, his adolescent affair with Eliot's poetry (recounted strikingly in a 1948 essay entitled 'Eliot and the Adolescent'[72]) was less lasting than his involvement with the work of Yeats or Spenser, with an 'Anima Mundi' that went beyond the Waste Land: 'anyhow Waste Lands are not only community phenomena, there must be one somewhere in each individual just as everyone contains in himself those places which Spenser described as the Cave of Despair, the House of Busyrane, and, thank God, the Gardens of Adonis'.[73] From this perspective, the experiments of MacNeice's early poetry are not false starts, but rather preliminary excursions into territory which the poet was to explore, in different ways, for the rest of his career.

[72] In *T. S. Eliot: A Symposium*, ed., [T.] Tambimuttu and R. Marsh (London, 1948), repr. in *Selected Literary Criticism*, 148–53.
[73] 'When I Was Twenty-One', 236.

'A Communist to Others'
A Symposium

In each volume of *Auden Studies* a number of writers will be invited to respond to a single work by Auden that seems particularly significant or problematic. For this volume we have chosen the first published version of 'A Communist to Others' which appeared in *The Twentieth Century* [Promethean Society] (September 1932). This is the text printed below, though five emendations have been made following a manuscript of the poem that Auden sent to Christopher Isherwood (these mainly restore letters or punctuation marks left out in the magazine). In 1933 'A Communist to Others' reappeared in the influential *New Country* anthology. Then, as three of our contributors mention, Auden cut and rewrote the poem before collecting it in *Look, Stranger!* (1936).[1]

A Communist to Others

Comrades who when the sirens roar
From office shop and factory pour
    'Neath evening sky;
By cops directed to the fug
Of talkie-houses for a drug
Or down canals to find a hug
    Until you die:

We know, remember, what it is
That keeps you celebrating this
    Sad ceremonial;
We know the terrifying brink
From which in dreams you nightly shrink
'I shall be sacked without,' you think,
    'A testimonial.'

---

[1] The 1936 version of the poem, beginning 'Brothers, who when the sirens roar', is reprinted in *EA* 120–3. 'A Communist to others' appears here by permission of Faber & Faber Ltd.

We cannot put on airs with you
The fears that hurt you hurt us too
    Only we say
That like all nightmares these are fake
If you would help us we could make
Our eyes to open, and awake
    Shall find night day.

On you our interests are set
Your sorrow we shall not forget
    While we consider
Those who in every county town
For centuries have done you brown,
But you shall see them tumble down
    Both horse and rider.

O splendid person, you who stand
In spotless flannels or with hand
    Expert on trigger;
Whose lovely hair and shapely limb
Year after year are kept in trim
Till buffers envy as you swim
    Your Grecian figure:

You're thinking us a nasty sight;
Yes, we are poisoned, you are right,
    Not even clean;
We do not know how to behave
We are not beautiful or brave
You would not pick our sort to save
    Your first fifteen.

You are not jealous yet, we know,
But we must warn you, even so
    So pray be seated:
It isn't cricket, but it's true
The lady who admires us, you
Have thought you're getting off with too,
    For you're conceited.

Your beauty's a completed thing
The future kissed you, called you 'King,'
> Did she? Deceiver!
She's not in love with you at all
No feat of yours can make her fall,
She will not answer to your call
> Like your retriever.

Dare-devil mystics who bear the scars
Of many spiritual wars
> And smoothly tell
The starving that their one salvation
Is personal regeneration
By fasting, prayer and contemplation;
> Is it? Well,

Others have tried it, all delight
Sustained in that ecstatic flight
> Could not console
When through exhausting hours they'd flown
From the alone to the Alone
Nothing remained but the dry-as-bone
> Night of the soul.

Coward; for all your goodness game
Your dream of Heaven is the same
> As any bounder's;
You hope to corner as reward
All that the rich can here afford
Love and music and bed and board
> While the world flounders.

And you, the wise man, full of humour
To whom our misery's a rumour
> And slightly funny;
Proud of your nicely balanced view
You say as if it were something new
The fuss we make is mostly due
> To lack of money.

Ah, what a little squirt is there
When of your aren't-I-charming air
    You stand denuded.
Behind your subtle sense of humour
You hide the boss's simple stuma
Among the foes which we enumer
    You are included.

Because you saw but were not indignant
The invasion of the great malignant
    Cambridge ulcer
That army intellectual
Of every kind of liberal
Smarmy with friendship but of all
    There are none falser.

A host of columbines and pathics
Who show the poor by mathematics
    In their defence
That wealth and poverty are merely
Mental pictures, so that clearly
Every tramp's a landlord really
    In mind-events.

The worst employer's double dealing
Is better than their mental-healing
    That would assist us.
The world, they tell us, has no flaws
There is no need to change the laws
We're only not content because
    Jealous of sisters.

Once masters struck with whips; of recent
Years by being jolly decent
    For these are cuter
Fostering the heart's self-adulation
Would dissipate all irritation
Making a weakened generation
    Completely neuter.

Let fever sweat them till they tremble
Cramp rack their limbs till they resemble
  Cartoons by Goya
Their daughters sterile be in rut
May cancer rot their herring gut
The circular madness on them shut
  Or paranoia.

Their splendid people, their wiseacres,
Professors, agents, magic-makers,
  Their poets and apostles
Their bankers and their brokers too
And ironmasters shall turn blue
Shall fade away like morning dew
  With club-room fossils.

Unhappy poet, you whose only
Real emotion is feeling lonely
  When suns are setting;
Who fled in horror from all these
To islands in your private seas
Where thoughts like castaways find ease
  In endless petting.

You need us more than you suppose
And you could help us if you chose.
  In any case
We are not proud of being poor
In that of which you claim a store
Return, be tender; or are we more
  Than you could face?

Comrades to whom our thoughts return
Brothers for whom our bowels yearn
  When words are over
Remember that in each direction
Love outside our own election
Holds us in unseen connection.
  O trust that ever.

Julian Symons

Then

The Twentieth Century, which first appeared in March 1931 and lasted until the end of 1934, was one of the thirties' odder magazines. The page size was large, the cover red, and the magazine announced itself as the journal of the Promethean Society, which was in favour of 'the formation of a new (twentieth century) *Weltanschauung*'.[1] The periodical was above all clamorously and insistently youthful, distrustful of organization and calling for 'the complete yet reasoned and reasoning liberty of the individual'.[2] Lawrence with a dash of Aldous Huxley, one might say, and the 'youth group' aspect of the magazine may have appealed to Auden. It was here that in September 1932 'A Communist to Others' was printed, that I read it, and was sufficiently impressed to learn it by heart.

Auden's early readers were divided between those who knew him or had heard tales about his unusual sexual and personal habits, and the larger number who like me knew of him only through the poems. To us the use of Christian names in the verse was baffling and irritating, many references obscure (who was Homer Lane? what was the Twickenham Baptist gang?), yet the tone was unmistakably urgent, the language strange and new, the imagery startling. Auden seemed to us evidently somebody not just in favour of that new *Weltanschauung*, but a man working actively to bring it about. For the many like me who thought social change not merely desirable but inevitable, much of Auden's work appeared prophetic. Some of the prophecies were hard to understand, but 'A Communist to Others' seemed straightforward: an appeal to join the Party. We never doubted that the poet was himself a Party member, and indeed that (mistaken) belief was reasonable enough.

The poem was for us a kind of complement to those early poems of Stephen Spender's like 'oh young men oh young comrades' and 'After they have tired of the brilliance of cities' that were in effect hymns to the brotherly love of the future. I don't think the homosexual currents in Spender and Auden disturbed many of us then, although a certain Rupert Brookeian gush about some of Spender's lines ('The beautiful generation that shall spring from our sides'[3]) rocked one back on one's

[1] Hugh Gordon Porteus, '"Art-for-Art's-Sake": I. Programme Notes for the Arts Group of the Prometheans', *The Twentieth Century*, 1. 5 (July 1931), 9.

[2] E. M. Barraud, 'Sanity in Sex: The Aims of the Sexology Group of the Prometheans', *The Twentieth Century*, 1. 3 (May 1931), 9.

[3] 'After they have tired of the brilliance of cities', *Poems* (London, 1933), 40.

heels occasionally. There was comradeship but no gush about Auden:

> Comrades who when the sirens roar
> From office shop and factory pour
> 'Neath evening sky.

Yes,

we could identify with that great army of workers going home or to the cinema (from an office in my case), and the fact that 'we' were not envisaged as a beautiful generation but as poisoned, not clean, not beautiful, not brave, was also convincing. We were, or felt ourselves to be, a depressed and ignored group in society, much more intelligent than those who ruled us by the luck of birth, money, education. For all such readers the poem's vision of an overturn in society was exhilarating, and the fact that it was put in extremely colloquial language provided somehow a further encouragement:

> It isn't cricket, but it's true
> The lady who admires us, you
> Have thought you're getting off with too,
>   For you're conceited.

> Your beauty's a completed thing
> The future kissed you, called you 'King,'
>   Did she? Deceiver!

The

poem had a further, wholly personal appeal for me. There was a strain in Auden's work at this time which suggested that all important thought came out of emotional frustration ('The foiled caresses from which thought was born'[4]), and hinted often that our social and personal troubles might be ended by the arrival of a magician, a healer, a ruler, whose regime would be authoritarian although benevolent. The most open expression of this view is in the Ode to John Warner of 1931 (included in *The Orators*), but it is expressed more subtly in many early poems, and in the prose sections of *The Orators* as well. In 'A Communist to Others' it appears in the form of contempt for liberals, psychologists, 'professors, agents, magic-makers'—as well, of course, as such natural objects of detestation as double-dealing employers and ironmasters. All these will be destroyed, the poem says, when the Frog turns into the Fairy Prince.

---

[4] 'Sleep on beside me though I wake for you' (1933), repr. in *EA* 148 (where the first line is 'Turn not towards me, lest I turn to you').

Now

In later years Auden condemned the poem often and vigorously. When it appeared in *Look, Stranger!* he changed the opening 'Comrades' to 'Brothers', and dropped several stanzas including the one saying 'We are not beautiful or brave'. Later the poem was excluded altogether from the canon, and Auden scribbled beside one text of it 'O God what rubbish'.[5]

How does the poem look to-day, the thirties now a mere footnote of failure in history, to a reader who still—rather unfashionably—regards Auden as the greatest twentieth-century poet writing in English? It is not so good a poem as I thought it when young, that's for sure. The most obvious weakness is the poem's divergence from the subject given in the title, into personal invective against Cambridge intellectuals, mystics, a ragbag containing the sort of people Auden didn't like. And there is something cosy and chummy about the name-calling which seems to be saying: 'This is all just fun, you know, no need to get het up about it, some of my best friends are Cambridge intellectual liberals', which is distressing. The 'message' of the poem becomes more blurred the longer you look at it, and I'm driven to the conclusion that the political opinions I read into it were never really there. Or there for no more than ten minutes. One of the shocks in Humphrey Carpenter's biography, at least for me, was the jackdaw nature of Auden's intellect, the fact that the apparently self-assured, confident poet was an erratic haphazard thinker, attaching himself to any bright idea that caught his eye, then abandoning it for another. Looking through spectacles now more than fifty years older than those through which I first saw the poem, the savagely satirical piece has turned into a bit of engaging light verse.

Yet that it *is* engaging, spirited, immensely skilful light verse, often acid and tangy as light verse should be, I have no doubt. The poem's enemies are those every self-respecting radical should retain throughout his life: business bosses ('Once masters struck with whips; of recent / Years by being jolly decent'), po-faced economists ('Proud of your nicely balanced view / You say as if it were something new / The fuss we make is mostly due / To lack of money'), the smiling psychiatrists who tell us that 'There is no need to change the laws / We're only not content because / Jealous of sisters.' 'A Communist to Others' is a much better poem in its entirety—that is, in its original form—than in the truncated

---

[5] Quoted in Carpenter, 330.

version that appeared in *Look, Stranger!* and later in *The English Auden*. It is a pity that this original poem has not been easily available in recent years. To read it you had to search out *The Twentieth Century* in a library, or to find *Poetry of the Thirties*, edited by Robin Skelton, a Penguin volume long out of print.

Valentine Cunningham

The chief, perhaps the only, problem in reading this poem is to decide who is speaking, and to whom. Who is the addresser, and who the addressee? To whom do the pronouns 'you' and 'we' refer?

The poem's earliest readers had few doubts. They simply assumed that the poet Auden or his narrating surrogate was here addressing some putative brothers or comrades in the proletariat. They assumed that Auden was the 'Communist' of the poem's original title and that he was talking to others of similar mind, either Communists or potential Communists, out there among the reading public and in the working class. 'The well-brought up young men discovered that people work in factories and mines, and they want to know more about these people. But it seems to me that instead of finding out about them, they write poems calling them Comrades from a distance.' Thus Allen Tate in 1937.[1] Doubtless Edmund Wilson too had this poem in mind when he talked of Auden as 'this brilliant and engaging' young student taking a 'bold and exhilarating step' in coming out 'so strongly for the class struggle'.[2]

In more recent times doubts have set in about such straightforward assumptions. Justin Replogle has offered this poem as the clearest example among early Auden works of the Poet being overwhelmed by his dialogic Other, the so-called Anti-Poet—'an Antipoet who finds this pretended brotherhood' claimed by the Poet to be 'preposterous'.[3] Replogle still adheres, though, to the notion that the poem's opening lines are uttered by the Poet *in propria persona*, before dialogical doubts and a counter-persona, the Anti-Poet, intervene. Edward Mendelson is much more radical. He throws all the authority of his intimate knowledge of Auden's writing against the idea of Auden or an Audenic narrator being the speaker: 'The voice of this poem is not Auden's but that of a Communist telling Auden what he needs to learn'.[4] Auden is being ventriloquial.

But Mendelson acknowledges that his reading still leaves us with a real difficulty: 'The ventriloquism is not entirely convincing. The Communist is supposedly a member of the working class, "a nasty sight"

[1] 'Sixteen Comments on Auden', *New Verse*, 26–7 (Auden Double Number, Nov. 1937), 27.
[2] 'The Oxford Boys Becalmed', *The New Republic*, 90. 1160 (24 Feb. 1937), 77–8.
[3] *Auden's Poetry* (London, 1969), 119.   [4] *Early Auden*, 143.

and proud of it, but he is well-informed in the intellectual fashions of the bourgeoisie—mysticism, psychoanalysis, Cambridge liberalism, and so on. D. H. Lawrence seems to figure far more prominently than Marx in his pantheon.'[5] And of course this is true. And it is very odd. But then, whichever way one reads the addresser and the addressee a sense of oddity prevails. For in the progress the reader makes gradually through the poem, his or her sense of who might at any one time be speaking and to whom, his or her grasp of who the pronouns 'we' and 'you' refer to, are continually being assailed and unsettled.

To be sure, stanza 1 appears to offer itself as if uttered by a voice we recognize as Audenic and bourgeois, directed at workers in their offices, shops, and factories—the ordinary people that thirties poetry constantly deplored for swallowing the bosses' and authority's cinematic drugs and for other escapist pastimes such as snogging along canal banks. The 'We' of stanza 2, however, comes with other tones, and ones that upset any neat equations implied by the first stanza. '"I shall be sacked without," you think, / "A testimonial."' But who so thinks? Well, the bourgeois schoolmaster of Edward Upward's story 'Sunday' did, for one. 'I might be sacked without a testimonial', he declared, only a few pages earlier than 'A Communist to Others' when it appeared in the *New Country* anthology.[6] Are we then to take this stanza's knowing 'We' to be the accusing voice of a proletarian reminding Auden–Upward types who are contemplating going over to the side of the workers and fearing for their nice jobs in consequence, that workers also have nightmares of joblessness? Any confidence we might have in doing that, though, falters at the next stanza, for its 'We' appears to be attachable either to an Auden or an Auden-accuser: at least until the last two lines of the stanza, with their suggestions of blindness ('If you would help us we could make / Our eyes to open')—an acceptance of unseeingness that sits more readily on a dithering Audenic narrator than on a worker-Communist from whom the period would expect—and usually got—greater confidence and faith in superior political vision.

If confusion is by now mounting seriously, stanza 4 exacerbates it, for the voice here could belong to either class of potential narrator—both poets and workers can be thought of as having been 'done brown', that is bemerded by the bourgeoisie, the sort of intellectuals and liberals who after this point in the poem become its main subject and its main addressees. And in the same confusing way, the poisoned, dirty 'we' of

[5] Ibid. 143–4.
[6] Michael Roberts, ed. (London, 1933), 185 and 209.

stanza 6 ('Not even clean') could, without further evidence of the kind that is unhelpfully not on offer, be taken as workers grimy with toil, or grubby poets like Auden himself who did not care to wash over-much. Just so, the 'You' who think 'us a nasty sight' could equally well be the Evelyn Waugh kind of observer who saw in the Welsh proletarian brass-bandsmen of *Decline and Fall* (1928) a frightening bunch of simian loonies, or the spruce games captains and school prefects who turned into Cyril Connolly's permanently adolescent leaders of Britain and who scorned all ragamuffin poets, bohemians, and bourgeois pinkoes.

What's more, if the 'we' of the poem is a worker, as Mendelson believes, he is, as Mendelson concedes, mightily and suspiciously *au fait* with the nuances of educated and bourgeois existence. He appears to know all about Goya and paranoia (stanza 18) and has clearly dipped into *King Lear* long enough to afforce the fury of his cursing in the same stanza ('Their daughters sterile be in rut'). And one would have to wonder just how he became so intimate with the characteristic prep-school rhetoric of the Audenesque manner ('Ah, what a little squirt is there' in stanza 13). Still, for all that wonder, the poverty of the poem's speaker is striking and looks suggestive: the wise man addressed in stanza 12 is rebuked for thinking 'our misery's a rumour / And slightly funny' and for believing that 'The fuss we make is mostly due / To lack of money.' But of course poverty is not limited to any one class, so that the insistence fails to help us here in limiting the addresser to being either a poor worker or a poor poet. And just to complicate our reading further, the speaker of stanza 21 claims to be 'poor / In that of which' the unhappy poet of stanza 20 claims 'a store'. So, it appears, the sort of poverty that engages the poem will not be confined just to money poverty; nor is it something that unhappy bourgeois poets (at least ones who can afford to toddle off and indulge in private escapist lives on far-off islands—like Graves and Laura Riding in Mallorca) have no interest in. The kind of poverty in question here makes the narrator akin to the unhappy poet, as well as serving to demarcate the one from the other, and so weights the emphasis in stanza 21 towards that narrator's being an Audenic figure on terms with the poet addressed in stanza 20. This emphasis is surely neutralized, however, by the last lines of stanza 21— 'or are we more / Than you could face?'—which chime in with the earlier ambivalent claim to griminess ('Not even clean') in stanza 6.

The poem ends with the same Comrades or Brothers being addressed in stanza 22 as in stanza 1. And the pronouns are as indeterminate in stanza 21 as they were in stanzas 2, 3, and 4. Words are indicated as the prerogative of the speaker in stanza 22. He expresses an interest in his Comrades 'When words are over', and since this pronouncement comes at the end of a poem, these words in question might be supposed to be the poem's own words just uttered, and therefore to indicate that the speaker has been and is a poet, or even *the* poet of this poem. But, obviously, discourse, words, are not the prerogative of only one kind of word-user, and since it has not been possible at any point in the poem finally to settle whether this poem's speaker is a poet rather than a worker, the claim, just by itself, that the speaker is in command of the words, the utterance, is no defining factor at all.

Clearly, then, 'A Communist to Others' is characterized by deep confusion. Its pronouns prove, strictly, unreadable, and so both its addresser and its addressee remain undecidable. Attempts at rationalizing the confusion can be made. In my *British Writers of the Thirties*, I have linked it to Auden's inability to resolve his own position in the period's wider dialectic between the fraught bourgeois 'I' of writers and the communal 'we' of the proletariat and the Communist Party that was held out by Communist critics and propagandists as the saving solution to the problems of selfhood prevailing in the modernist and late-capitalist world.[7] The confusion is revealingly endorsed in Auden's well-known shifts over the first addressee of the poem (at different times 'All', 'Comrades', 'Brothers') and also confirmed by his later disgusted rejection of the poem ('O God what rubbish'[8]). But evidence of the confusion is by no means limited to such manœuvres and indications: it begins at the earliest stages of the poem's textual life and pervades its whole textual space. It has been glossed by Stan Smith like this: 'The speaker is simultaneously an outsider despising the bourgeois world and, in his intimate knowledge of its flaws and vanities, the insider-poet himself, a self-delighting traitor in the camp'.[9] What cannot be proved, however, is that this simultaneity is anything other than helplessly contradictory and, as it emerges in the process of reading the poem, perpetually misleading and frustrating. Here is no 'careful manipulation of personae',[12] but rather an instructively messy wash of undecided and indecipherably clashing tones, ideolects, personae, utterly apt to the confusions and contradictions of Auden's wavering social allegiances, his well-known uncertainties as to political and moral direction at the time of writing this poem.

[7] (Oxford, 1988), 221–4.   [8] See above, Symons n. 5.
[9] *Inviolable Voice: History and Twentieth Century Poetry* (Dublin, 1982), 139.
[10] Ibid.

Stan Smith

Auden's Others

Sometimes even Auden got it right. Unlike 'Spain' and 'September 1, 1939', this is not the fine but flawed poem one wants to defend against its author's censure. Nevertheless, it is an interesting and symptomatic poem, which tells us a lot about the linguistic versatility and the ideological confusion of the early Auden.

Its vocabulary ranges through several registers of slang and a variety of jargons. This lexical scope proposes a political constituency. Within it, ouvrierist populism and Leninist élitism jostle for dominance. It addresses 'the masses' in an ersatz demotic which casts them as anti-intellectual and escapist. But it indicates to all rival intelligentsias that it is more knowing than they, and that its knowledge can interpret, place, and subdue theirs. It would actually like to weld a political and discursive *combinatoire* out of its diverse addressees. By adopting the abrupt 'tailed rhyme' familiar from the Burns stanza (compare the first version of 'The Witnesses', written around the same time), Auden invokes a radical and democratic ancestry appropriate to the poem's Scottish provenance. But the intemperate flyting associated with the device here suggests impotence rather than cool confidence. Arrogance is repeatedly undercut by deeper insecurities of tone. The political uncertainties generate some of the verbal richness.

'Cops', 'talkie-houses', 'find a hug', and 'done you brown' share a different social register from 'buffers', 'bounder', 'jolly decent', 'it isn't cricket', and (twice) the Senior Common Room use of 'splendid'. And whereas the former propose an intimate and sympathetic complicity, the latter are familiarly contemptuous and parodic. Slangy idioms such as 'little squirt' and 'smarmy' are under renegotiation. Coinages of a 'superior' class to categorize its 'inferiors', they are here turned against that class, in a crafty inversion. The vernacular of 'put on airs', 'fake', 'kept in trim', 'nasty sight', 'getting off with', 'goodness game', 'corner', 'wiseacres', 'aren't-I-charming' occupies a border zone, acceptable to polite usage as the kind of self-conscious colloquialism it is amusing and fashionable to scatter around smart conversation. Even the 'sophisticated' jargons of spiritual regeneration (the Oxford Group), contemporary psychology, and idealist philosophy are deployed with cocktail-party knowingness.

Some words are at a watershed, their meaning dependent on the register we attribute to them, which in turn reveals what *we* are. 'Petting' may have its traditional meaning of 'sulks'. Or it could be a racily up-to-date Americanism for which the *OED Supplement* records a first usage in 1931: 'frequent and often indiscriminate indulgence . . . in hugging, kissing, and fondling'. Classically educated traditionalists may think of Achilles in his tent. Movie-going moderns will connect the poet's self-fondling thoughts with the mental masturbation of mystics and philosophers, contrasted with hugging proletarians and the yearning bowels of muscular leftists.

The poem is linguistically promiscuous. Highbrow vogue-words consort with the rough trade of factory, street, and picture-house. This is not just a matter of the company they keep. Individual words themselves are prone to semantic degeneration, their slumming become habitual. Others set out to con us, pretending to higher status than they merit. 'Stuma' sounds like a medical term of classical provenance, but it's not in the *OED*. 'Stumer' or 'stumor' is: 1890s slang for 'A forged or dishonoured cheque; a counterfeit bank-note or coin; a sham'. 'Stuma' enacts its meaning here: itself a sham coinage, counterfeiting another, more lowly word, it is unhonoured by the dictionary. For 'stumer' the 1933 *OED Supplement* gives 1920s meanings of a racehorse fraudulently run to lose, and a failure or 'dud'. In the 1950s it still meant the latter in Lancashire dialect, and my students inform me that it is still in regular use in Glasgow and the Scottish Lowlands. Auden would have heard it on the playing-fields of Helensburgh. His 'simple stuma', it turns out, is far from simple.

The *OED* reveals further sneaky *doubles entendres*. A columbine could be 'a dove-like person', 'a type of innocence or gentleness'. This fits one meaning of 'pathic'—'one who suffers or undergoes something'. But the most obvious reference is to Harlequin's mistress, 'a coquet, in love with everybody'. This ambivalence—a meretricious innocence—supports the strong meaning of 'pathic', appropriate to the Cambridge of Anthony Blunt: 'a man or boy upon whom sodomy is practised; a catamite'. And this complicates the homo-erotic impulse behind the Brüderschafting and the risqué play on biblical idiom at the end. Anger here projects inner anxiety. Similar projections occur in the assaults on all the rival authorities of the poem, each in turn indicted for the hubris or imposture of which the speaker might also be accused.

The continuous negotiation of registers suggests a deeper instability in the poem's sense of its intended audience. The poem moves promiscuously from addressee to addressee, unable to rest with any particular 'other'. The title sets up a simple antithesis but, as Derrida has suggested, such binaries always comprise a dominant and a subordinate partner. In Auden's poem this relationship keeps changing, power surging backwards and forwards between speaker and changing addressees. One representative 'communist' addresses indeterminate but plural 'others'. Heroic singleness confronts multitude, sustained by a collectivity which promises solidarity beyond solitude. Yet Shelley's words to the men of England, of their masters, 'Ye are many, they are few',[1] gives way throughout Auden's poem to a more disturbing anxiety: 'you' (the others) are many, 'we' (the communists) are few. The splendid person is disabused of his conceit by the rhetorical question which inserts an unsettling third, 'the future', into the exchange. But the conceit of the communist is similarly under threat. He never runs out of opponents to 'enumer'. The mystic is rebuked by the dramatic reversal that follows another rhetorical question in the enjambment of stanzas 9 and 10. His ecstasy is not unique: 'Others have tried it...'. Echoes of T. E. Lawrence or Saint-Exupéry are less significant here than the expansive vagueness of 'Others'. This intrusion of otherness besets and destabilizes the whole discourse. Every duet the speaker sets up is displaced in turn. For each 'we' and 'you' there is a 'they' to break up the tête-à-tête.

This multitudinous other proliferates from stanza to stanza, and there is no reason why it should ever stop. It is cut short, rather than concluded, in stanza 19's terse list of yet undescribed opponents. The imposed rhetorical resolution afforded by prophecy rescues the poem from the Shandean impasse in which its roll-call of enemies has trapped it, just as history will intervene to solve the communist's problems by extinguishing those enemies. This *performative* dimension is a recurrent stylistic device for providing an imaginary resolution to insoluble political dilemmas. The communist's unsureness is revealed in the very strategies he adopts to conceal it—his abrupt changes of rhetoric, from plaintive appeal to disdain, insecure mock-apologia turning round into aggressive challenge, scornful indictment slipping into intemperate abuse and cursing. The curse, though it may seem a prophet's *métier*, is really the genre of those excluded from power and the apparatus of retribution. This is not the 'nicely balanced' cadence of the master but the wishful subjunctive of the slave, invoking some external agency to turn its 'Let' and 'May' into 'Shall'.

The confident claims to knowing are never embodied in a knowledge.

---

[1] Percy Bysshe Shelley, 'The Mask of Anarchy' (1819), l. 155.

In stanza 2 the workers are required to *remember* what the communist has yet to persuade them of—that 'we know'. This 'we' constantly makes the large claims it denounces in its opponents. But the claim to knowledge in stanzas 7–8 does not differ from the mystic's claims in 9–10. The dismissals of his 'dream' and of the wise man's 'nicely balanced view' as concealed self-interest are no different from the latter's critique of the communists, or the liberal's 'Freudian' reading of discontent as sibling rivalry in stanza 15. Projection is of the very essence of this politics, and it is reciprocal.

The 'knowledge' claimed in stanza 2 is two different, but elided, things. The ambiguous tense of the redoubled 'hurt' (present or past) conceals the slip from a shared *experience* of suffering to the intellectual *understanding* of it. Does the speaker *still* feel their hurt, or has his new knowledge freed him from it? He never explains how taking thought transforms real oppression into fake nightmares, nor how this differs from the liberal's demonstration 'That wealth and poverty are merely / Mental pictures'. The communist *does* 'put on airs' with the workers, offering assurances like those of the 'magic-maker'. Yet his arrogance is undercut by a humbling dependency. History hinges on that conditional in stanza 3, where the succession of pronouns enacts a dream of conversion.

In stanzas 2–3 'we' is the confident subject and 'you' the passive object of knowledge. Stanza 3 initially separates 'we' and 'you' as subject and object at opposite ends of the first line, but unites them as common objects of 'hurt'. The modest claim of 'only we say', facilitates the shift in which 'you' becomes the subject and 'us' the object of a putative action. The final 'we' and 'our' incorporate 'you' into the collective subject of this still merely hypothetical making: 'If *you* would help *us we together* could make...'. Since, however, the communist has already proclaimed his own wide-awakeness, this mock humility stands self-condemned as rhetoric. The imaginary community of communist and others it invents is broken at once, leaving 'you' again the object of 'our interests', 'your sorrow' the object of 'we shall not forget', as the 'we' wanders off to contemplate new objects, those who have for centuries reduced the workers to objects, but whose downfall will shortly become the object of the workers' seeing.

Throughout, the revolution of its pronouns mimics the political transformations the poem envisages. In conceding grammatical precedence to the 'splendid person', the speaker seems to acknowledge him as the arbiter of values, picker and chooser. Even in knowing, where he lays claim to a monopoly with the workers, the communist defers to the splendid person: 'you are right', 'we do not know', 'you would not pick our sort'. But this is ironic apologetic, biding its time. Stanza 7 claims a more important knowledge, with real consequences. There is a struggle for control of the main verb in these stanzas. Stanza 7 contains five 'yous', of which four are subjects of the verb. The exception is crucial. For while 'you' seems to be the dominant subject, all its acts are finally reduced to *objects* of knowledge, subordinate to the interjected 'we know' which inserts a superior subject into the sentence. This subject not only knows but turns 'you' into a threatened object of the verb 'warn', and his opponent's knowledge into mere opinion: 'you're thinking us', 'you have thought'. The final twist lies in the grammatical inevitability with which the tables are turned: 'we *must* warn you'. In stanza 8, the grammatical peripety has been effected: 'you' and 'your' are all in object positions except in the one line that declares their death warrant: 'Your beauty's a completed thing'.

The 1936 version in *Look, Stranger!* ends on the apparently impersonal, 'objective' prophecy. At the high point of Auden's leftism, in the year of the Popular Front, such an ending deliberately steels the will for struggle. The 1932 version by contrast closes in the real world of historical indeterminacy and fractious special-pleading. The most destabilizing 'other' in the poem is addressed in these final three stanzas, which problematize the status of the utterance itself. In rounding on the 'unhappy poet' the text undercuts its own authorship and authority. If the poet too is an 'other' of the communist, then who is speaking here, and with what authority? Of course, the poem may wish to distinguish the happy political from the unhappy romantic poet (evoked with equal ambiguity in 'Spain', complete with his sunsets and solitude). It may even wish to dissemble its own status as a poem. But if feeling lonely is the poet's 'only / Real emotion', the speaker lays himself open to the suspicion that it's his real condition too, a lonely orator haranguing indifferent or hostile multitudes. In which case, all the rhetoric is only sublimation and evasion of a romantic posture, as various 'others' have suggested within the text, and as Communist Party critics such as Caudwell were to propose in print.

How does the political poet's rejection of bourgeois mediocrity differ from the romantic's? Is his yearning bowel not just another version of endless petting? In the cajoling tone of 'You need us more than you suppose / And you could help us if you chose' the need is all with the speaker, though it is projected on to the addressee. The four times repeated 'you' takes priority over the dependent and plaintive 'us' (which again moves into the conditional for its vision of help and hope). Confronting the supposedly worthless poet, the communist is uncharacteristically humble and apologetic in admitting to impoverished feeling. The appeal to 'Return, be tender' transforms the despised poet into a saviour. That this may be going too far is recognized by the sudden snarl of that last challenging question. The question is really self-addressed. 'We' and 'you' face each other interchangeably as communist and poetic *alter ego*, as in the reproachful mirror of 'September 1, 1939'. It is 'our thoughts' that return in answer to the appeal, 'our bowels' that experience a sudden flux of tenderness.

Only an impersonal third force, 'Love', can hold all these duets in its collectivizing grip, imposing an 'unseen connection' on all the personal tendernesses, elections, derelictions, and acts of trust. The circular madness descends upon the poem as a hermeneutic closed circle. There is no outside to this 'knowledge', which returns repeatedly on itself, as the thought of the poet returning makes the poet's thoughts return to those comrades with whom he began. Much easier, then, in the 1936 version, to break this circle by dropping the last three stanzas, to end with an imaginary future in which this whole order will 'fade away like morning dew'. But in purging the 'comrades' Auden also expelled any sense of the historical agency that might achieve such a break. For all the demagoguery, this is the image of Auden's politics: a helpless poet, an absent proletariat, a disconnected future. Auden's final solution, in his reaction against his thirties stance, is, ironically, a drolly Stalinist one: a suppressed poem, a past rewritten and expunged, the silence of a text reduced to non-person.

Mick Imlah

Many poems of the 1930s make distinctive use of the pronoun 'we': 'A Communist to Others' is their prototype. The Marxist, iconoclastic 'we' created here became, in the hands of a small number of writers under Auden's influence, simply their version—anti-athletic, misogynist, exclusively cosmopolitan—of the clubbishness they deplored in other circles (Rex Warner: 'Come with us, if you can, and, if not, go to hell';[1] and Cecil Day-Lewis, with his boyish invocation of 'Wystan and Rex my friend'[2]). As a result, in the second half of the decade, the public-school–communist 'we' loses its mischievous thrust in the shadow of a more urgent and less voluntary historical force; in poems like Louis MacNeice's 'The Sunlight on the Garden'[3] it is revealed as an emblem of doomed shared enjoyments. Here, when MacNeice makes a plural of Mark Antony's farewell—'We are dying, Egypt, dying'—it is the pronoun that is dying, as well as each of its disintegrated components.

In Auden's case, transformation of the pronoun is compressed into a few months. He is quick to discover a 'we' that has personal as well as communal meaning, in the light of the visionary picnic experience of June 1933, described by Edward Mendelson in *Early Auden*, whereby he learned 'what it means to love one's neighbour as oneself'.[4] Less than a year after 'A Communist to Others', Auden is writing (in the summer of 1933) 'A Summer Night', which places the poet with his selected companions squarely on the bourgeois side of the barricades, preferring not to ask 'what doubtful act allows / Our freedom in this English house, / Our picnics in the sun'.[5] The richer social poetry of the thirties comes, after all, from the experience of privilege under pressure. There isn't much richness, though, in 'A Communist to Others', and Auden's 'we' is a large part of the problem. It is, of course, the appropriate pronoun for a

[1] 'Hymn', *Poems* (London, 1937), 40.
[2] 'The Magnetic Mountain', *Collected Poems 1929–1936* (London, 1948), 111.
[3] *Collected Poems of Louis MacNeice*, ed. E. R. Dodds (London, 1966), 84–5. (The allusion is to *Antony and Cleopatra*, 4. 15. 18.)
[4] Mendelson quotes Auden's prose account of the experience which was part of his Introduction to Anne Fremantle's anthology, *The Protestant Mystics* (1964), repr. *FA* 49–78. The party comprised Auden, a fellow master, and two matrons from the Downs School near Malvern: 'We were talking casually about everyday matters when, quite suddenly and unexpectedly, something happened. I felt myself invaded by a power which, though I consented to it, was irresistable and certainly not mine. For the first time in my life I knew exactly . . . what it means to love one's neighbour as oneself. I was also certain, though the conversation continued to be perfectly ordinary, that my three colleagues were having the same experience.' See *Early Auden*, 160–1.   [5] Repr. in *CP76* 104.

poem spoken by a Communist; but the reader is not advised whether to
listen for an individual, with a personality distinct from Auden's and
from other Communists', or to the anonymous chorus of revolution.
Auden would have seen the value of the plural pronoun as an escape from
'private seas' into public poetry; but where the level of dramatization
is so uncertain, some effects which are intended as archetypal are not
sufficiently detached from their author.[6] The calculated non-con-
descension to the working class ('All those . . .' was revised to 'Comrades
. . .' in manuscript) suggests a bond more willed than natural, while
'Brothers for whom our bowels yearn' conveys a quasi-erotic attraction
(and separation) rather than social and economic proximity or intellectual sympathy. A poem which was really designed—either directly or
dramatically—as an appeal to factory workers would hardly dwell, as
this does, on (for instance) the shortcomings of liberal thinking at
Cambridge University. And so on. The poem vacillates between the
coldness of the general will and the overheated imagery of individual
malice; and if it isn't Auden speaking, it fails just as clearly to imitate
anyone else.

In addition to problems with the address, the special importance for
such writing of the act of publication leads Auden to disregard an
unusual number of local defects (which, incidentally, the half-hearted
revision for book publication in *Look, Stranger!* does nothing to amend).
First there is the punctuation. The younger Auden was habitually
slovenly in this respect, but here his negligence inflicts serious structural
damage. The fourteenth, fifteenth, and twentieth stanzas are falsely
punctuated as complete sentences; and this can't be fixed by alternative
punctuation. Clumsy syntax is more certainly a failing the farther poetry
gets from the lyrical (and it can't get much farther than this): it is a
product here of the same superficiality of attention that breeds errors of
detail like the fading fossils of the nineteenth stanza (the one thing
fossils don't do is fade).

Then there are three instances of apparently unconscious repetition.
The address 'O splendid person' is duplicated later by 'splendid
people', referring to a different group;[7] the 'poets and apostles' of the

[6] In his *British Writers of the Thirties* (Oxford, 1988), Valentine Cunningham sees the
poem's vague plural voice alternatively as a product of Auden's failure to develop a
satisfactory socialist 'I' for himself, 221–4.

[7] This ironical phrase was a favourite of Auden's at this time; cf. a book review in
Scrutiny, 1. 2 (Sept. 1932), which said of public schools: 'They fail because they are only
for the splendid people', 193. It was taken up by some of those under Auden's influence,
e.g. Rex Warner: 'The splendid body is private and calls for more . . .' ('Hymn', 39).

nineteenth stanza are too close to the 'unhappy poet' of the twentieth not to be prosaically distinguished from him; and 'humour' is used as a rhyme-word in consecutive stanzas (the twelfth and thirteenth) without effective variation. This is bad writing by standards lower than we would ever think of applying to Auden.

These marks of carelessness are especially unfortunate because the form Auden has chosen depends more than most on the precise calculation of effects. His stanza is really a light-verse vehicle, close to the familiar Burns stanza (which Auden might have thought an appropriately populist vehicle) but more long-winded. It fits not one (like Burns), or two (like Auden's later, better 'The Witnesses'), but three lines into the space between the clinching shorter lines, and so defuses its own charge. Furthermore these intervening lines are dully rhymed, sometimes with three abstract, Latinate words (self-adulation/irritation/generation; direction/election/connection; intellectual/liberal/all). As well as going against the colloquial or at least conversational grain of the genre (resembling more the fustian of Burns's English poems than the fire of his Scots), this simply isn't inventive enough to make the verse work.

The most promising stanza, from the technical point of view, is the eighteenth: Goya/paranoia has the right muscular surprise as a rhyme, and 'the circular madness on them shut' exploits the swing and closure of the form; but this is also, coincidentally, the point in the poem where the tone (throughout a dodgy fluctuation between game and earnest) goes most badly awry. It works, in dramatic writing, to have a character curse like Lear if he has Lear's cause, or like Caliban if he is evidently impotent; it works, in light verse, to invoke destruction, if your weapons are metaphoric like Betjeman's 'friendly bombs' (the cabbages he'd drop on Slough),[8] or if your targets are satirically individuated like Pope's dunces. But Auden's Communist does not have a personal context for his curses, and his punishments are relished as much for their nastiness as for their justice. The implication is that with history on his side the Communist can project cruelties without responsibility; but part of Auden's own personality betrays him here. In a poem which is anxious to imply some sort of organic conscience, the most specific violence is directed against women's sexuality—used incidentally as vengeance on their fathers. 'May cancer rot their herring gut' means to

---

[8] 'Slough', *A Continual Dew* (London, 1937).

refer back to these fathers, but it attaches itself instead to the rutting daughters of the preceding line. If the two lines were reversed, the ambiguity would be avoided and the offence diminished; but misogyny has imaginative precedence even over a Marxism that triumphs by disease. The poem is out of control.

Collecting W. H. Auden

ROBERT A. WILSON

BOOK collecting is a challenge. If the challenge is too easy, for instance, assembling a complete collection of the works of Thomas Pynchon or Robert Lowell, there will be little excitement because these collections can be completed with no greater difficulty than the expenditure of a relatively small sum of money. In both cases, there are no great rarities to pursue. On the other hand, if the challenge is too hard, there is no incentive. Take, for instance, collecting the work of Vladimir Nabokov. His first book, a volume of poems issued in St Petersburg before the Russian Revolution of 1917, is known to exist in only two copies in the Western world, and both of these are lodged permanently in institutional libraries. Thus a collection of Nabokov is unlikely ever to be complete, a fact which will frustrate the true collector. Furthermore, a long and satisfying chase can be made only in pursuit of a sufficiently large quantity of material. Thus, most twentieth-century authors and poets are not ideal targets for the spirited and devoted collector, although there are, of course, some exceptions. They are by and large the giants of the century: Yeats, Pound, Lawrence, Joyce, Stein, and Eliot spring readily to mind. But these authors have been collected so avidly for the last two decades that prices have risen to staggering heights for the rarities and the supply even of middle-range items in fine condition has been virtually exhausted.

At least one titan does remain as a possibility for a beginning collector, namely, W. H. Auden. More and more he is regarded as the last of this century's great writers. One line of descent in English poetry clearly passes from Yeats to Pound to Eliot to Auden. For the collector, Auden is an ideal choice. He was prolific, working in every genre of literature except fiction. As well as being a great poet, he was also a major critic, an essayist on world affairs and religious subjects, an editor of anthologies, a translator, a librettist of considerable success and distinction, and a discoverer of new talent. The Yale Younger Poets series has issued annually for nearly 75 years a volume of poetry by a young poet who has not previously had a book published. From 1948 to 1959 Auden edited the series, and he was responsible for the publication of first books by Adrienne Rich, W. S. Merwin, Daniel Hoffman, John Ashbery, James Wright, and John Hollander, to mention only some of the most famous of his choices. His, surely, was the most perspicacious eye ever to oversee the series.

The central part of Auden's canon (listed in section 'A' of Bloomfield's and Mendelson's *Bibliography*, which is the principal tool for collectors) includes some 64 primary items. This figure is nearly doubled if one counts both the British and the American editions of Auden's books. While many of these are still relatively easy to come by, my experience as a dealer suggests they are beginning to disappear. Quite a few will no longer be found very easily, and Auden's first book, the *Poems* (1928) printed by Stephen Spender on a hand press, may never turn up at all for most collectors (I still don't have one myself!). In thirty years as a professional book dealer, I have known only four copies to come on the market. The situation is not hopeless; only about half of the probably 35 or so copies that the teenage Spender printed for his older friend have been accounted for, but it remains a considerable challenge.

Hand-printed books, pamphlets, and other limited edition items have a continuing allure for the collector once the major volumes have been assembled. Their interest, perhaps less obvious at first, increases as the search progresses and the collection grows more elaborate. For example, there are the four legitimate pamphlets printed by Frederic Prokosch in the thirties in editions of 22 copies each: *Poem* (1933), *Two Poems* (1934), *Our Hunting Fathers* (1935), and *Sonnet* (1935). Prokosch was then a Yale undergraduate and subsequently made a respectable career as a poet and novelist. But after World War II he succumbed to a temptation that had, decades earlier, ensnared Thomas J. Wise, the leading bibliographer and book expert of his day. He produced nicely printed pamphlets by major authors, all bearing dates many years earlier than the years in which they were first 'discovered'. Unfortunately for Prokosch, book collectors and dealers had become far more sophisticated since Wise's era, and suspicion arose immediately at the sudden appearance of so many pamphlets by such major authors as Yeats, Pound, Eliot, Stein, and Auden. People who were knowledgeable about the *œuvres* of these authors could not accept Prokosch's claim that he had caused these pamphlets to be printed in 1939, but that all copies had been lost in a suitcase that disappeared during his flight from Europe at the beginning of the war and had only recently, and miraculously, been recovered. Chemical analysis of the papers, as well as the identification of typefaces that had not come into use until after the end of the war undid Prokosch, who now admits the printed dates are false. Such productions must be relegated to the section of ephemera rather than being given status as bona fide items in an author's *œuvre*. There are six of these forged Auden pamphlets, discussed in an Appendix to the Bloomfield and Mendelson *Bibliography* and, more fully, in Nicolas Barker's *The Butterfly Books: An Enquiry into the Nature of Certain Twentieth Century Pamphlets*,[1] which examines all Prokosch's pamphlets in detail.

Auden also attracted a number of printers who specialized in producing artistic broadsides. These can be more a headache than a joy for most collectors, and certainly for institutional librarians. They present nearly insurmountable storage problems because of size and fragility. Few people have enough wall space to display them framed, and many collectors eschew them altogether. They are seldom issued in large quantities. In Auden's case, the first one, *Night Mail*, was issued in 1938 to accompany a documentary film made by the British General Post Office Film Unit. It was given out at screenings of the film, at exhibitions, shows, and schools. In all likelihood, a rather substantial quantity were printed, but few have survived. Most were probably discarded by their uncaring recipients. I have never seen one of these for sale or in any of the Auden collections that I know of. However, many equally elusive items have mysteriously surfaced from time to time; there is always hope.

Another broadside came from DePauw University—*Reflections in a Forest*. It was distributed in an edition of 500 copies at a reading there by Auden in 1957. Once again, copies are very elusive, probably as a result of the way the broadside was issued as well as the cumbersome format. Yet another broadside, *But I Can't*, is, numerically at least, the rarest Auden item in existence. It was published in an edition of only ten copies in Cambridge, Massachusetts, in 1966 at the hefty price of $400. Most people would regard this, like similar productions of the publisher, as a deliberately created 'instant rarity'. Even so, for absolute rarity, it has a close challenger in *Brussels in Winter*, a tiny broadside printed at Pearson College in New Haven during a reading by Auden there. The text was pre-set on a small hand press which was then cranked by Auden, thereby validating the imprint at the foot of the broadside, 'Printed by his own hand'. The number of copies is not given, but it was probably

[1] (London, 1987).

about twelve. Auden's own copy, now in my possession, was laid into a cloth folder bearing the arms of the College. This broadside is so scarce that it eluded Bloomfield and Mendelson in both editions of their *Bibliography*. Other broadsides, about half a dozen, while all limited to some degree, can usually be found without too much difficulty.

There are also some pamphlets that will make the chase more exciting if only because they are very infrequently offered in dealers' catalogues. The first of these, *Epithalamium*, was issued in 1939 at Princeton, New Jersey, for the wedding of Giuseppe Borgese and Elizabeth Mann, Auden's sister-in-law. Mrs Borgese could not recall how many had been printed, but it was probably not more than 100. So far only two copies have made their way into Auden collections. Another pamphlet appeared two years later, *Three Songs for St. Cecilia's Day*. Of this, 250 copies were issued as the personal Christmas card of Caroline Newton, a friend and patron of Auden's. A third pamphlet, *Litany and Anthem for S. Matthew's Day*, appeared in 1946. 500 copies of this were printed for the dedication of St Matthew's Church in Northampton, England. Again, while the number of copies printed was fairly substantial, the pamphlet was probably discarded after the service by many of the less than astute worshippers. It is certainly seldom offered in rare-book dealers' catalogues.

Finally, there is a 1963 memorial pamphlet for Louis MacNeice, Auden's close friend and collaborator. This contains the text of Auden's remarks at MacNeice's memorial service, but was not distributed then because it could not be printed in time. Instead, copies were mailed to a list of MacNeice's friends, the list being supplied to Faber and Faber by his widow. Presumably the large majority of these friends were in literary circles, so most of these copies probably still exist and are being tightly clasped by the recipients. Whatever the reason, copies seldom appear, and always bear a triple-digit price-tag.

One late pamphlet, *Portraits*, produced in 1966 at the Apiary Press in Northampton, Massachusetts, is virtually unobtainable. It was produced by a printing student of Leonard Baskin's as her final exercise. The edition consisted of only 20 copies. To my knowledge, none has ever been offered for sale.

When one considers that Auden made his impact early, scoring a major success with his third published book—*The Orators*—in 1932, it is odd that he had very few invitations to issue signed limited editions of his work. He was not loathe to do this (as for instance was Nabokov) and generally acceded to all such requests. But, aside from the signed broadsides, there are only three such items. The first, *The Old Man's Road*, appeared in 1956. It was an edition of 50 signed copies, accompanied by an unsigned regular edition of 700. The second, *Marginalia*, appeared in 1966 in an edition of 150 copies, of which 45 were *hors commerce*. Of these, 26 were lettered, as opposed to being merely numbered like the balance of the edition. The final one, *Two Songs*, published by me in 1968 in the Phoenix Book Shop's 'Oblong Ocatvo' series, consisted of 126 copies, of which 100 were numbered and signed, for sale, and 26 lettered and signed, not for sale, being equally divided between publisher and author for their personal use. The printer also provided an overrun of 24 copies. These were not signed and were not sold. Naturally, the 26 lettered copies seldom appear, as Auden gave all of his to such close friends as Marianne Moore and Reinhold Niebuhr.

Auden was often asked to provide introductions for other authors' books or to edit anthologies, which resulted in a very large canon of secondary items. Additionally, items by him that had previously appeared in magazines were quite often published in book form in various anthologies. These are grouped in two sections by his bibliographers: those which Auden personally authorized and saw through the press, and those for which he or his agent merely gave permission to reprint from the magazine. There are over 200 such items listed in the *Bibliography*, among them several very elusive ones, as well as many that are, in themselves, interesting or amusing. For instance, one can imagine the anguish of the fifteen-year-old Auden when he opened a copy of *Public School Verse* for 1924, his first appearance in anything more than a school magazine, only to find his name misspelled as 'W. H. Arden'. Two years later, at the precocious age of seventeen, he co-edited the prestigious annual volume *Oxford Poetry* for 1926, thereby making his début as an anthology editor, a role he was to play frequently throughout his career. (He also contributed to *Oxford Poetry* in this and the two succeeding years.) In 1932 a rather thick anthology was issued entitled *An Outline for Boys and Girls and Their Parents*. Auden contributed the section called 'Writing'. When I asked him to sign my copy of this, he remarked that it was the first piece of writing for which he had received payment!

Auden began contributing to periodicals—at first just to school magazines—in the early 1920s, and continued to do so until his death. The number of such contributions is large. Nearly 800 of them are presently known: enough to give any collector pause, if only from sheer bulk, to say nothing, in many cases, of scarcity. There are, however,

2220202 COLLECTING W. H. AUDEN

many items in this category that have not yet been published in book form, and are important to any collector wanting a complete representation of Auden's output.

Since Auden was involved in music for most of his life, there are also numerous musical items to look for. First, of course, are the published libretti for the various operas. These exist sometimes only as separate pamphlets, sometimes as full scores. His most famous work in this genre, co-authored with Chester Kallman (who co-authored most of the libretti), was for Igor Stravinsky's *The Rake's Progress*, which had its première in Venice in 1951. In addition, many of Auden's poems have been set to music by such dissimilar composers as Luciano Berio, Sir Arthur Bliss, Benjamin Britten, Ned Rorem, and Lukas Foss.

Auden's international reputation resulted in an extraordinarily large number of foreign translations of his work, numbering some 400 separate items in at least three dozen different languages, including such esoteric ones as Albanian, Catalan, Flemish, Frisian, Gujarati, and Slovenian. Any addicted collector will naturally want at least a few examples from this branch of Auden's published work.

A large, diverse, and often fascinating group of what Auden's biblio-graphers call 'Odds and Ends' includes dust-jacket blurbs for other authors, notes or long statements in programmes for various types of performances (including *son et lumière*), brief excerpts quoted by other authors, and perhaps most interesting of all, three pamphlets each entitled *Oratio Creweiana*. One of the duties of the Professor of Poetry at Oxford is to deliver, every second year, the Creweian Oration, in Latin. Auden delivered three such addresses during his tenure. They were published by the University, without attribution to Auden, in editions of 1,500 copies, the Latin text facing the English. These are extremely hard to find; perhaps because they are anonymous they go unnoticed.

These details barely suggest the fascination and challenge of assembling a collection of Auden's work. It can be a lifetime occupation if you have a lifetime to spare. The marvellous thing is that the collector can set his own parameters. Unlike a stamp collector who is obliged to fill in pre-printed blank spaces, the book collector can add or eliminate anything that he feels he wants to without destroying the symmetry of his collection. And above all, every inch of the collection will provide enjoyable reading. At the risk of inviting competition for the items I still lack in my own collection, I urge anyone interested in poetry and book collecting to start an Auden collection. But start now because, as Auden would say, 'It is later than you think.'

W. H. Auden: A Bibliographical Supplement

EDWARD MENDELSON

W. H. Auden: A Bibliography 1924–1969, 2nd edn. (Charlottesville, Virginia, 1972), compiled by B. C. Bloomfield and Edward Mendelson, described Auden's publications from the start of his career through the end of 1969. This supplementary list extends the record to the end of 1987 and includes items mistakenly omitted from the *Bibliography*. This list is a summary only, without the full detail presented in the *Bibliography*. It lists Auden's books, and his contributions to books and periodicals, but does not include interviews, published extracts fom private letters, recordings, broadcasts, or other forms of publication. A future edition of the *Bibliography* will include such items, as well as full descriptions of the books briefly listed here.

Reset editions of books that Auden published before 1970 are included in this list, using the reference number under which the original edition appeared in the *Bibliography*. Simple reprints of books by Auden published before 1970 (and listed in the *Bibliography*) are not noted, nor are new impressions or editions of books published before 1970 to which Auden contributed. I have used a simplified transcription of title-pages and have listed imprints in conventional style (place: publisher, date). As in the normal practice of descriptive bibliography, capitalization of titles has been reduced to the level of prose.

In the list of periodical contributions, volume and part numbers are given in arabic numerals; the 1972 *Bibliography* used roman for volumes and arabic for parts. Places of publication are listed for periodicals that may be difficult to identify in library catalogues.

A few books that appeared in the 1972 *Bibliography* in the list of anthologies have been elevated to section **B** and listed in this supplement. Although Auden's contributions to these books were first published in periodicals, it seems clear that the editors of each of these books asked Auden to contribute to the book itself (or to a symposium that would eventually become that book), and that the editors, and not Auden, then submitted Auden's contribution to the periodical in which it appeared.

Auden died in the early morning of 28 September 1973. His contributions to periodicals that appeared in October and November 1973 (with the exception of one excerpt from an essay written for a book; see **C917** below) were submitted by Auden himself before his death. All items published afterwards were submitted for publication either by his Estate or, in the case of translations from Swedish and other languages, by his co-translators.

An imperfect but I hope useful division has been made between publications, other than books, that Auden himself (or his co-translators) prepared for the press near the end of Auden's life and early and unfinished work prepared for publication by others and printed posthumously. Section **D** of the following list, which does not correspond to **D** in the *Bibliography*, includes posthumous work published by scholars and critics using manuscripts of early or abandoned poems and prose. This list is offered mainly for the convenience of readers; it excludes quotations of fragments of unpublished work, and its citations are as brief as possible. The next edition of the *Bibliography* will include a more extensive listing.

One item, a printing of the poem 'School children', is known only in the form of a cutting from the unidentified periodical in which it appeared. The periodical, perhaps similar in format to *Vogue* and other fashion magazines, was printed on glossy paper measuring 32.2 cm tall by about 25 cm wide (the cutting consists of the outer two-thirds of the page; the inner section seems to have contained an advertisement). The reverse side of the page contained an ornamental border and the first page of a poem (not by Auden) titled 'Gargoyle and His Christmas B[ells]', so the date of the periodical was perhaps December 1937. The text of Auden's poem is similar to the text in *Another time*, except for the title in two words and the variant first line 'All the captivities are here; the cells are as real:'. The periodical was probably not printed for general distribution in Britain, because the poem also appeared in the *Listener*, 21 July 1937. The cutting belonged to James and Tania Stern, who were living in Paris in 1937; possibly the periodical was printed in America or in Europe for a continental readership.

The United States Copyright Office has an entry for a work by Auden listed as 'Education and decline of classic preparation', described as appearing in *Mademoiselle*, 50. 3 (Jan. 1960). Nothing by Auden (and nothing by anyone else that fits that summary title) appeared in that issue or in issues around the same time. Possibly the magazine planned to publish such a piece but omitted it during production; or perhaps the piece never arrived. No essay by Auden has been located that fits the title.

I have excluded two books that have no textual authority. One is *Madrigal* (an unauthorized pamphlet printing of the poem; see *Bibliography*, A22), printed in London by M. C. Caine at a press that he called The Scargill Press, and dated on the colophon 1 April 1982, the date of the retirement of Joe Gormley as president of the National Union of Mineworkers. The colophon also states that twelve copies were printed; the copy in Edinburgh University Library is marked 'Fourteenth copy'. The other excluded item is a volume of *Five poems* (all taken from *Collected poems*) printed in 1983 in an expensive limited edition of 122 copies by Labyrinth Editions, Cedar Falls, Iowa.

A brief poem mistakenly attributed to Auden appeared in *London review of books*, 5. 24 (22 Dec. 1983–18 Jan. 1984), 2, under the title 'Letter to an editor' (the first line is 'Robert Lowell . . .'). The poem was in fact written by Chester Kallman. See letter by Edward Mendelson, ibid., 6. 2 (2–15 Feb. 1984), 4.

This list incorporates the contents of an earlier list 'Addenda to Bloomfield and Mendelson *W. H. Auden: A Bibliography*', *Library*, 6th ser., 4. 1 (Mar. 1982), 75–9.

BOOKS BY AUDEN

A16a [*Night mail.*] Post Office Film Display. Royal Institution, Hull. January 17, 1938. *Poem for the Post Office film 'Night mail.'* [Text of the poem on both sides of a single leaf, followed by 'W. H. AUDEN.']

This broadside edition is a different setting from the undated broadside listd as **A16**; the only copy located is stamped '1st PROOF' and may therefore vary from the published edition—if such an edition ever existed. Other broadside editions of the poem may have been printed for distribution at various showings of the film.

A20c W. H. Auden and Christopher Isherwood. *Journey to a war.* London: Faber & Faber, [1973].

A new paperback edition, to which Auden added his 'Second thoughts' (pp. 7–8); the shorter poems are revised to conform to the text in *Collected shorter poems 1927–1957,* and the 'Commentary' is newly revised. (On p. 266 of the 'Commentary' the fourth and fifth stanzas are printed in reverse order.)

A25b Benjamin Britten (opus 27). *Hymn to St. Cecilia*, for S.S.A.T.B. Words by W. H. Auden . . . Winthrop Rogers Edition. London: Boosey & Hawkes, [1942].

The vocal score, with the text printed separately on the first two leaves.

An undated (but mid-1940s) American edition (New York: Boosey, Hawkes, Belwin) has a reset cover-title.

A31d W. H. Auden. *The enchafèd flood* or the romantic iconography of the sea. London, Boston: Faber & Faber, [1985].

Reset paperback edition of the British edition (**A31b**).

A57.1 *Brussels in winter*. Printed by his own hand at the Pierson College Press 6 December 1967. [Auden's signature in ink.] [New Haven, 1967.]

Small broadside with the text of the poem taken from *Collected shorter poems 1927–1957*; printed in an edition of perhaps ten copies. Set in type by students at Pierson College, Yale University, on the occasion of Auden's visit to the campus. Auden operated the press and signed the copies.

A59b *Selected poems*, by W. H. Auden. London: Faber & Faber, [1972].

Second edition of *Selected poems*, 1968 (**A59**). The book is nowhere identified as a second edition, but is in fact entirely reset, with the text taken from the second Faber impression of *Collected shorter poems 1927–1957*; many typographical errors in the first edition are thus corrected, and a minor variant is introduced in 'A walk after dark'. The contents of this book are not the same as those of *Selected poetry of W. H. Auden* listed below (**A66**).

A62c W. H. Auden. *Secondary worlds*. The T. S. Eliot memorial lectures delivered at Eliot College in the University of Kent at Canterbury October 1967. London, Boston: Faber and Faber, [1984].

Reset paperback edition of the British edition (**A62a**).

A63b W. H. Auden. *City without walls and other poems*. New York, Random House [1970].

First American edition, preceded by the 1969 British edition listed in the *Bibliography*. Some minor textual errors are corrected. A simultaneous paperback issue was announced but was never printed. The second impression (1970) has corrections.

A65 *A certain world*, a commonplace book. W. H. Auden. New York: The Viking Press, A William Cole Book, [1970].

Some copies of the sewn sheets without the cloth binding, but in the dust-jacket, were distributed at the American Booksellers' Association convention in Washington, June 1970.

The British edition (London: Faber & Faber, [1971]) includes thirteen pages of 'Addenda' consisting entirely of quotations from other writers.

A66 *Selected poetry of W. H. Auden*, second edition, chosen for this edition by the author. New York: Vintage Books, a division of Random House, [1971].

The second American edition of *W. H. Auden, a selection by the author*, 1958 (**A58**); issued in paperback. Reprinted in a clothbound edition (New York: The Modern Library, [1972]). Text as the first American edition, slightly corrected, with additional poems. The second Vintage paperback impression (1973) has minor corrections.

A67 *Natural linguistics* (for Peter Salus). [Text of the poem, signed by Auden in ink.] . . . published by Poem-of-the-Month Club, Ltd, 27

Brynmaer Road, S.W.11 . . . Copyright (1970) Poem-of-the-Month Club Ltd.

A broadside edition of the poem, distributed to subscribers to the club.

A68 *Academic graffiti.* W. H. Auden. Illustrated by Filippo Sanjust. London: Faber & Faber, [1971].

The American edition (New York: Random House, [1972]) has the same text.

A69 W. H. Auden. *Epistle to a godson and other poems.* New York: Random House, [1972].

The British edition (London: Faber & Faber, [1972]) has a reset text as the American edition with some corrections, and a revision to 'A shock'.

A70 *Love's labour's lost / Verlor'ne Liebesmüh'.* Comedy set to music by Nicolas Nabokov. Libretto by W. H. Auden and Chester Kallman after Shakespeare's play / Musikalische Komödie von W. H. Auden und Chester Kallman nach William Shakespeare, deutsch von Claus H. Henneberg. Musik von Nicolas Nabokov. Particell mit englischem und deutschem Text. Berlin, Wiesbaden: Bote & Bock, [1972].

Vocal score of the opera.

A71 *Forewords and afterwords,* by W. H. Auden. Selected by Edward Mendelson. New York: Random House, [1973].

Reprinted in paperback in 1974 with the imprint: New York: Vintage Books, a division of Random House. The British edition [London: Faber & Faber, [1973]) has the text as the American edition, and was reprinted in paperback in 1979.

A72 *Nocturne.* W. H. Auden. For E. R. Dodds. [Text of the poem.] To commemorate the sixty-seventh anniversary of the author's birth, one hundred copies of this poem were printed at the Jonathan Edwards College Press in New Haven, Connecticut, on the 21st day of February, 1974. . .

One hundred copies were printed.

A73 *Auden poems. Moore lithographs.* Selections from poems by Auden, lithographs by Henry Moore. [London:] Petersburg Press, [1974].

The poems were selected by Nikos Stangos with Auden's approval; all are reprinted from earlier volumes of Auden's work. Three hundred copies were printed.

A74 *Thank you, fog,* last poems by W. H. Auden. London: Faber & Faber, [1974].

The American edition (New York: Random House, [1974]) has a reset text, as the British edition but with slight corrections.

A75 W. H. Auden. *Sue.* Sycamore Broadsheet 23. [Oxford: Sycamore Press, 1977.]

A text of this abandoned poem written in 1937, reconstructed by John Fuller and Edward Mendelson from Auden's rough drafts.

A76 *Paul Bunyan*. An operetta in two acts and a prologue. Libretto by W. H. Auden. Set to music by Benjamin Britten. Op. 17. London: Faber Music Limited, in association with Faber and Faber Limited, [1976].

Libretto of the operetta first performed in 1941. A vocal score was published by Faber Music Limited in 1978.

A77 W. H. Auden. *Collected poems*. Edited by Edward Mendelson. London: Faber & Faber, [1976].

The American edition (New York, Random House, [1976]) has the text of the British edition; the second and third impressions of the American edition are corrected.

Three reset editions were published for subscribers by The Franklin Library, Franklin Center, Pennsylvania. The first, sold in 1976 to subscribers of 'The first edition society' (and with 'The first edition society' on the title-page), was officially published before the first British and American trade editions, but was in fact set from an advance copy of the first British edition and printed after the American trade edition was printed; it includes a note by Stephen Spender. The second Franklin Library edition, 1978, was part of the series 'The greatest books of the twentieth century'; the text includes minor corrections. The third Franklin Library edition, 1980, was part of the series 'The 100 greatest masterpieces of American literature'; its text includes further corrections. The title-pages of the second and third Franklin Library editions include the line 'A limited edition'.

A78 *The English Auden*. Poems, essays and dramatic writings 1927–1939. Edited by Edward Mendelson. London: Faber & Faber, [1977].

Printer's errors introduced after the page proof stage are corrected on an errata slip. The first impression was withdrawn in 1978 and replaced by a corrected impression identifiable by the photo credit to Eric Bramall printed on the copyright page. The paperback issue (1986) has further corrections.

The American edition (New York: Random House, [1978]) has the text of the British edition, slightly corrected. The American subtitle reads: Poems, essays, and dramatic writings, 1927–1939.

A79 W. H. Auden. *Selected poems*. New edition. Edited by Edward Mendelson. New York: Vintage Books, a division of Random House, [1979].

An errata slip was inserted in copies of the first impression. The second (1980) and sixth (1985) impressions are corrected.

The British edition (London & Boston: Faber and Faber, [1979]) was issued in cloth and paperback bindings. The third impression (1982) is corrected. Some copies of the first cloth issue were printed with the imprint of a book club: London: Book Club Associates, [1979]. The British title-pages lack the subtitle 'New edition'.

A80 W. H. Auden. *Three unpublished poems*. Introduction by Edward Mendelson. [New York:] The New York Public Library, 1986.

An edition of 222 copies printed for the benefit of the rare book room of the New York Public Library. Contains 'To Robert Russell', 'The evolution of the dragon', and 'Daydreams of a tourist', all printed from manuscripts in the New York Public Library.

BOOKS EDITED OR WITH CONTRIBUTIONS BY AUDEN

B19.1 *Poems of to-day*, third series, published for the English Association. London: Macmillan, 1938.

Contains seven poems by Auden reprinted from earlier publications. The text of 'Blues: Stop all the clocks, cut off the telephone . . .' is not the text in *The ascent of F6* (1936), but is apparently the first appearance of the rewritten version prepared in June 1937 and later reprinted in *Another time*. The acknowledgements in the collection mention the *Listener* as the source of the poem, but it seems never to have been printed there. It is possible that the editors of the collection obtained the text directly from Auden, who mistakenly thought it had appeared in the *Listener*, or from an editor of the *Listener* at a time when that editor believed the poem would be printed in the magazine's pages.

B22.1 *Pastor Hall*, by Ernst Toller. Translated from the German by Stephen Spender & Hugh Hunt. *Blind man's buff*, by Ernst Toller and Denis Johnston. New York, Random House, [1939].

The song 'Further than the eye can follow . . .' (p. 60) is translated by Auden.
A British edition (*Pastor Hall*, a play in three acts by Ernst Toller, translated by Stephen Spender. London: John Lane The Bodley Head, [1939]) did not include the second play, *Blind man's buff*; the song translated by Auden appears on pp. 97–8.

B23.1 *We moderns.* Gotham Book Mart 1920–1940 . . . [New York: Gotham Book Mart, 1939].

Contains 'Louis MacNeice' (p. 48). This pamphlet was issued as the bookshop's Catalogue no. 42.

B40.1 *Religion and the intellectuals*, a symposium with [names of contributors in eight lines]. PR Series number three. [New York: Partisan Review, 1950].

Contains Auden's contribution (pp. 22–31); reprinted from Auden's contribution to this symposium in *Partisan review*, Feb. 1950 (**C363**).

B65.1 Nino D'Ambra. *Nulla vogliamo del sogno.* Milano: G. Intelisano, 1957.

Contains 'Prefazione', English text followed by Italian translation, pp. 5–6.

B90.1 *The contemporary poet as artist and critic*, eight symposia edited by Anthony Ostroff. Boston and Toronto: Little, Brown, [1964].

Contains 'A change of air' (pp. 168–9) and Auden's reply to a symposium on the poem (pp. 183–7). The poem and essays first appeared in *Kenyon review*, Winter 1964, but the symposium was conceived for this volume.

B90.2 *Half-way to the moon*, new writing from Russia, edited by Patricia Blake and Max Hayward. London: Weidenfeld and Nicolson, [1964].

Contains Auden's translations of poems by Andrei Voznesensky, Evgeni Vinokurov, and Bella Akhmadulina (pp. 40–3).

B93.1 *Of poetry and power*, poems occasioned by the presidency and by the death of John F. Kennedy, foreword by Arthur Schlesinger, Jr., edited with an introduction by Erwin A. Glikes and Paul Schwaber. New York: Basic Books, [1964].

Contains 'Elegy for J.F.K.' (p. 111).

B96.1 *Hiroshima plus 20*, prepared by *The New York times*, introduction by John W. Finney. New York: Delacorte Press, [1965].

Contains 'The bomb and man's consciousness' (pp. 126–32). A slightly revised version of 'The corruption of innocent neutrons', *New York times*, 1 Aug. 1965 (**C663**). Auden further revised the text of the original version when it was reprinted (under its original title) in an anthology, *Using prose*, 2nd edn., ed. Donald W. Lee and William T. Moynihan (New York, Toronto: Dodd, Mead, 1967), 197–202.

B̄98.1 Ford Foundation. *Berlin confrontation*. Künstler in Berlin / artists in Berlin / artistes à Berlin. Berlin: Gebr. Mann, [1966].

Contains 'The cave of making' (pp. 98–100).

B116 *G. K. Chesterton, a selection from his non-fictional prose*, selected by W. H. Auden. London: Faber & Faber, [1970].

Contains 'Foreword' (pp. 11–18).

B117 James E. Miller, Jr., Robert O'Neal, Helen M. McDonnell. *Man in literature*, comparative world studies in translation. Introduction: W. H. Auden. [Glennview, Ill.:] Scott, Foresman, [1970].

Contains 'Translation' (pp. 8–11).

B118 *The ballad of Barnaby*. W. H. Auden. Music by students of the Wykeham Rise School in Washington, Connecticut, realization by Charles Turner. New York: G. Schirmer, [1970].

Contains 'The ballad of Barnaby' (p. [v]).

B119 Paul Valéry. *Analects*, translated by Stuart Gilbert, with an introduction by W. H. Auden. Bollingen Series XLV, 14. [Princeton:] Princeton University Press, [1970].

Contains 'Introduction' (pp. vii–xvii).
The British edition (London: Routledge & Kegan Paul, [1970]) has the identical text.

B120 *I am an impure thinker*. Eugen Rosenstock-Huessy. Introduction by W. H. Auden. Norwich, Vermont: Argo Books, [1970].

Contains 'Foreword' (pp. vii–viii).

B121 Nobel symposium 14. *The place of value in a world of facts*, proceedings of the fourteenth Nobel Symposium, Stockholm, September 15–20, 1969, edited by Arne Tiselius and Sam Nilsson. Stockholm: Almqvist & Wiksell; New York: John Wiley & Sons, Wiley Interscience Division, [1970].

Contains 'Freedom and necessity in poetry' (pp. 135–42). The imprint listed above is that of the Swedish issue; the imprint of the American issue lists Almqvist & Wiksell after John Wiley & Sons.

B122 Johann Wolfgang von Goethe. *The sorrows of young Werther.* *Novella.* Translated from the German by Elizabeth Mayer and Louise Bogan, poems translated by W. H. Auden, foreword by W. H. Auden. New York: Random House, [1971].

Contains 'Foreword' (pp. ix–xvi), and translated poems (pp. 195–6, 199–201).

B123 *Federal participation HemisFair '68.* [Washington:] U.S. Department of Commerce, February 1971.

Contains 'US', Auden's narration for the documentary film shown at the Confluence Theatre, US Pavilion, at HemisFair '68 in San Antonio (pp. 52–3).

Another, apparently more accurate, version of the text was mimeographed as a three-page press release distributed by the US Expositions Staff publicity office at the fair in 1968.

B124 Malcolm de Chazal. *Plastic sense,* edited and translated by Irving J. Weiss. [New York:] Herder and Herder, [1971].

Contains 'Foreword' (pp. 7–11).

B125 *10 poets 10 poems,* collected by O. G. Bradbury. London: Graphix Press, Ealing School of Art, [1971].

Contains 'Old people's home' (pp. 7–9).

A reset second edition of this book was published as: *Ten good poems,* an anthology by Oliver G. Bradbury. [Norwich:] e.g. Publications, Norwich School of Art, 1972 [for 1973].

B126 W. H. Auden / V.Kh. Odn. *Pesni* (izbor). Skopje: [Fakel], 1971.

This volume of fifteen poems in English and in Macedonian translations by Bogomil Ǵuzel includes three texts that Auden gave the translator when he visited Skopje in 1971: 'Prologue at sixty' (pp. 82–8), 'Talking to myself' (pp. 90–6; published here for the first time), and 'Moon landing' (pp. 98–100). The title-page cited above is transliterated.

B127 *Selected poems.* Ondra Lysohorsky. Selected and introduced by Ewald Osers, translated from the Lachian and the German by Ewald Osers, Hugh McKinley, Isobel [for Isabella] Levitin and W. H. Auden, Lydia Pasternak. London: Jonathan Cape, [1971]. Available in the United States from Grossman Publishers, Inc.

Contains seven poems translated by Levitin and Auden.

B128 *Austria, people and landscape.* Stella Musulin. With a foreword by W. H. Auden. London: Faber & Faber, [1971].

Contains 'Foreword' (pp. 17–21).

The American edition (New York, Washington: Praeger Publishers, [1972]) is titled *Austria and the Austrians,* but has the same text.

B129 *Selected poems*: Gunnar Ekelöf. Translated by W. H. Auden and Leif Sjöberg. With an introduction by Göran Printz-Påhlson. [Harmondsworth:] Penguin Books, [1971].

Contains 'Foreword' (pp. 7–10) and translations of poems.

The American edition (New York: Pantheon Books, A Division of Random House, [1972]) has the identical text.

B130 *Attacks of taste.* Compiled and edited by Evelyn B. Bryne & Otto M. Penzler . . . New York: Gotham Book Mart, 1971.

Contains statement by Auden (p. 5).

B131 *Poems for Shakespeare*, edited with an introduction by Christopher Hampton. London: The Globe Playhouse Trust Publications, 1972.

Contains 'Talking to mice' (pp. 27–30).

B132 Music by Pablo Casals / poem by W. H. Auden. *Hymn to the United Nations*, for four-part chorus of mixed voices with piano (or organ) accompaniment. New York: Tetra Music Corporation . . ., [1972].

Contains 'Hymn to the United Nations' (see **C830** and **C831**).

B133 Kurt Weill . . . *Die sieben Todsünden der Kleinbürger / The seven deadly sins*, ballet chanté, Text Bert Brecht . . . Englische Übersetzung: English translation: W. H. Auden und Chester Kallman. Klavierauszug von: Vocal score: Wilhelm Brückner-Rüggeberg. Edition Schott 6005. Mainz: B. Schott's Söhne . . ., [1972].

The Auden–Kallman translation is printed beneath Brecht's German in this vocal score (see also **B147**).

B134 *Sense & inconsequence*, satirical verses by Angus Stewart, with a foreword by W. H. Auden. London: Michael de Hartington, [1972].

Contains 'Foreword' (pp. [9–10]).

B135 *The spirit of man*, an anthology compiled by Robert Bridges, with an introduction by W. H. Auden. [London:] Longman, [1972].

Contains 'Introduction' (pp. [5–9]).

B136 *George Herbert*, selected by W. H. Auden. [Harmondsworth:] Penguin Books, [1973].

Contains 'Introduction' (pp. 7–13).

B137 *A tribute to W. H. Auden*, by Alan Brownjohn, Charles Causley [*et al.*]. [Ilkley, Yorks.:] For the Ilkley Literature Festival, printed by the Scolar Press, 1973.

Contains 'Lullaby' (p. [ix–x] of a printed pamphlet; and, in a facsimile of Auden's manuscript, on the first of a set of single leaves of facsimiles of poems commissioned for the tribute).

B138 *A choice of Dryden's verse*, selected and with an introduction by W. H. Auden. London: Faber & Faber, [1973].

Contains 'Introduction' (pp. 7–12).

B139 *Goldsworthy Lowes Dickinson* and related writings. E. M. Forster. Foreword by W. H. Auden. [London:] Edward Arnold, [1973].

Contains 'Foreword' (pp. vii–x).

B140 *Selected songs of Thomas Campion*, selected and prefaced by W. H. Auden, introduction by John Hollander. Boston: David Godine, 1973.

Contains 'Preface' (pp. 9–14).
Published in an edition of 250 numbered copies and a trade edition issued in cloth and paperback; some copies of the clothbound issue (with a different dust-jacket) were distributed in Britain by The Bodley Head in 1974.

B141 *A keepsake from the new library at the School of Oriental and African Studies*, 5 October 1973. [London: B. C. Bloomfield, Mansell Information, 1973.]

Contains 'No, Plato, no' (p. [5]).

B142 *New movements in the study and teaching of English*, edited by Nicholas Bagnall. London: Temple Smith, [1973].

Contains 'How can I tell what I think till I see what I say?' (pp. 206–11).

B143 Joseph Brodsky: *Selected poems*, translated and introduced by George L. Kline, with a foreword by W. H. Auden. [Harmondsworth:] Penguin Books, [1973].

Contains 'Foreword' (pp. 9–12).
The American edition (New York: Harper & Row, [1974]) has the identical text.

B144 *G. K. Chesterton, a centenary appraisal*, edited by John Sullivan. London: Paul Elek, [1974].

Contains 'The gift of wonder' (pp. 73–80).
The American edition (New York: Barnes & Noble, [1974]) has the identical text.

B145 *William Empson, the man and his work*, edited by Roma Gill . . . London and Boston: Routledge & Kegan Paul, [1974].

Contains 'A toast' (p. 1).

B146 *Evening land / Aftonland*, by Pär Lagerkvist, translated by W. H. Auden and Leif Sjöberg . . . Detroit: Wayne State University Press, 1975.

The translations in this book are largely Sjöberg's work.
The British edition (London: Souvenir Press, A Condor Book, [1977]) has the identical text.

B147 *The rise and fall of the city of Mahagonny*. Bertolt Brecht. Translated by W. H. Auden and Chester Kallman. Boston: David R. Godine, [1976].

Translated in 1960.
A Canadian issue (Toronto: Oxford University Press, 1975 [for 1976]) differs only in the title-page. The text is reprinted (with editorial changes), together with the Auden–Kallman translation of *The seven deadly sins* (see **B133**) in Brecht's *Collected plays*, volume two part three, ed. John Willett and Ralph Manheim (London: Eyre Methuen, [1979]).

B148 *Norse Poems*. W. H. Auden, Paul B. Taylor. [London: Athlone, 1981.]

The complete text of the translations partially published as *The Elder Edda* (**B115**). Reprinted in paperback by Faber and Faber in 1983.

CONTRIBUTIONS TO PERIODICALS

Addenda

C0.1 Dawn: Far into the vast the mists grow dim . . . *Gresham*, Gresham's School, Holt, 10. 2 (16 Dec. 1922), 23.

Unsigned. Reprinted by John Fuller in *Notes & queries*, NS 20. 9 (Sept. 1973), 333.

C0.2 Nightfall: Cool whisper of the trees . . . *Gresham*, 10. 5 (9 June 1923), 65.

Unsigned. Reprinted by John Fuller in *Notes & queries*, NS 20. 9 (Sept. 1973), 333.

C29.1 Apology. *Badger*, Downs School, 1. 1 (Spring 1933), 1–2.

Unsigned; this introduction to the school magazine is almost certainly by Auden, possibly with Geoffrey Hoyland.

C40.1 What is wrong with architecture? *Architectural review*, 74. 441 (Aug. 1933), 66.

A review of *Architecture in the balance*, by F. Towndrow, and *The architecture of a new era*, by R. A. Duncan.

C40.2 Apologia. *Badger*, 1. 2 (Autumn 1933), 1–2.

Unsigned; this introduction to the school magazine is almost certainly by Auden, possibly with Geoffrey Hoyland.

C40.3 Lament: The dawn of day had scarce broke through . . . *Badger*, 1. 2 (Autumn 1933), 34.

Signed 'Anon.' Almost certainly by Auden, this is a topical poem about a junior matron at the school.

C49.1 Prologue. *Badger*, 2. 3 (Spring 1934), 1–2.

Unsigned; this introduction to the school magazine is probably but not certainly by Auden, possibly with Geoffrey Hoyland.

C55.1 [Review of] *Modern poetic drama*, by Priscilla Thouless. *Listener*, 11. 278 (9 May 1934), 808.

Unsigned. Cf. letters by Laurence Kitchin, ibid. (30 May 1934), 930, and by E. Cannell, with a response by Auden, ibid. (28 June 1934), 1102.

C61.1 Apologia. *Badger*, 2. 4 (Autumn 1934), 1–2.

Unsigned; this introduction to the school magazine is probably but not certainly by Auden, possibly with Geoffrey Hoyland.

C68.1 Prologue. *Badger*, 3. 5 (Spring 1935), 1.

Unsigned; this introduction to the school magazine is probably but not certainly by Auden, possibly with Geoffrey Hoyland.

C98.1 Four stories of crime. *Daily telegraph*, 17 Nov. 1936, p. 8.

A review of *Cards on the table*, by Agatha Christie, *Death meets the coroner*, by John Knox Ryland, *Thirteen guests*, by J. Jefferson Farjeon, and *The clue of the bricklayer's aunt*, by Nigel Morland.

C105.1 Crime tales and puzzles. *Daily telegraph*, 5 Jan. 1937, p. 8.

A review of *Murder in the family*, by James Ronald, and *A puzzle for fools*, by Patrick Quentin. Extensively quoted in Cameron McCabe [pseud. of Ernest Borneman], *The face on the cutting-room floor* (London: Gollancz, 1937), 295–6, 301, 319.

C107.1 Song for the lost. By Ernst Toller, adapted by W. H. Auden. *Common sense*, 6.2 (Feb. 1937), 9.

Reprinted in *Pastor Hall* (**B16**).

C120.1 Johnny (a cautionary tale by request): His name was John, a charming child . . . *Badger*, 5. 10 (Autumn 1937), 68–73.

Signed 'Rather anon.' Almost certainly by Auden.

C142.1 In defense of gossip. *American lady*, 1. 1 (Sept. 1938), 83–6.

'[R]eprinted by courtesy of the author and The Listener.'

C151.1 Ports of call. By W. H. Auden and Christopher Isherwood. *Harper's bazaar*, London, 19. 3 (Dec. 1938), 40–1, 96, 98.

A reprint of 'Escales' (**C143**).

C175.1 Young British writers—on the way up . . . by . . . W. H. Auden and Christopher Isherwood. *Vogue*, New York, 94. 4 (15 Aug. 1939), 94, 156–7.

Isherwood, asked about this essay during the 1970s, said he had no recollection of it, but assumed that it was mostly his work.

C216.1 Luther: With conscience cocked to listen for the thunder . . . *Christian century*, 57. 40 (2 Oct. 1940), 1208.

C261.1 La trahison d'un clerc. *Perspectives*, Ann Arbor, 5. 2 (Jan. 1942), 12; supplement to *Michigan daily*, 17 Jan. 1942.

On 'Primary literature and coterie literature', a paper by Van Wyck Brooks later included in modified form in his *Opinions of Oliver Allston*.

C261.2 W. H. Auden speaks of poetry and total war. *Chicago sun*, 14 Mar. 1942, p. 14.

C266.1 Lecture notes. *Commonweal*, 37. 3 (6 Nov. 1942), 61.

Signed 'Didymus'. A regular column which continued until the issue of 4 Dec. 1942.

C266.2 Lecture notes. *Commonweal*, 37. 4 (13 Nov. 1942), 84–5.

Signed 'Didymus'.

C266.3 Lecture notes. *Commonweal*, 37. 5 (20 Nov. 1942), 108–9.

Signed 'Didymus'.

C266.4 Lecture notes. *Commonweal*, 37. 6 (27 Nov. 1942), 133–4.

Signed 'Didymus'.

C266.5 Lecture notes. *Commonweal*, 37. 7 (4 Dec. 1942), 157–8.
Signed 'Didymus'.

C268.1 An unbiased biography of Yeats and his world. *Chicago sun*, 7
Feb. 1943, Book Week (1. 15), p. 6.
A review of *Life of W. B. Yeats* [*sic*, for *W. B. Yeats, 1865–1939*], by Joseph Hone.

C352.1 Poetry and freedom. *American letters*, 1. 7 (June 1949), 3–12.
'A speech sponsored by the Schools of English, University of Virginia.' Talk delivered
27 Feb. 1948.

C376.1 Some December books chosen for the trade book clinic.
Publishers' weekly, 159. 1 (6 Jan. 1951), 69–70, 72.
Auden's choice of one month's well-designed books, with his comments.

C408.1 Presentation of arts and letters grants of the Institute . . . in
literature . . . To Theodore Roethke . . . *Proceedings of the American
Academy of Arts and Letters and the National Institute of Arts and Letters*,
New York, ser. 2, no. 3 (1953), 16.
A brief unsigned citation, first printed in the program of *The American Academy of Arts
and Letters & the National Institute of Arts and Letters ceremonial . . .* May 28, 1952 . . . New
York, p. [9].

C461.1 Presentation of arts and letters grants and American Academy
in Rome Fellowship . . . in literature . . . To Richmond Lattimore . . .
[and] To Ruthven Todd . . . *Proceedings of the American Academy of Arts
and Letters and the National Institute of Arts and Letters*, ser. 2, no. 5
(1955), 17.
Two brief unsigned citations, first printed in the program of *The American Academy of
Arts and Letters and the National Institute of Arts and Letters ceremonial . . .* May 26, 1954
. . . New York, p. [6].

C483.1 The history of science: All fables of adventure stress . . . *New
poems*, 1956 (London: Michael Joseph), pp. 34–5.

C512.1 Presentation of arts and letters grants and American Academy
in Rome fellowship in literature . . . To James Baldwin [and] To
Henry Russell Hitchcock . . . *Proceedings of the American Academy of
Arts and Letters and the National Institute of Arts and Letters*, ser. 2, no. 7
(1957), 96.
Two brief unsigned citations.

C514.1 Guy Burgess [letter to the editor]. *Sunday times*, 6975 (20 Jan.
1957), 4.
Reply to a letter by Stephen Spender, ibid. (13 Jan. 1957), 2.

C516.1 The holy spirit in the Church. *Meridian*, 1. 1 (Spring 1957), 6.
Excerpt reprinted from Auden's introduction to Charles Williams's *The descent of the
dove*.

C545.1 Daniel in the lion's den: Welcome, good people, watch and listen . . . *Seventeen*, 17. 12 (Dec. 1958), 56–7.

Reprinted from the recording of *Daniel* listed in the note to section E of the *Bibliography*.

C575.1 You: Really, must you . . . *Badger*, 33 (Autumn 1960), 26–7.

C634.1 Fantasies of the famous: or, every man his own Walter Mitty. W. H. Auden. *Sunday telegraph*, 151 (22 Dec. 1963), 12.

C637.1 One circumlocution: Sometimes we see astonishingly clearly . . . *Open space*, San Francisco, [6 (30 June 1964)], 17.

Signed 'Wystan'.

C645.1 'Pray that your loneliness may spur you into finding something to live for, great enough to die for'. [Excerpts from] The diaries of Dag Hammarskjöld. [Translated by W. H. Auden and Leif Sjöberg.] *Observer*, 9037 (13 Sept. 1964), 35.

C654.1 Behaviour, action and enchantment. *Breakthrough*, London, 10 ([Feb. 1965]), 17–24.

Signed 'Didymus'.

C654.2 The cave of making: For this and for all enclosures like it the archetype . . . *Harper's bazaar*, New York, 98th year, 3039 (Feb. 1965), 118–19.

This text includes the 'Postscript' to the poem.

C673.1 Warum ein Meisterwerk neu schreiben? Von W. H. Auden und Chester Kallman. *Salzburger Journal*, 1966 [cover-title: *Salzburger Festspiele 1966*], 19–20.

On *The Bassarids*.

C700.1 Auden on education. *Breakthrough*, 16 ([Feb. 1967]), 25–6.

C707.1 Andrei Voznesensky. The cashier. Translated by W. H. Auden. *London magazine*, NS 7. 3 (June 1967), 8–9.

C723.1 Induction of newly elected members of the Academy . . . John Crowe Ransom. *Proceedings of the American Academy of Arts and Letters and the National Institute of Arts and Letters*, ser. 2, no. 18 (1968), 68–9.

A citation, preceded by the words: 'As the poet Wystan Hugh Auden has written of him . . .'; the citation was specially written for this occasion.

C731.1 Hávamál. *65°* [i.e., *Sixty-five degrees*], Reykjavík, 2. 2 (Spring 1968), 11–14.

Twenty-eight quatrains from the translation by Auden and Paul B. Taylor, printed in full in *The elder edda* as 'The words of the high one'. An erratum slip with a correction to the text is pasted on p. 1 of the magazine. Cf. letter by Tryggvi Gíslason, ibid., 2. 2 (Summer 1968), 3.

C743.1 Ode to Terminus: The high priests of telescopes and cyclotrones [*sic*] . . . *Ensemble*, München, [1] (1969), 50, 52, 54.

Facing a German translation by Hans Egon Holthusen.

C749.1 The worship of God in a secular age: some reflections. *Preacher's quarterly*, 15. 1 (Mar. 1969), 1–6.

Reprinted from a 4-page mimeographed leaflet with the same title (except for the spelling *reflexions*) prepared in 1966 by the World Council of Churches, Division of Ecumenical Action, Geneva. Auden sent this essay (without a title) to a conference on 'The worship of God in the secular age', held at Taizé, France, 2–6 Sept. 1966; he did not attend the conference itself.

1970

C770 A bad night (a lexical exercise): In his dream zealous . . . *Armadillo*, Sarasota, Fla., [1] (1970), 14.

The publisher advertised a 400-copy edition of this magazine that was to reproduce the original manuscripts, but never printed it. This periodical was first advertised under the title *New work*.

C771 [Bertolt] Brecht. *The rise and fall of the city of Mahagonny*, scene 18–end. Translators, W. H. Auden and Chester Kallman. *Delos*, Austin, 4 (1970), 29–44.

C772 The garrison: Martini-time: time to draw the curtains and . . . *Third hour*, 9 (1970), 9.

C773 Shorts [16 short poems]: How many ravishing things whose innocent beauty astounds us . . . *New York quarterly*, 1 (Winter 1970), 14–15.

C774 Gunnar Ekelöf (1907–1968). [Three] poems. Translated by W. H. Auden and Leif Sjöberg. *Nimrod*, Tulsa, Okla., 14. 2 (Winter 1970), 1–3.

C775 Nikola Šop. Cottages in space. [Translated by] Branko Brusar and W. H. Auden. *Bridge*, Zagreb, 19–20 ([Jan.–Apr.] 1970), 9–15.

C776 Moon landing: It's natural the Boys should whoop it up for . . . *London magazine*, NS 9. 10 (Jan. 1970), 56–7.

C777 Smelt & tasted: The nose and palate never doubt . . . [and] Heard & seen: Events reported by the ear . . . *Windless orchard*, Fort Wayne, Ind., 1 (Feb. 1970), 1–2.

C778 Concerning the unpredictable. *New Yorker*, 46. 1 (21 Feb. 1970) 118, 121–5.

A review of *The unexpected universe*, by Loren Eiseley.

C779 Neglected books [chosen by various authors]: W. H. Auden. *American scholar*, 39. 2 (Spring 1970), 318.

On *Rhymes of a Pfc*, by Lincoln Kirstein.

C780 The song of Rig. Translated from the Icelandic with notes by Paul B. Taylor, W. H. Auden and Peter H. Salus. *Atlantica & Iceland review*, Reykjavík, 8. 1 ([Spring] 1970), 8, 20–3, 25.

'Translator's note', by Auden alone, appears on p. 19.

C781 Gunnar Ekelöf. Two poems. Translated by W. H. Auden and Leif Sjöberg. *Denver quarterly*, 5. 1 (Spring 1970), 133–5.

C782 Gunnar Ekelöf. Two poems. Translated by W. H. Auden and Leif Sjöberg. *Shenandoah*, 21. 3 (Spring 1970), 108–9.

C783 The garrison: Martini-time: time to draw the curtains and . . . *Shenandoah*, 21. 3 (Spring 1970), 109.

C784 Gunnar Ekelöf (1907–1968). [Two poems.] Translated by W. H. Auden and Leif Sjöberg. *Michigan quarterly review*, 9. 2 (Spring 1970), 104.

C785 Natural linguistics (for Peter Salus): Every created thing has ways of pronouncing its ownhood . . . *Candelabrum*, London, 1. 1 (Apr. 1970), 11.

C786 A Russian aesthete. *New Yorker*, 46. 7 (4 Apr. 1970), 133–8.

A review of *Against the current*, by Konstantin Leontiev.

C787 Auden in the looking glass. *Atlantic*, 225. 5 (May 1970), 62–6.

Excerpts from *A certain world* (A65).

C788 Gunnar Ekelöf (1907–1968). Xoanon. Translated by W. H. Auden and Leif Sjöberg. *Poetry northwest*, Seattle, 11. 2 (Summer 1970), 46–7.

C789 Old people's home: All are limitory, but each has her own . . . *New York review of books*, 15. 2 (23 June 1970), 4.

C790 Ondra Lysohorsky. Four poems. [Translated by] Isobella Levatin [*sic*, for Isabella Levitin] and W. H. Auden. *Poetry*, 116. 5–6 (Aug.– Sept. 1970), 273–8.

C791 The garrison: Martini-time: time to draw the curtains and . . . *Badger*, 43 (Autumn 1970), 22.

The poem is dated Feb. 1970.

C792 G. K. Chesterton's non-fictional prose. *Prose*, 1 ([Fall 1970]), 17–28.

The foreword to Auden's selection (B116).

C793 Gunnar Ekelöf (1907–1968). Two poems. Translated by W. H. Auden and Leif Sjöberg. *Southern humanities review*, 4. 4 (Fall 1970), 356–7.

C794 Gunnar Ekelöf (1907–1968). [Two poems.] Translated by W. H. Auden and Leif Sjöberg. *Transatlantic review*, 37–8 (Autumn–Winter 1970–1), 125–6.

C795 Lame shadows. *New York review of books*, 15. 4 (3 Sept. 1970), 10, 12–13.

A review of *Tonio Kröger and other stories*, by Thomas Mann.

C796 Robert to the rescue. *New Yorker*, 46. 30 (12 Sept. 1970), 153–9.

A review of *The letters of Robert Browning and Elizabeth Barrett, 1845–1846*, ed. Elvan Kintner.

C797 Portrait with a wart or two. *New York review of books*, 15. 8 (5 Nov. 1970), 11–12.

A review of *Belloc: a biographical anthology*, ed. Herbert van Thal.

C798 The aliens: Wide though the interrupt be that divides us, runers and counters . . . *New Yorker*, 46. 40 (21 Nov. 1970), 58.

C799 They had forgotten how to laugh and how to pray. *Columbia forum*, 13. 4 (Winter 1970), 46–8.

An excerpt from Auden's address at the Columbia University Seminar on the Nature of Man, 15 Jan. 1970.

C800 Policy on insurance: cancel [letter to the editor]. *New York times*, 11 Dec. 1970, p. 46.

C801 [A review of] *Hogarth on the high life: the 'Marriage à la mode' series*, from Georg Christoph Lichtenberg's commentaries. *New Yorker*, 46. 43 (12 Dec. 1970), 196.

Unsigned.

1971

C802 Louise Bogan. 1897–1970 [commemorative tribute]. *Proceedings of the American Academy of Arts and Letters and the National Institute of Arts and Letters*, ser. 2, no. 21 (1971), 63–7.

C803 Gunnar Ekelöf (1907–1968). [Two poems.] Translated by W. H. Auden and Leif Sjöberg. *Soundings*, State University of New York at Stony Brook, [8] (1971), 16–17.

C804 The artist's private face. *Sunday times*, 7700 (3 Jan. 1971), 43.

A review of *The letters of Thomas Mann*, sel. and tr. Richard and Clara Winston.

EDWARD MENDELSON 221

C805 An encounter: The Year: 452. The Place: the southern . . . *New statesman*, 81. 2078 (15 Jan. 1971), 86.

C806 W. H. Auden on George Orwell. *Spectator*, 226. 7438 (16 Jan. 1971), 86–7.
A review of *The collected essays, journalism and letters of George Orwell*, ed. Sonia Orwell and Ian Angus.

C807 The anomalous creature. *New York review of books*, 16. 1 (28 Jan. 1971), 20.
A review of *The fall into time*, by E. M. Cioran.

C808 Forgotten laughter, forgotten prayer. *New York times*, 2 Feb. 1971, p. 37 [early editions, p. 35].
An excerpt from the address published in *Columbia forum*, Winter 1970 (**C799**).

C809 The mountain allowed them pride. *New York times*, 7 Feb. 1971, section 7 (*book review*, 76. 6), pp. 10, 12.
A review of *Deborah*, by David Roberts.

C810 Lines to Dr. Walter Birk on his retiring from general practice: When you first arrived in Kirchstetten, trains had . . . *New York review of books*, 16. 2 (11 Feb. 1971), 13.

C811 Well done, Sir Walter Scott! *New Yorker*, 47. 1 (20 Feb. 1971), 117–23.
A review of *Sir Walter Scott: the great unknown*, by Edgar Johnson.

C812 Talking to dogs: From us, of course, you want gristly bones . . . *Harper's*, 242. 1450 (Mar. 1971), 110.

C813 He descended into Hell in vain. *New York review of books*, 16. 4 (11 Mar. 1971), 17–18.
A review of *A spy for God: the ordeal of Kurt Gerstein*, by Pierre Joffroy.

C814 [Untitled essay.] *Podium*, Wien, 1 (Apr. 1971), 31–4.
In German. 'Dieser Vortrag wurde bei der Veranstaltung LYRIK 70 auf Schloß Neulengbach gehalten' (editorial note).

C815 Talking to dogs: From us, of course, you want gristly bones . . . *London magazine*, NS 11. 1 (Apr.–May 1971), 58–9.

C816 Craftsman, artist, genius. *Observer*, 9377 (11 Apr. 1971), 9.
On Stravinsky.

C817 Bonjour Chazal. *New York review of books*, 16. 8 (6 May 1971), 22–3.
The introduction to Malcolm de Chazal's *Plastic sense* (**B124**).

C818 Academic graffiti [eighteen clerihews]: St. Thomas Aquinas . . . *New Yorker*, 47. 12 (8 May 1971), 40.

C819 Nikola Šop. Space scene with the rooster. Translated by Branko Brusar and W. H. Auden. *Encounter*, 36. 6 (June 1971), 42–4.

With a note on the poet by Auden (p. 42).

C820 [Ondra Lysohorsky.] Three poems. Translated by W. H. Auden & Isobella Levatin [*sic*, for Isabella Levitin]. *Two tone*, Salisbury, Rhodesia, 7. 2 (June 1971), 4–5.

Lysohorsky's name is mentioned nowhere in this curious publication.

C821 The megrims. *New York review of books*, 16. 10 (3 June 1971), 25–6.

A review of *Migraine*, by Oliver Sacks.

C822 A bad night (a lexical exercise): In his dream zealous . . . *Isis*, Oxford, 6 June 1971, p. 26.

C823 Gunnar Ekelöf. Five poems. Translated from the Swedish [by] W. H. Auden and Leif Sjöberg. *Stand*, Newcastle upon Tyne, 12. 3 ([July] 1971), 4–6.

C824 Saying no [letter to the editor]. *New York review of books*, 16. 12 (1 July 1971), 41.

On W. S. Merwin's refusal of the Pulitzer Prize; followed by Merwin's reply.

C825 An encounter: The Year: 452. The Place: the southern . . . *Horizon*, New York, 13. 4 (Autumn 1971), 112.

C826 Precious five: Be patient, solemn nose . . . *New York quarterly*, 8 (Autumn 1971), 44–6.

Reprinted to accompany an 'imitation' of the poem by Michael Newman.

C827 Gunnar Ekelöf . . . (1907–1968). Two poems. Translated by W. H. Auden and Leif Sjöberg. *Sewanee review*, 79. 4 (Autumn 1971), 600–1.

C828 Lines to Dr. Birk on his retiring from general practice: When you first arrived in Kirchstetten, trains had . . . *Workshop new poetry*, London, 13 ([Sept.] 1971), 3–4.

C829 Talking to mice: Plural the verdicts we cast on the creatures we have to shake hands with . . . *New York review of books*, 17. 3 (2 Sept. 1971), 6.

C830 Hymn to the United Nations: Eagerly, musician . . . *New York times*, 25 Oct. 1971, p. 40.

'It is reprinted with the permission of the United Nations . . .' The text also appears in the course of a dispatch in *Times*, London, 25 Oct. 1971, p. 4.

C831 United Nations hymn: Eagerly, musician . . . *Secretariat news*, United Nations, New York, 26. 17 (29 Oct. 1971), 16.

An account (not by Auden) of the writing and composition of the work appears on p. 10.

C832 Ode to the Medieval poets: Chaucer, Langland, Douglas, Dunbar with all your . . . *Poetry*, 119. 2 (Nov. 1971), 63–4.

C833 Too much mustard. *New York review of books*, 17. 7 (4 Nov. 1971), 19.

A review of *The complete immortalia*, ed. Harold H. Hart, and *The Gambit book of popular verse*, ed. Geoffrey Grigson.

C834 W. H. Auden on the young Mr Goethe. *Spectator*, 227. 7485 (11 Dec. 1971), 849–50.

A review of *The autobiography of Johann Wolfgang von Goethe*, tr. John Oxenford. This review includes Auden's poem 'How wonderfully your songs begin . . .', reprinted in *City without walls*.

1972

C835 The diary of a diary. *New York review of books*, 17. 12 & 18. 1 (27 Jan. 1972), 19–20.

A review of *Kathleen and Frank*, by Christopher Isherwood.

C836 A Worcestershire lad. *New Yorker*, 47. 53 (19 Feb. 1972), 111–14.

A review of *The letters of A. E. Housman*, ed. Henry Maas.

C837 Down with the 'melting pot'. *Times*, London, 23 Feb. 1972, 'Europe in 1975' [special section], p. xiv.

By comparing translated versions published simultaneously in other European news-papers, Peter Sharratt demonstrates that one word is lacking from the English text (see *Encounter*, 38. 5 [May 1972], 88–90).

C838 Pseudo-questions: Who could possibly approve of Metternich . . . *Vanderbilt poetry review*, Nashville, 1. 1 (Spring–Summer 1972), 25.

C839 Chester Kallman: a voice of importance. *Harper's*, 244. 1462 (Mar. 1972), 92–3.

A review of Kallman's *The sense of occasion*.

C840 A genius and a gentleman. *New York review of books*, 18. 4 (9 Mar. 1972), 17–18.

A review of *Letters of Giuseppe Verdi*, ed. Charles Osborne.

C841 Pär Lagerkvist. Two poems. Translated from the Swedish by W. H. Auden with Leif Sjöberg. *Times literary supplement*, 71st year, 3654 (10 Mar. 1972), 273.

C842 Telling it the way it was. *Observer*, 9424 (12 Mar. 1972), 29.

A review of *Historical memoirs of the Duc de Saint-Simon*, vol. 3, ed. Lucy Norton.

C843 I'll be seeing you again, I hope. *New York times*, 18 Mar. 1972, p. 31.

About his departure from New York. Letters about a crossword clue mentioned in this piece were printed 5 Apr. 1972, p. 44, and 11 Apr. 1972, p. 40.

C844 A shock: Housman was perfectly right . . . *New Yorker*, 48. 4 (18 Mar. 1972), 40.

C845 A poet of the actual. *New Yorker*, 48. 6 (1 Apr. 1972), 102–4.

A review of Anthony Trollope, by James Pope Hennessy.

C846 Harry Martinson. The dream city. Translated by W. H. Auden and Leif Sjoberg [*sic*]. *Times literary supplement*, 71st year, 3658 (7 Apr. 1972), 382.

C847 Doing oneself in. *New York review of books*, 18. 7 (20 Apr. 1972), 3.

A review of *The savage god*, by A. Alvarez.

C848 Mr Auden and the Laureateship [letter to the editor]. *Times*, London, 31 May 1972, p. 15.

Reported in *New York times*, 1 June 1972, p. 32.

C849 Wilson's Sabine farm. *Books and bookmen*, 17. 9 (201) (June 1972), 6–8.

A review of *Upstate*, by Edmund Wilson.

C850 Gunnar Ekelöf. [Two poems.] Translated by W. H. Auden and Leif Sjöberg. *Chelsea*, New York, 30–1 (June 1972), 110–11.

C851 Cecil Day Lewis's distinguished contemporary W. H. Auden contributes a salute to an old friend. *Sunday times*, 7773 (4 June 1972), 40.

An obituary tribute.

C852 Par [*sic*] Lagerkvist. Eight poems. Translated from the Swedish by W. H. Auden and Leif Sjöberg. *Prism international*, 12. 1 (Summer 1972), 136–8.

C853 Par [*sic*] Lagerkvist. [Poem.] Translated by W. H. Auden and Leif Sjöberg. *Shenandoah*, 23. 4 (Summer 1972), 76.

C854 Talking to myself: Spring this year in Austria started off benign . . . *New Yorker*, 48. 18 (24 June 1972), 32.

C855 Short one [*sic*] for the cuckoo: No one now imagines you answer idle questions . . . *Atlantic*, 230. 2 (Aug. 1972), 55.

C856 The poet of no more—W. H. Auden offers some personal reflections on Tennyson. *Listener*, 88. 2263 (10 Aug. 1972), 181.

A review of *Tennyson*, by Christopher Ricks. Reply by Jean Naish, ibid., 17 Aug. 1972, p. 212.

C857 A Saint-Simon of our time. *New York review of books*, 19. 3 (31 Aug. 1972), 4, 6–7.

A review of *In the twenties: the diaries of Harry Kessler*, tr. Charles Kessler.

C858 Special issue of *Agenda* on rhythm. W. H. Auden. *Agenda*, 10. 4–11. 1 (Autumn–Winter 1972–3), 9.

Contribution to a symposium.

C859 A shock: Housman was perfectly right . . . *Decal*, Cardiff, [1 (Autumn 1972)], 4.

C860 Harry Martinson. *From* Li Kan speaks beneath the tree. Translated by W. H. Auden and Leif Sjöberg. *Denver quarterly*, 7. 3 (Autumn 1972), 14–16.

C861 Erik Lindegren. The rain. [And] Erik Lindegren. The suit K. [And] Harry Martinson. The insects. Translated by W. H. Auden and Leif Sjöberg. *Michigan quarterly review*, 11. 4 (Fall 1972), 282–5.

C862 Pär Lagerkvist. Poem. Translated by W. H. Auden and Leif Sjöberg. *Western humanities review*, 26. 4 (Autumn 1972), 350.

C863 Three poems. Pseudo-questions: Who could possibly approve of Metternich . . . Loneliness: Gate-crashing ghost, aggressive . . . Stark bewölkt (for Stella Musulin): I'm no photophil who burns . . . *Atlantic*, 230. 3 (Sept. 1972), 88–9.

C864 Harry Martinson. The dream city. Translated from the Swedish by W. H. Auden and Leif Sjöberg. *American–Scandinavian review*, 60. 3 (Sept. 1972), 278.

C865 Other people's babies. *Observer*, 9449 (3 Sept. 1972), 33.

A review of *The rise and fall of the British nanny*, by Jonathan Gathorne-Hardy.

C866 Poem: O who can ever praise enough . . . *Poetry*, 121. 1 (Oct. 1972), 1.

Reprint of **C104** as part of the magazine's sixtieth anniversary number.

C867 An odd couple. *New York review of books*, 19. 6 (19 Oct. 1972), 6, 8–9.

A review of *Munby, man of two worlds*, by Derek Hudson.

C868 A curse: Dark was that day when Diesel . . . *Daily telegraph magazine*, 416 (20 Oct. 1972), 15.

C869 Ode to the diencephalon: How *can* you be quite so uncouth? After sharing . . . *New statesman*, 84. 2170 (20 Oct. 1972), 555.

C870 A kind of poetic justice. *Observer*, 9457 (29 Oct. 1972), 38.

A review of *The new Oxford book of English verse 1250–1950*, ed. Helen Gardner.

C871 Harry Martinson. The world clock. Translated by W. H. Auden with Leif Sjöberg. *New statesman*, 84. 2175 (24 Nov. 1972), 773.

C872 Evangelist of the life force. *New Yorker*, 48. 40 (25 Nov. 1972), 190, 193–4, 196, 198–9.

A review of *Bernard Shaw: collected letters 1898–1910*, ed. Dan H. Laurence.

C873 Ode to the diencephalon (after A. T. W. Simeons): How *can* you be quite so uncouth? After sharing . . . *New York review of books*, 19.9 (30 Nov. 1972), 10.

C874 Happy birthday, Dorothy Day. *New York review of books*, 19. 10 (14 Dec. 1972), 3–4.

A review of *A harsh and dreadful love: Dorothy Day and the Catholic Worker movement*, by William D. Miller.

C875 'Love's labour's lost' as a libretto. [By] W. H. Auden / Chester Kallman. *Tagebuch*, Musikverlag Bote & Bock, Berlin, 31 (Dec. 1972), 7–8.

1973

C876 Ondra Lysohorsky. The bundle. Translated by W. H. Auden. *Dimension*, Austin, 6. 3 (1973), 515.

C877 Nocturne (for E. R. Dodds): Do squamous and squiggling fish . . . *Journal of Hellenic studies*, 93 (1973), 2.

C878 Harry Martinson. Li Kan speaks from under the tree. Translated by W. H. Auden and Leif Sjöberg. *New directions in prose and poetry*, 27 (1973), 77–90.

C879 Marianne Moore, 1887–1972 [commemorative tribute]. *Proceedings of the American Academy of Arts and Letters and the National Institute of Arts and Letters*, ser. 2, no. 23 (1973), 94–7.

C880 Werner Aspenstrom [*sic*, for Aspenström]. Vladov pulled a sledge. Translated by W. H. Auden with Leif Sjoberg [*sic*]. *Soundings*, State University of New York at Stony Brook [10] (1973), 4.

C881 Pär Lagerkvist. With old eyes I look back. Translators, W. H. Auden and Leif Sjöberg. *Mundus artium*, 6. 1 (1973), 15, 17, 19.

Swedish text on facing pages. Reprinted without the Swedish, ibid., 12–13 (1980–1), 326–8.

C882 Labour of love, [by] W. H. Auden and Chester Kallman. *Opera*, 24. 2 (Feb. 1973), 114–15.

On *Love's labour's lost* (**A70**).

C883 Renderings. *New statesman*, 85. 2185 (2 Feb. 1973), 164–5.

A review of *English biblical translation*, by A. C. Partridge.

C884 Unpredictable but providential (for Loren Eiseley): Spring with its thrusting leaves and jargling birds is here again . . . *Times literary supplement*, 72nd year, 3700 (2 Feb. 1973), 112.

C885 Veni, vici, VD. *New York review of books*, 20. 2 (22 Feb. 1973), 34.

A review of *The dark fields of Venus*, by Basile Yanovsky.

C886 Pär Lagerkvist. The spear has been cast. An accident like a poppy. His shadow fell. Translated by W. H. Auden and Leif Sjöberg. Who has walked here . . . ? Translated by W. H. Auden and Pär Lagerkvist. *Denver quarterly*, 8. 1 (Spring 1973), 44–6.

C887 Aubade (after Eugene [*sic*] Rosenstock-Huessy): Beckoned anew to a world . . . *Four quarters*, Philadelphia, 22. 3 (Spring 1973), 20–1.

C888 Aubade: Beckoned anew to a World . . . *Oxford poetry magazine*, 1 (Mar. 1973), 6–7.

C889 [Letter to the editor.] *Scientific American*, 228. 3 (Mar. 1973), 8.

A reply to an article by Gunther S. Stent on 'Prematurity and uniqueness in a scientific discovery', in the Dec. 1972 issue. Auden's letter is followed by Stent's response, pp. 8–9.

C890 Cavafy [letter to the editor]. *New York times*, 11 Mar. 1973, section 7 (*book review*, 78. 10), 51.

Reply to a review of a volume of translations of Cavafy's poems.

C891 Larkin's choice. *Guardian*, 29 Mar. 1973, p. 16.

A review of *The Oxford book of twentieth-century English verse*, ed. Philip Larkin. Replies by Simon Edwards and Anthony Rudolf, 2 Apr. 1973, p. 10; a third letter by Robin Milner-Gulland on the same page replies to an unrelated letter mentioning Auden by Sally Jacobson, 29 Mar. 1973, p. 14.

C892 A curse: Dark was that day when Diesel . . . *Harper's*, 146. 1475 (Apr. 1973), 11.

C893 The poems of Joseph Brodsky. W. H. Auden. *New York review of books*, 20. 5 (5 Apr. 1973), 10.

The foreword to the selection (**B143**), followed here by the introduction by George L. Kline.

C894 Werner Aspenström. Strindberg answers an ornithological question. Translated by W. H. Auden and Leif Sjöberg. *New statesman*, 85. 2195 (13 Apr. 1973), 554.

C895 Unpredictable but providential (for Loren Eiseley): Spring with its thrusting leaves and jargling birds is here again . . . *New Yorker*, 49. 8 (14 Apr. 1973), 40.

C896 Rhyme and reason. *Observer*, 9486 (20 May 1973), 36.
A review of *The Oxford book of children's verse*, ed. Iona and Peter Opie.

C897 Between crossfires. *New Yorker*, 49. 14 (26 May 1973), 130–5.
A review of *Hammarskjöld*, by Brian Urquhart.

C898 Harry Martinson. From 'Li Kan speaks from under the tree'. Translated by W. H. Auden and Leif Sjöberg. *Western humanities review*, 27. 3 (Summer 1973), 274–7.

C899 Artur Lundkvist. [Four poems.] Translated by W. H. Auden with Leif Sjöberg. *London magazine*, NS 13. 2 (June–July 1973), 81–3.

C900 Indestructible. *New Statesman*, 85. 2202 (1 June 1973), 812–13.
A review of *Conversations with Klemperer*, ed. Peter Heyworth.

C901 Progress is the mother of problems (G. K. Chesterton). *New York review of books*, 20. 11 (28 June 1973), 20–2.
A review of *The ancient concept of progress*, by E. R. Dodds.

C902 Praiseworthy. *New statesman*, 85. 2206 (29 June 1973), 972.
A review of *The church hymnary: third edition.*

C903 Aubade (in memoriam Eugene Rosenstok-Huessy [*sic*]): Beckoned anew to a World . . . *Atlantic*, 232. 1 (July 1973), 70.

C904 Responses to the Near East. *New Yorker*, 49. 19 (2 July 1973), 72–5.
A review of *Flaubert in Egypt*, ed. Francis Steegmuller.

C905 Thank you, fog: Grown used to New York Weather . . . *Times literary supplement*, 3725 (27 July 1973), 846.

C906 'Love's labour's lost'. [Letter signed by] W. H. Auden and Chester Kallman. *Opera*, 24. 8 (Aug. 1973), 758–9.
A reply to a review (by John McCann in the Apr. 1973 number) of the first performance of the opera.

C907 A lullaby: The din of work is subdued . . . *New Yorker*, 49. 24 (6 Aug. 1973), 32.

C908 Johannes Edfelt. [Two poems.] Translated by W. H. Auden with Leif Sjöberg. *Little magazine*, New York, 7. 3 (Fall 1973), 17.

C909 Johannes Edfelt. Six prose poems. Translated by W. H. Auden with Leif Sjöberg. *Shenandoah*, 25. 1 (Fall 1973), 41–3.

C910 Pär Lagerkvist. Two poems. Translated by W. H. Auden and Leif Sjöberg. *Southern humanities review*, 7. 4 (Fall 1973), 377.

C911 Werner Aspenström. [Two poems.] Translated by W. H. Auden with Leif Sjöberg. *Texas quarterly*, 16. 3 (Autumn 1973), 114–15.

C912 Reading. Books which mean much to me. *Mademoiselle*, 77. 5 (Sept. 1973), 24.

C913 A Russian with common sense. *New Yorker*, 49. 28 (3 Sept. 1973), 62–6.

A review of *The letters of Anton Chekhov* ed. Avrahm Yarmolinsky.

C914 On my mind. 'I have a ferocious bee in my bonnet'. *Vogue*, New York, 162. 4 (Oct. 1973), 189.

C915 Address to the beasts: For us who, from the moment . . . *New Yorker*, 49. 33 (8 Oct. 1973), 44.

C916 Posthumous letter to Gilbert White: It's rather sad we can only meet people . . . *New York review of books*, 20. 16 (18 Oct. 1973), 53.

C917 Auden's last post for the poets. *Sunday telegraph*, 660 (21 Oct. 1973), 20.

Excerpts from Auden's contribution to *New movements in the study and teaching of English*, ed. Nicholas Bagnall (B142).

C918 An odd ball in an odd country in an odd time. *New York review of books*, 20. 17 (1 Nov. 1973), 8–10.

A review of *St. John of the Cross: his life and poetry*, by Gerald Brenan.

C919 No, Plato, no: I can't imagine anything . . . *New York review of books*, 20. 17 (1 Nov. 1973), 9.

C920 Where are the arts going? W. H. Auden. *Observer*, 9510 (4 Nov. 1973), *magazine*, p. 9.

Contribution to a symposium.

1974

C921 Artur Lundkvist. Eight poems. Translated by W. H. Auden with Leif Sjöberg. *New directions in prose and poetry*, 29 (1974), 164–71.

C922 Artur Lundkvist. The horse. Translated by W. H. Auden with Leif Sjoberg [*sic*]. *Soundings*, State University of New York at Stony Brook, [11] (1974), 52.

C923 Johannes Edfelt. Places of rest. Translated by W. H. Auden with Leif Sjoberg [*sic*]. *Soundings*, State University of New York at Stony Brook, [11] (1974), 60.

C924 Artur Lundkvist. A love of wood. Translated by W. H. Auden and Leif Sjöberg. *Stand*, 15. 4 (1974), 28.

C925 Harry Martinson. The cable ship. Translated by W. H. Auden and Leif Sjöberg. *Stand*, 15. 4 (1974), 70.

C926 Pär Lagerkvist. The morning of creation. Translated by W. H. Auden and Leif Sjöberg. *Denver quarterly*, 9. 1 (Spring 1974), 34–8.

C927 Pär Lagerkvist. Poems. Translated by W. H. Auden with Leif Sjöberg. *Michigan quarterly review*, 13. 2 (Spring 1974), 138–9.

C928 Pär Lagerkvist. [Three poems.] Translated from the Swedish by W. H. Auden with Leif Sjöberg. *Nimrod*, 18. 2 (Spring–Summer 1974), 47.

C929 Shorts. *Intellectual digest*, 4. 7 (Mar. 1974), 42.

Thirteen selections from 'Shorts II' in *Epistle to a godson*, reprinted without change.

C930 Lullaby: The din of work is subdued . . . *Listener*, 91. 2352 (25 Apr. 1974), 536.

See textual correction, ibid. (9 May 1974), 602.

C931 Oton Župančič. Tittlinghey-Tittlingpugh. [Translated by Branko Brusar and W. H. Auden.] *Matica*, Zagreb, 24. 5 (May 1974), 36.

One of a group of thirteen poems for children by Croatian poets, translated by Auden and Brusar around 1967. Eleven poems were printed in *Matica* in 1974–5; the full set exists as a carbon-copy typescript in the Berg Collection, New York Public Library, with the title 'The child's concept of poetry, translated by Branko Brusar and W. H. Auden'.

C932 Two poems. Nocturne: Do squamous and squiggling fish . . . A curse: Dark was that day when Diesel . . . *New Yorker*, 50. 11 (6 May 1974), 42.

C933 The gift of wonder. *Tablet*, 228. 6985 (18 May 1974), 481–3.
Auden's contribution to *G. K. Chesterton: a centenary appraisal* (**B144**).

C934 Jovan Jovanović Zmaj. Pete as a doctor. Translated by B. S. Brusar and W. H. Anden [*sic*]. *Matica*, 24. 6 (June 1974), 41.

C935 Address to the beasts: For us who, from the moment . . . Posthumous letter to Gilbert White: It's rather sad we can only meet people . . . Archaeology: The archaeologist's spade . . . *London magazine*, NS 14.3 (Aug.–Sept. 1974), 5–10.

C936 Gustav Krklec. A crazy day. Translated by Branko Brusar and W. H. Auden. *Matica*, 24. 8 (Aug. 1974), 38.

C937 Nocturne (for E. R. Dodds): Do squamous and squiggling fish . . . *Listener*, 92. 2368 (15 Aug. 1974), 221.

C938 Harry Martinson. The rhinoceros. [And] Werner Aspenström. [Three poems.] Translated by W. H. Auden and Leif Sjöberg. *Antaeus*, 15 (Autumn 1974), 119–23.

C939 Harry Martinson [and] Werner Aspenstrom [*sic*]. Four poems in translation. Translated by W. H. Auden and Leif Sjöberg. *Sewanee review*, 82. 4 (Fall 1974), 682–4.

C940 Artur Lundkvist. The magpie. Translated by W. H. Auden with Leif Sjöberg. *Transatlantic review*, 50 (Autumn–Winter 1974), 90.

C941 Desanka Maksimović. Dolls doing sums. Translated by Branko Brusar and W. H. Auden. *Matica*, 24. 9 (Sept. 1974), 33.

C942 Dobriša Cesarić. Two rabbits. Translated by Branko S. Brusar and W. H. Auden. *Matica*, 24. 10 (Oct. 1974), 38.

C943 Thank you, fog: Grown used to New York weather . . . *Vogue*, New York, 164. 4 (Oct. 1974), 145.

C944 A contrast: How broad-minded were Nature and My Parents . . . No, Plato, no: I can't imagine anything . . . *Times literary supplement*, 3787 (4 Oct. 1974), 1077.

C945 Igo Gruden. Joe inhabits a little house. Translated by Branko S. Brusar and W. H. Auden. *Matica*, 24. 11 (Nov. 1974), 35.

C946 Grigor Vitez. If trees could walk. Translated by Branko Brusar and W. H. Auden. *Matica*, 24. 12 (Dec. 1974), 38.

C947 [Harry Martinson. Three poems.] Translated from the Swedish by W. H. Auden and Leif Sjöberg. *Christian Science monitor*, 4 Dec. 1974, home forum, p. 1.

C948 Archaeology: The archaeologist's spade . . . A thanksgiving: When pre-pubescent I felt . . . *New York review of books*, 21. 20 (12 Dec. 1974), 27.

C949 Death at random. *New York review of books*, 21. 20 (12 Dec. 1974), 28–9.
A review of *Twentieth century book of the dead*, by Gil Elliot.

1975

C950 Branko Ćopić. The three floor patient. Translated by Branko S. Brusar and W. H. Auden. *Matica*, 25. 1 (Jan. 1975), 37.

C951 Slavko Janevski. Grand-dad and grand-son. [Translated by Branko Brusar and W. H. Auden.] *Matica*, 25. 2 (Feb. 1975), 33.

C952 Harry Martinsen [*sic*]. Song of the thrush. Translated by W. H. Auden and Leif Sjoberg [*sic*]. *Christian Science monitor*, 11 Feb. 1975, home forum, p. 1.

C953 Dušan Radović. The lion. Translated by Branko S. Brusar and W. H. Auden. *Matica*, 25. 3 (Mar. 1975), 37.

C954 Pär Lagerkvist. Two poems. Translated from the Swedish by W. H. Auden and Leif Sjöberg. *Malahat review*, 34 (Apr. 1975), 36.

C955 Dragan Lukić. Every day. Translated by W. H. Auden and B. S. Brusar. *Matica*, 25. 4 (Apr. 1975), 36.

C956 Harry Martinson. Out at sea. The cable ship. Translated from the Swedish by W. H. Auden with Leif Sjöberg. *Books abroad*, 49. 3 (Summer 1975), 421.

C957 Werner Aspenström. Three poems. Translated by W. H. Auden with Leif Sjöberg. *Literary review*, Fairleigh Dickinson University, 19. 1 (Fall 1975), 108–11.

1979

C958 A translation of 'The sun song' [by] W. H. Auden [and Paul B. Taylor]. *Comparative criticism*, 1 (1979), 129–39.

Translated from the Old Icelandic; reprinted in *Norse poems* (1981).

C959 Erik Lindegren. [Three poems.] A translation . . . by W. H. Auden and Leif Sjöberg. *Comparative criticism*, 1 (1979), 153–4.

1980

C960 Nikola Šop. Honeymoon in heaven (Angelica ars amandi). Translated by B. S. Brusar and W. H. Auden. *Most*, Zagreb, NS [2?]. 1–2 (1980), 92–101.

This periodical is a continuation of *Bridge*, the title under which it may be catalogued in some libraries.

C961 Harry Martinson. [Three poems.] Translated by W. H. Auden and Leif Sjöberg, revised by W. J. Smith and Leif Sjöberg. *Poetry east*, 1 (1980), 35–7.

1983

C962 W. H. Auden 'on Chaadayev', edited by George L. Kline. *Russian review*, 42. 4 (Oct. 1983), 409–16.

A review of *Philosophical letters and Apology of a madman*, by Peter Yakelovich Chaadayev; written for *New Yorker* probably in Mar. 1973, but not printed there.

POSTHUMOUS PRINTINGS OF WORK NOT PREPARED FOR PUBLICATION BY AUDEN

D1 Edward Mendelson. Auden in New York: 1939–1941. *Adam*, 379–84 (1973–4), 27–33.

Includes 'Ballade of a disappointed man' (p. 29); this poem is also quoted in: Katie Louchheim, 'The truth is not the proper thing to tell', *Washington post*, 5 Nov. 1978, *magazine*, p. 21.

D2 Pride and prayer. *Episcopalian*, Philadelphia, 139. 3 (Mar. 1974), 6–8.

This and the two following items from the same journal comprise about three-fourths of the text of an early version of the essay 'Work, carnival and prayer', from a draft typescript written in 1971. The first two instalments appeared without the authorization of Auden's Estate. The magazine changed format after the third instalment, and the projected fourth part did not appear.

D3 Auden on work, agriculture & science. *Episcopalian*, 139. 4 (Apr. 1974), 12–14.

See note to **D2**.

D4 Auden on laughter and carnival. *Episcopalian*, 139. 5 (May 1974), 20–2.

See note to **D2**.

D5 Five early poems: These also told their secrets to the hazels . . . Father and mother, twin-lights of heaven . . . You who have come to watch us play and go . . . Bourgeois why are you looking so gay . . . 'Sweet is it', say the doomed, 'to be alive though wretched' . . . *Times literary supplement*, 3853 (16 Jan. 1976), 52–3.

Prefatory note by Edward Mendelson.

D6 The prolific and the devourer (part I). *Antaeus*, 21–2 (Spring–Summer 1976), 7–23.

The first part of a book written in 1939; reprinted in *The English Auden* (from which an advance excerpt of the same piece appeared in *New York times*, 29 Jan. 1978, section 7 (*book review*), pp. 3, 39. (See **D17**.)

D7 An unpublished poem: Renewal of traditional anger in peace . . . *Pearl*, Odense, 2 (Autumn 1976), 1.

Written around Jan. 1930.

D8 Easter Monday: Spring, a toy trumpet at her lips . . . *Oxford poetry now*, 2 (Michaelmas 1976), 2–3.

Previously unpublished poem written Apr. 1927.

D9 An unpublished early poem: The month was April, the year . . . *New statesman*, 93. 2397 (25 Feb. 1977), 263–4.

Written Apr. 1933; this text is an advance excerpt from *The English Auden.*

D10 Passenger shanty: The ship weighed twenty thousand ton . . . *Times literary supplement*, 3942 (14 Oct. 1977), 1199.

Written Jan. 1938; this text is an advance excerpt from *The English Auden.*

D11 A chorus by W. H. Auden: O quick and furtive is the lovers' night . . . *Sunday times*, 8054 (30 Oct. 1977), 41.

From an early version of *On the frontier*, this text is an advance excerpt from *The English Auden.*

D12 In the year of my youth when yoyos came in . . . *Review of English studies*, NS 29. 115 (Aug. 1978), 281–309.

The text of a long unpublished poem in Cantos written in 1932, transcribed by Lucy S. McDiarmid with an introduction (pp. 267–81) and notes (pp. 310–12). One hundred offprints in wrappers were prepared for the transcriber.

D13 Brian Finney. *Christopher Isherwood, a critical biography*. London: Faber & Faber, 1979.

Includes Auden's poem for Isherwood, 'Who is that funny-looking man so squat with a top-heavy head . . .' (pp. 287–9).

D14 Sean Day-Lewis. *C. Day-Lewis, an English literary life*. London: Weidenfeld & Nicolson, 1980.

Includes 'This morning any touch is possible . . .', Auden's 1928 epithalamium to Day-Lewis (pp. 307–8), and 'Time flies, Cecil; hardly a week ago . . .', a verse-letter written Feb. 1929 (pp. 309–11).

D15 Lyrics for *Man of La Mancha*. *Antaeus*, 40–1 (Winter–Spring 1981), 11–30.

Lyrics (some unpublished) written late in 1963 for the musical play *Man of La Mancha*, a play first conceived as having song lyrics by Auden and Chester Kallman. Disagreements over the tone of the play led to the departure of Auden and Kallman from the collaboration, and the version eventually produced had lyrics by another hand. The collaboration was announced in *New York times*, 4 Aug. 1963, section 2, p. 1. Rex Harrison recalled Auden's contribution in an interview, 'Lady's man moves on', *Observer*, 24 Jan. 1965, p. 22. Revised texts of two of the lyrics appear in *City without walls* as 'Song of the ogres' and 'Song of the devil'. Two further lyrics appear in *Thank you, fog* as 'Two *Don Quixote* lyrics' ('The golden age' and 'Recitative by Death'). Some further passages are quoted in Dale Wasserman, 'Tilting with "Man of La Mancha"', *Los Angeles times*, 5 Mar. 1978, Calendar, p. 60. The *Antaeus* texts present the full original texts, with a prefatory note by Edward Mendelson. (Kallman's planned contribution seems never to have been written.)

D16 Ode [to the George Washington Hotel]: In this epoch of high-pressure selling . . . *New York times*, 8 Mar. 1981, section 7 (*book review*), p. 11.

Written in 1939; prefatory note by Edward Mendelson.

D17 The prolific and the devourer. *Antaeus*, 42 (Summer 1981), 7–65.

The complete text of a prose book written in 1939. Prefatory note by Edward Mendelson. Some copies of this issue of the magazine were bound in cloth and a dust-jacket and sold at $9.95.

D18 Pride: When Little Claus meets Big Claus in the road . . . *Yale review*, 71. 1 (Winter 1982), 172.

Written probably in 1926; prefatory note by Edward Mendelson.

D19 Lachlan Mackinnon. *Eliot, Auden, Lowell, aspects of the Baudelairean inheritance*. London: Macmillan, 1983.

Includes quotations from juvenilia from the E. R. Dodds bequest in the Bodleian, including complete texts of 'The sawmill', 'Prayer', 'March song', 'The old mine' [first version], 'Like other men when I go past', and 'The old mine' [second version] (pp. 52–6).

D20 Edward Callan. *Auden: a carnival of intellect*. New York: Oxford University Press, 1983.

Includes 'Il bar internationale [*sic*, for internazionale]' (p. 225).

D21 Dorothy J. Farnan. *Auden in love*. New York: Simon & Schuster, 1984.

Includes 'To Chester Kallman b. Jan. 7, 1921' (pp. 25–7), a letter-poem to Kallman, Christmas 1941 (pp. 65–6), and 'Ode' [to the George Washington Hotel] (pp. 93–5).

D22 Poems by W. H. Auden (1927–1928), introduced by Nicholas Jenkins. *Oxford poetry*, 1. 3 (Spring 1984), 84–94.

[Ten previously unpublished poems:] The houses rolled into the sun . . . Out of sight, assuredly, not out of mind . . . Narcissus: I shall sit here through the evening . . . Truly our fathers had the gout . . . We, knowing the family history . . . Deemed this an outpost, I . . . This is the address of the lost soul . . . The weeks of blizzard over . . . The colonel to be shot at dawn . . . 'Grow thin by walking and go inland' . . .

D23 Poem: Love is this and that . . . *Babel*, München, 4 (Winter 1984–5), 80.

Written in 1930.

D24 Lucy McDiarmid. Auden's 1931 epithalamion and other generous hours. *Modern language quarterly*, 46. 4 (Dec. 1985), 407–28.

Includes 'As the magnum is smashed on the stern when the liner is loosed' (pp. 425–8).

D25 Paris: The poets have taken their quick myopic walks . . . *Oxford poetry*, 2. 3 (Winter 1985[–6]), 86.

Poem written 1938; note by Nicholas Jenkins (pp. 86–7). The poem and note are headed 'On the way to China: an unpublished poem by W. H. Auden'.

D26 *'If Christ be not risen . . .'*, *essays in resurrection and survival*. St Mary's Annual for 1986, edited by Elizabeth Russell and John Greenhalgh. [London:] St Mary's Bourne Street, [1986].

Contains 'Words and the word' (pp. 67–71), the text of a sermon Auden preached at Christ Church, Oxford, 24 Oct. 1965; not the same as other works with the same title.

NOTES ON CONTRIBUTORS

KATHLEEN BELL is the Editor of *The W. H. Auden Society Newsletter*. Her contribution to this volume is part of her planned edition of the complete correspondence between Auden and the Doddses.

JOHN BRIDGEN was Rector of Barrow cum Denham, Suffolk, until 1983. He is now working on a memoir of his own and Frank McEachran's mutual friend, the public schoolmaster, naturalist, and poet, Humphrey Moore.

KATHERINE BUCKNELL received her Doctorate from Columbia University and was a Junior Research Fellow at Worcester College, Oxford. She is currently preparing an edition of Auden's juvenilia.

DAVID CONSTANTINE teaches German at Queen's College, Oxford. He has published three volumes of poetry, a novel, and several academic works—including in 1988 a study of the poet Hölderlin.

VALENTINE CUNNINGHAM is Fellow and Tutor in English Literature at Corpus Christi College, Oxford. He is the editor of *The Penguin Book of Spanish Civil War Verse* (1980) and *Spanish Front: Writers on the Civil War* (1986). His *British Writers of the Thirties* was published in 1988.

JOHN FULLER is a fellow of Magdalen College, Oxford, where he is Tutor in English. He published *A Reader's Guide to W. H. Auden* in 1970. His *Selected Poems 1954–1982* appeared in 1985 and his third novel, *The Burning Boys*, in 1989.

MICK IMLAH published his first book of poems, *Birthmarks*, in 1988; it was a Poetry Book Society Recommendation and was nominated for a Whitbread Prize.

NICHOLAS JENKINS is a graduate of Magdalen College, Oxford. He is currently preparing a critical edition of *The Double Man*.

PETER MCDONALD is Fellow and Lecturer in English at Pembroke College, Cambridge. His *Louis MacNeice: The Poet in His Contexts* will be published shortly by the OUP. He won an Eric Gregory Prize in 1987, and his first collection of poems, *Biting the Wax*, appeared in 1989.

EDWARD MENDELSON who teaches English and Comparative Literature at Columbia University, is Auden's literary executor. His edition of the Auden–Isherwood plays, the first volume in *The Complete Works of W. H. Auden*, was published in 1988 by the Princeton University Press and in 1989 by Faber & Faber.

NAOMI MITCHISON has described her friendship with Auden in *You May Well Ask: A Memoir 1920–1940* (1979). She is the author of many volumes of fiction, autobiography, biography, social and political commentary, poems, children's stories, and other works.

STAN SMITH is the author of *W. H. Auden* (1985), *Edward Thomas* (1986), and *W. B. Yeats: A Critical Introduction* (1990). He is Professor of English at Dundee University and co-director of the Auden Concordance Project. He is currently working on Auden's Scottish connection (Helensburgh 1930–2).

JULIAN SYMONS was founder and editor of *Twentieth Century Verse* (1937–9). He is the author of *Bloody Murder*, a history of the crime story, and *The Thirties* (a personal view of the period), as well as two collections of essays, *Critical Occasions* and *Critical Observations*.

ROBERT A. WILSON was, until his retirement in 1988, the proprietor of the Phoenix Book Shop in New York City. He is the author of *Modern Book Collecting* (New York, 1980) and compiler of the bibliographies of Gregory Corso, Denise Levertov, and Gertrude Stein.

INDEX

This index is not complete for 'A Bibliographical Supplement'. Readers should also consult the appropriate sections between pp. 203 and 235 where many first-time publications are listed, for instance, in section 'D', works which appeared after Auden's death.

Lawrence, D. H. 37, 127, 137, 178, 183, 197
Lawrence, T. E. 144, 188
Lear, Edward 140; *see also* Auden, 'Edward Lear'
Leavis, F. R. 63–4
Lehmann, John 72, 73
Leibniz, Gottfried Wilhelm von 125
Lessing, Gotthold Ephraim 125
Levitin, Isabella 211 ff.
Lindegren, Erik 225 ff.
Listener, The 63, 106, 204
Llewellyn, Richard, *How Green Was My Valley* 112
Lorca, F. Garcia 69
'Lords of Limit' 126–30
Lothian, Lord (Philip Henry Kerr) 104
Lundkvist, Artur 229 ff.
Lunn, Arnold 30, 37–8
Lunn, Henry S. 37–8
Lysohorsky, Ondra 211 ff.

McDiarmid, Lucy S. 234–5
McEachran, Frank 117 ff., *The Civilized Man* 119, 126–9, 133; *The Life and Philosophy of Johann Gottfried Herder* 119, 124; 'A Pattern for Reality' 132; 'The Tragic Element in Dante's *Commedia*' 119
Machine, the 99–100, 109–10
Mackinnon, Lachlan 235
Maclean, Donald 84
MacNeice, Louis 56, 68, 96, 106, 108–9, 111–12, 147 ff., 200, 209; 'Adam's Legacy' 163, 166; *Autumn Sequel* 157, 162; *Blind Fireworks* 147, 150, 156, 158, 162, 164–7, 169; 'Child's Terror' 159; 'Epitaph for Louis' 167–8; 'Experiences with Images' 148–9, 158, 162, 164; 'En Avant: A Poem Suggested by Marco Polo' 161–2, 169; 'Laburnam (May 1929)' 165–6; *Modern Poetry* 148, 150, 152, 156–8, 161, 165, 169; 'Neurospastoumenos' 166–7; 'Sentimentality' 154–56; *The Strings Are False* 148, 152–3, 157, 162–3, 170; 'Summer Remembered' 160–2; 'The Sunlight on the Garden' 192; 'Threnody' 169–70; 'Twilight of the Gods' 163–4, 166–7; 'The ways are green and gorgons creep' 149; 'When I Was Twenty-One' 148, 150, 170–1
Madge, Charles 61–3, 79

Malinowski, Bronislaw 26–7
Mann, Erika 67
Mann, Golo 78
Mann, Thomas 67, 220
Marlborough School 147, 150, 157
Marlburian, The 147 ff.
Martinson, Harry 224 ff.
Marx Brothers 108
Marx, Karl 122, 131–3, 183
Marxism 130, 195; *see also* communism, Auden (communism) (socialism)
Mayer, Elizabeth 79, 211
Mead, Margaret 112–13
Medley, Robert 118
Medley, Robert 69
Melville, Herman 47, 139; *see also* Auden, 'Herman Melville'
Mendelson, Edward 17, 18, 32, 60, 120, 127, 130, 132, 150, 182, 184, 192
Merwin, W. S. 198, 222
Miller, Charles 79
Milton, John, *Samson Agonistes* 86
Mitchison, Naomi 17, 19, 20, 30, 37–8, 63
modernism 147, 152, 168, 170
Montreal 107
Moore, Henry 207
Moore, Humphrey 120
Moore, Marianne 80, 201, 226
Mozart, Wolfgang Amadeus, *Don Giovanni* 78
Musulin, Stella 211, 225

Nabokov, Nicolas 207
Nabokov, Vladimir 197, 200
Napoleon III 144–5
Nazi-Soviet Pact 95, 104
Nazism 36, 62, 67
Negative Capability 145
Neulengbach 221
New Country 61–2, 173, 183
New Republic, The 98
New School for Social Research 111, 113
New York 106, 133
Newton, Caroline 200
Nicolson, Harold 81
Niebuhr, Reinhold 102, 132–3, 201
Nietzsche, Friedrich 126–7

OED 187
Opie, Iona and Peter 228
Orwell, George 92, 221